THE

SOUTH SINCE THE WAR

THE

SOUTH SINCE THE WAR

AS SHOWN BY

FOURTEEN WEEKS OF TRAVEL AND OBSERVATION

IN

GEORGIA AND THE CAROLINAS

BY

SIDNEY ANDREWS

ABRIDGED WITH A
NEW INTRODUCTION
BY

HEATHER COX RICHARDSON

LOUISIANA STATE UNIVERSITY PRESS

BATON ROUGE

DESIGNER: Andrew Shurtz

TYPEFACE: Whitman

PRINTER AND BINDER: McNaughton & Gunn

LIBRARY OF CONGRESS CATALOGING-IN-PUBLICATION DATA

Andrews, Sidney, 1837–1880.

The South since the war : as shown by fourteen weeks of travel and observation in Georgia and the Carolinas / Sidney Andrews ; abridged with a new introduction by Heather Cox Richardson

p. cm.

Unabridged ed. originally published : Ticknor and Fields, 1866.

ISBN 0-8071-2957-7 (pbk. : alk. paper)

1. Southern States—Description and travel.

2. Reconstruction (U.S. history, 1865-1877).

3. African Americans—History—1863-1877.

4. North Carolina—Description and travel.

5. South Carolina—Description and travel.

6. Georgia—Description and travel.

I. Richardson, Heather Cox.

II. Title.

F216.A56 2004

917.5'044—dc22

CONTENTS

INTRODUCTION Heather Cox Richardson vii

I. Conditions and Prospects of the City in Which Rebellion Began 1

II. Manners and Customs in the Interior of South Carolina 6

III. The Situation with Respect to the Negro 10

IV. Scenes in the Track of Sherman's Army 14

V. Organization of the South Carolina Convention 18

VI. The Leaders of the Convention and the Repeal of the Secession Ordinance . 23

VII. Action of the Convention on the Slavery Question 27

VIII. The Basis of Representation 32

IX. The Great Contest between the Upper and Lower Sections of South Carolina . 36

X. Minor Work of the State Convention 39

XI. Summary of Four Weeks' Observations 42

XII. The Great Military Prison of North Carolina 47

XIII. Affairs in Western North Carolina 51

XIV. The North Carolina Freedmen's Convention 56

XV. The Organization and Personnel of the North Carolina State Convention . 65

XVI. Debate and Action in Respect to the Ordinance of Secession 69

XVII. Action in Regard to Slavery and the Freedmen 74

XVIII. The War-Debt Question and the Minor Work of the Convention . . . 79

XIX. Affairs in Central North Carolina 82

xx. Summary of Three Weeks' Observations in North Carolina 86

xxi. The Great Military Prison of South Carolina 92

xxii. Life and Labor in the South Carolina Low-Country 98

xxiii. Life and Labor in the South Carolina Up-Country 105

xxiv. Social Characteristics of the South-Carolinians 109

xxv. First Glimpses of Georgia 114

xxvi. Organization and Personnel of the Georgia State Convention 118

xxvii. Secession and Slavery 122

xxviii. Asking Pardon for Jeff Davis 124

xxix. Amending the State Constitution 127

xxx. The Minor Work of the Convention 129

xxxi. How Repudiation Was Accomplished 130

xxxii. Review of the Proceedings of the State Convention 136

xxxiii. A Visit to the Home of Judge Lynch 140

xxxiv. The Great Military Prison of Georgia 147

xxxv. Matters in Southwestern Georgia 153

xxxvi. The State Elections 157

xxxvii. Matters in Western Georgia 159

xxxviii. Matters in Northwestern Georgia 164

xxxix. Matters in Central Georgia 168

xl. Matters in Eastern Georgia 173

xli. Matters in Southeastern Georgia 178

xlii. Summary of Five Weeks' Observations in Georgia 183

xliii. Some General Conclusions on the Situation in Georgia and the Carolinas . 188

INDEX 199

Sidney Andrews's *The South since the War*

IN LATE SUMMER and fall 1865, northern journalist Sidney Andrews spent fourteen weeks touring South Carolina, North Carolina, and Georgia. His job was to tell readers of the *Chicago Tribune* and the *Boston Advertiser* what the war had done to the South and what the region and its inhabitants were like in the aftermath of the fighting.

Northerners were not merely curious about the world of their former foes; by the time Andrews set out they were worried that white southerners were not willing to accept the results of the war. Some white southerners acknowledged the death of the Confederacy and, recognizing that cooperation with the North would bring economic as well as political recovery, quietly acquiesced in northern demands. Others, encouraged by President Andrew Johnson's leniency toward the former Confederate states, clung to the legitimacy of the Confederacy by defending its debt, demanded the admission of wartime leaders to Congress, and insisted on retaining control over ex-slaves. Some even went so far as to refuse to acknowledge emancipation.

Constitutional conventions organized under Johnson's plan of reconstruction were scheduled for the fall, and northerners waited anxiously to see the mindsets delegates brought to their deliberations. Andrews was there to report on the conventions. "I went South to study the political situation," he wrote at the end of his southern tour, "my object being to gather information at first hand and to keep my reports free from the bias and prejudice of Northern sojourners." Despite Andrews's claims to neutrality, however, it was all but impossible for any northern reporter to tour the South five months after the Civil War had ended without some preconceived ideas about what he would find.

Born and reared in Massachusetts before moving to northern Illinois, Andrews had no doubt about the superiority of northern over southern society. Continually comparing his southern surroundings with the North, he presented a bleak picture of the war-torn South. He condemned southern railroads, businesses, convention delegates, schools, clothing, and especially housekeeping as inferior to their northern counterparts. Nettled by southerners' traditional scorn for what they believed was the North's small-minded materialism, Andrews argued that the South's conditions revealed the viciousness of the southern way of life. Detailing the squalor of a southern home, he attacked the old myth of the South's superior civilization. "Let us call things by their right names," he suggested, "—then shall we say *Southern barbarism.*"

Like most of his contemporaries in the North, Andrews believed that the reason for the North's supremacy was the fundamental superiority of its free-labor economy over that of the southern slave system. In the North, every individual could work his way to economic security, but in the South, slavery degraded both black slaves and white workers, who could not compete with cheap slave labor. Wealthy and powerful aristocrats controlled government in their interests while the poor whites—"clay-eaters" and "crackers," as Andrews termed them—struggled to survive. Horrified and disgusted by this hierarchical society, Andrews constantly pointed out class tensions in the South and happily recorded evidence that the power of the South's wealthy planters appeared to be fading.

Optimistic northerners like Andrews hoped that as free labor replaced slavery in the South, the region's stratified society would disappear and equality of opportunity would erase class lines. But accomplishing this transformation would not be easy. "The whole labor system of the State is in an utterly demoralized condition," Andrews wrote of South Carolina. "How soon it can be thoroughly reorganized, and on just what basis that reorganization will take place, are questions of no easy answering. The labor question, and not reconstruction, is the main question among intelligent thinking men." Andrews concluded that the North must teach white southerners to respect the rights of their black neighbors. At the same time, it must teach black southerners to work hard and wait patiently for whites to recognize their freedom.

Andrews believed that the free-labor system could flourish in the South because black Americans were good workers, as long as they were treated fairly. This point he repeated again and again, both explicitly and with anecdotes of ex-slaves who were anxious to find jobs. Tellingly, in his initial discussion of southern race relations Andrews repeated the insistence of a number of whites that African Americans were lazy and could not survive as free men. Andrews answered this argument by listing freedpeople who were gainfully employed, then permitted Pompey, a twelve-year-old boy, to have the last word. "I's free nigger now," said Pompey, "and I's goin' to work."

Andrews supported black laborers' economic aspirations despite his own deep racism, which made him dismiss rural freedmen as "idle, vicious, improvident, negligent, and unfit to care well for his own interests . . . a hard, coarse, unlovely fact." Andrews's actions as well as his words revealed northerners' profound and pervasive disrespect for black Americans after the Civil War. He unselfconsciously recorded his own intrusive questioning of African Americans who were unable safely to ignore him, during which he regularly replaced black people's actual names with generic ones: "John" or "Auntie." Although horrified by mob violence against freedmen and determined that they should have equal economic, if not political, rights, Andrews neither accorded them the same personal respect he automatically offered to whites nor did he notice his own prejudice.

For all his racism, though, Andrews reserved his harshest criticism for southern whites. He dismissed poor whites, locked into poverty and struggling with disease, as lower specimens of humanity than poor blacks, who at least aspired to a better life. Of the better classes of whites, his opinion was not much better. On the one hand, he lauded the courage and pride of angry white southerners as good qualities to foster in the reunited nation, and praised those few men who accepted the results of the war and were striving to bring progress to the South. On the other hand, he angrily recounted that white southerners not only deliberately tortured Union soldiers in Confederate prison camps, but also refused to accept the results of the war and were systematically obstructing the establishment of a free-labor system in their region. Andrews's visits to the Confederate prisons of Salisbury, Florence, and Andersonville filled him with pity for the thousands of Union soldiers who died there and outrage at what he believed was the callousness and deliberate malice that exacerbated the prisoners' suffering. But these sites were relics of the war, and their day was past. Still dangerous were those white southerners who refused to surrender their belief in states' rights and, occasionally, even refused to accept emancipation. Andrews repeatedly recorded conversations in which white southerners boasted they still whipped or cheated their black tenants, turning them away from the fields on which they had worked all summer with nothing to get them through the upcoming winter.

To his dismay these attitudes were well represented in the state constitutional conventions Andrews attended. In South Carolina delegates denied that black Americans were citizens or had rights; North Carolina's delegates harped on the idea of a "white man's government"; Georgia's delegates clung to the doctrine of states' rights and denied the principle of human equality by providing for separate legislation for ex-slaves. These convention delegates contrasted painfully with those of the North Carolina Freedmen's Convention of October, who, with great dignity, made a "moral appeal to the hearts and consciences" of white southerners to allow freedpeople fair wages and basic human rights.

Ultimately, Andrews concluded that there must be a thorough reconstruction of southern society before the South could be safely readmitted to the Union. Everything he saw at the conventions convinced him that most white southerners still hated the national government and remained dangerously committed to the ideal of southern independence. Observing the southern people at large had convinced him that blacks and whites were almost completely at odds. Ex-slaves did not trust their white neighbors, who often cheated and abused them, and the freedpeople hoped for the national government's protection to enable them to participate fairly in a free-labor society. At the same time, unrepentant white southerners had been encouraged by President Andrew Johnson's generous pardons for Confederates and by his order overturning Sherman's famous Order No. 15, which had granted valuable abandoned lands in coastal South Carolina and Georgia to black persons working them. These white southerners were now counting on the president's leniency to permit them to reestablish firm control over the region without recognition of either the supremacy of the national government or the fundamental principle of equal rights.

This, Andrews insisted, must not be permitted to happen. If it did, he warned, angry white southerners would force their black neighbors into peonage and even might reestablish slavery by imprisoning black men for minor crimes and then taking advantage of the Thirteenth Amendment's clause permitting criminals to be enslaved. Andrews himself believed that black suffrage would permit freedmen to defend their interests and protect themselves from discriminatory legislation, and his effort to push his readers toward the same conclusion anticipated the Republican Party's later campaign to justify black suffrage.

Andrews was prescient in both his hopes and his fears. In 1867, Congress established the principle of black voting with the Military Reconstruction Act, and three years later, the ratification of the Fifteenth Amendment placed black suffrage into national law. Ultimately, southern constitutions and postwar legal codes bowed to the principle of equal rights and did not explicitly distinguish between the black and the white populations. But while the Republican Congress that met as Andrews finished his tour did not permit President Johnson to dictate the terms of southern reconstruction, much of what Andrews feared eventually came to pass. Most black southerners had been reduced to various forms of economic dependency by the turn of the century, and in many states by the 1890s, the convict leasing system, which allowed employers to "lease" prisoners from the state, replicated some of the worst features of slavery. Andrews, it seems, was an American Cassandra, permitted to see the future but unable to change it.

I have edited Andrews's long manuscript and abridged it enough to make it widely useful. Many of my deletions are not material. Andrews often qualified his statements with "I presume," and "I suppose"; I have cut almost all of these qualifiers. Their frequency also made me choose not to replace his words with ellipses because I quickly discovered that they spilled like pepper over every page, making the text difficult to follow. I have also deleted duplicate paragraphs that appeared in different chapters. More materially, I have edited Andrews's detailed accounts of debates in the southern constitutional conventions; scholars interested in the politics of those conventions should refer to an unedited version of the text. I have also trimmed discussions that paraphrased things Andrews said elsewhere, notably his descriptions of the prison camps. I have tried neither to lose any of Andrews's themes nor to distort his sense of their relative importance. In no case have I rearranged material or deleted words that would change the meaning of Andrews's sentences. The few words or sentences I had to add for continuity are bracketed, and in my additions I tried to use Andrews's own phrases taken from the deleted section. Finally, it should be noted that this account of the South uses the derogatory stereotypes and language of its time. It is preserved here to provide context for Andrews's work, not because it reflects the views of either the editor or the publisher.

Heather Cox Richardson

THE

SOUTH SINCE THE WAR

{ 1 }

Conditions and Prospects of the City
in Which Rebellion Began

CHARLESTON, SEPTEMBER 4, 1865

A CITY of ruins, of desolation, of vacant houses, of widowed women, of rotting wharves, of deserted ware-houses, of miles of grass-grown streets, of acres of pitiful and voiceful barrenness is Charleston, wherein Rebellion loftily reared its head five years ago, on whose beautiful promenade the fairest of cultured women gathered with passionate hearts to applaud the assault of ten thousand upon the little garrison of Fort Sumter! Be sure the pride of these men and women has been laid low. They have eaten wormwood, and their souls have worn sackcloth. Here is enough of woe and want and ruin and ravage to satisfy the most insatiate heart,—enough of sore humiliation and bitter overthrow to appease the desire of the most vengeful spirit.

Who kindled the fire of December 1861, whereby a third of the city was destroyed? No one knows. "It was de good Jesus hisself," said an old negro to me when I asked him the question,—"it was de Almighty Hand workin fru de man's hand." The people were never able to discover the agency of the fire; though no one doubts that it was the work of an incendiary,—"some man," say the ex-Rebels, "who wanted to do you Federals a good turn."

We never again can have the Charleston of the decade previous to the war. The beauty and pride of the city are as dead as the glories of Athens. Five millions of dollars could not restore the ruin of these four past years; and that sum is so far beyond the command of the city as to seem immeasurable wealth. One marks now how few young men there are, how generally the young women are dressed in black. The flower of their proud aristocracy is buried on scores of battle-fields.

The Charleston of 1875 will doubtless be proud in wealth and intellect and rich in grace and culture. Yet the place has not in itself recuperative power for such a result. If Northern capital and Northern energy do not come here the ruin must remain a ruin; and if this time five years [hence] finds here a handsome and thriving city, it will be the creation of New England, not necessarily the pattern of New England, for the influences from thence will be moulded by and interfused with those now existing here; but yet, in the essential fact, the creation of New England.

On the steamship by which I came from New York, leaving out the foreign element, our passengers were from Charleston and from Massachusetts. We had nearly as many Boston men as Charleston men. "I hate all you Yankees most heartily in a general sort of way," remarked [one] of these Southerners; "but I find you clever enough personally, and I expect it'll be a good thing for us to have you come down here with your money, though it'll go against the grain with us pretty badly."

There are many Northern men here already, though one cannot say that there is much Northern society, for the men are either without families or have left them at home. Walking out yesterday with a former Charlestonian,—a man who left here in the first year of the war and returned soon after our occupation of the city,—he pointed out to me the various "Northern houses"; and this appeared to include at least half the stores on each of the principal streets. "The presence of these men," said he, "was at first very distasteful to our people, and they are not liked any too well now; but we know they are doing a good work for the city."

I fell into some talk with him concerning the political situation, and found him of bitter spirit toward what he denominated "the infernal radicals." When I asked him what should be done, he answered: "You Northern people are making a great mistake in your treatment of the South. We are thoroughly whipped; we give up slavery forever; and now we want you to quit reproaching us. Let us back into the Union, and then come down here and help us build up the country."

To bring here the conveniences and comforts of our Northern civilization, no less than the Northern idea of right and wrong, justice and injustice, humanity and inhumanity, is the work ready for the hand of every New England man and woman who stands waiting.

Business is reviving slowly, though perhaps the more surely. The resident merchants are mostly at the bottom of the ladder of prosperity. They have idled away the summer in vain regrets for vanished hopes, and most of them are only just now beginning to wake to the new life. While they vacillate, Northern men are springing in with hands swift to catch opportunity. It pains me to see the apathy and indifference that so generally prevails; but the worst feature of the situation is, that so many young men are not only idle, but give no promise of being otherwise in the immediate future.

Many of the stores were injured by the shelling. A few of these have been repaired, and are now occupied,—very likely by Northern men. A couple of dozen, great and small, are now in process of repair; and scores stand with closed shutters or gaping doors and windows. The doubt as to the title of property, and the wise caution of the President in granting pardons, unquestionably has something to do with the stagnation so painfully apparent; but very much of it is due to the hesitating shiftlessness of the Southern merchant.

I queried of the returning merchants on the steamship how they were received in the North. An Augusta man complained that he could get no credit, and that there was a disposition to be grinding. Another told me that he asked for four months, was given three, and treated like a gentleman everywhere. One man said he had many friends in the North, and they all knew him for a thorough Rebel; he expected some taunts, but was courteously received, "even in Boston."

I judge that such of the merchants as first went North and settled with their creditors made more favorable terms than those who went later. If it be said that those were men who had loved the Union, while these are men who had not; that those were men of keen sense of commercial honor and integrity, while these are men who cared less for an adjustment; that those are men who deserved favors, while these are men who have forfeited all claim to special consideration,—if this be said, the pith of the matter will probably be hit so far as regards most of those who now complain of their reception.

Yet there are men who deserved better than they have received. These are they who, whatever their views on the questions at issue in the war, meant to pay all their debts. Most of them are men who loved the Union and hated secession. That there were such men in all parts of the State is beyond question. These men, having no faith in the Confederacy, put everything they could into cotton or rosin or turpentine,—hoping to save something from the general wreck they saw impending,—only to find in the end that they are scarcely richer than those who invested everything in Confederate bonds.

It is not clearly understood how thoroughly Sherman's army destroyed everything in its line of march,—destroyed it without questioning who suffered by the action. That this wholesale destruction was often without orders, does not change the fact of destruction. The Rebel leaders were, in their way, just as thorough as our army in destroying property. They did not burn houses and barns and fences as we did; but, during the last three months of the war, they burned immense quantities of cotton and rosin.

The action of the two armies put it out of the power of men to pay their debts. Thousands of men who were honest in purpose have lost everything but honor. The cotton with which they meant to pay their debts has been burned, and they are without other means. What is the part of wisdom in respect to such men? It certainly cannot be to strip them of the last remnant. Many of them will pay in whole or in part, if proper consideration be shown them. It is no question of favor to any one, but a pure question of business,—how shall the commercial relations of the two sections be reestablished?

Yet when all this is said in favor of one class of merchants, it must be added, that by far, a larger class is showing itself unworthy of anything but stringent measures. I asked of one of the leading merchants this morning, "Are your people generally disposed to settle their accounts?" His answer was, "Those who expect to continue business must of course do so." "How about the others?" I queried. "I'm afraid there isn't so much commercial honor as there should be," he replied. I am told of one firm which represented itself entirely ruined, when subsequent investigation showed that it had five thousand pounds sterling to its credit in Liverpool; and of another which offered only thirty cents on the dollar, when its property in New York alone will cover over seventy cents on the dollar of its entire indebtedness.

That Rebellion sapped the foundations of commercial integrity in the State is beyond question. That much of the Northern indebtedness will never be paid is also beyond question. What is desirable is, that creditors should become cognizant of all the facts in the case before fixing terms. For the rascal there is but one set of terms, for the honest man there should be every possible consideration.

The city is under military rule; but the iron hand rests very lightly. Soldiers do police duty, and there is some nine-o'clock regulation; but, so far as I can learn, anybody goes anywhere at all hours of the night without molestation. "There never was such good order here before," said an old colored man to me. The main street is swept twice a week, and all garbage is removed at sunrise. "If the Yankees was to stay here always and keep the city so clean, I don't reckon we'd have 'yellow jack' here anymore," was a remark I overheard on the street. "Now is de fust time sence I can 'mem'er when brack men was safe in de street af'er nightfall," stated the negro tailor in whose shop I sat an hour yesterday.

On the surface, Charleston is quiet and well behaved; and I do not doubt that the more intelligent citizens are wholly sincere in their expressions of a desire for peace and reunion. The city has been humbled as no other city has been; and I can't see how any man, after spending a few days here, can desire that it shall be further humiliated merely for revenge. Whether it has been humiliated enough for health is another thing. Said one of the Charlestonians on the boat, "You won't see the real sentiment of our people, for we are under military rule; we are whipped, and we are going to make the best of things; but we hate Massachusetts as much as we ever did." This idea of making the best of things is one I have heard from scores of persons. I find very few who make any special profession of

Unionism; but they are almost unanimous in declaring that they have no desire but to live as good and quiet citizens under the laws.

For the first two months of our occupancy of the city scarcely a white woman but those of the poorer classes was seen on the street, and very few were even seen at the windows and doors of the residences. That order of things is now, happily, changed. There doesn't yet appear to be as much freedom of appearance as would be natural; but very many of what are called the "first ladies" are to be seen shopping in the morning and promenading in the evening. They, much more than the men, have contemptuous motions for the negro soldiers; and scorn for Northern men is frequently apparent in the swing of their skirts when passing on the sidewalk.

One doesn't observe so much pleasantness and cheerfulness as would be agreeable; but the general demeanor is quite consonant with the general mourning costume. A stroller at sunset sees not a few pale and pensive-faced young women of exquisite beauty; and a rambler during the evening not unfrequently hears a strain of touching melody from the darkened parlor of some roomy old mansion, with now and then one of the ringing, passionate airs with which the Southern heart has been fired during the war.

Down in the churchyard of St. Philip's, one of the richest and most aristocratic of churches in this proud city, is a grave which every stranger is curious to see. It is the grave of the father of the Rebellion, and on the marble slab there is cut the one word,—

"CALHOUN."

This churchyard symbolizes the city of Charleston. Children and goats crawl through a convenient hole in the front wall, and play at will among the sunken graves and broken tombstones. There is everywhere a wealth of garbage and beef-bones. A mangy cur was slinking among the stones, and I found a hole three feet deep which he had dug at the foot of one of the graves. Children were quarrelling for flowers over one of the more recent mounds. The whole yard is grown up to weeds and brush, and the place is desolate and dreary as it well can be. Time was when South Carolina guarded this grave as a holy spot. Now it lies in ruin with her chief city.

{11}

Manners and Customs in the
Interior of South Carolina

ORANGEBURG C.H., SEPTEMBER 7, 1865

FROM Charleston to Orangeburg Court House is seventy-seven miles. Route, South Carolina Railroad. Time, seven and a half hours. Fare, five dollars. There is one train per day each way. Our train consisted of five freight-cars, the baggage-car, a box freight-car with seats for negroes, and one passenger-coach. Our one car was uncomfortably full when we started; but only eleven of the passengers came through.

"What sort of accommodations can I get at Orangeburg?" I asked of a friend in Charleston.

"You're not going to stop up there? O you can't do it! The accommodations are awful: push right on to Columbia."

I wasn't to be put down that way, for I had consulted a gazetteer, and learned that "Orangeburg is a pleasant and thriving town on the northeast bank of the north fork of the Edisto River. It is in the midst of a farming district, and is the center of a large cotton trade. Population two thousand seven hundred." That was before the war, and I knew the place had been partly burned; but I felt confident that my friend exaggerated.

We left the city at seven and a half o'clock in the morning [and] got here at three o'clock in the afternoon. There were five passengers with baggage. Twenty-five negroes crowded around us, and troubled the hot air with harsh clamor. "Give yer baggage here, sir." "Luf dis yer nig tote yer plun'er, Mass'r." "Tuk a hack up town, Mass'r?"

There was the man I wanted. He proved to be a strapping boy of thirteen or fourteen, who tossed my valise to the top of his head and strode off with both hands swinging.

I found the "hack" to be a rickety old short-boxed spring wagon, with two rough board seats, on the back one of which was a worn-out cushion, over both being a canvas supported on sticks nailed to each corner of the box. This establishment was drawn by a scrawny lame mule, and we were seventeen minutes in accomplishing the half-mile up to the hotel.

I was a little distrustful about the hotel; and learning from the driver that boarders were sometimes taken at another house, I stopped there and asked the white girl of fifteen, whom I found on the piazza, if they could give me meals and lodgings for about three days. She thought they could, but would call her mother. So much of the house and grounds as I could see presented an inviting appearance, and I indulged in visions of a pleasant chamber and many dreamy hours on the broad piazza. Presently "mother" appeared. She was a plump woman of thirty-three, perhaps.

"Yes, sir, we have a couple of rooms, and we sometimes take transient boarders," said she.

"I am stopping three or four days in town, and had much rather be at a pleasant private house than at the hotel," I said.

"Are you a Yankee or a Southerner?"

"O, a Yankee, of course," I answered, smiling, though I saw breakers ahead.

"No Yankee stops here! Good day, sir!" And she turned and walked into the house.

The negro boy, who stood with my valise on his head, volunteered the remark, "Haf to go to de hotel, sah"; and I followed him back to the "hack."

At the "hotel" was a negro boy washing the steps from the piazza into the basement. I told him what I wanted. He would call the Missus. She was somewhere in the lower part of the house; and after her head came into sight above the level of the floor on which I stood, she stopped and washed her hands in the dirty water with which the boy had just finished scrubbing the stairway, smoothing her hair with them and wiping them on her apron.

I made known my desires, paid my driver his charge of seventy-five cents, and was shown by Robert—him of the wash-rag and scrubbing-brush—to room No. 8, the figure being at least a foot in length and rudely done in white chalk.

The room is about fourteen feet square, has one window fronting the southeast, and is in the third story. Lath and plaster there are not. The partitions are of rough unmatched pine, with strips of cloth over the larger cracks, and a cheap wall paper on the boards all round. The ceiling is also of wood, and was once painted white, but is now, like the wall paper, of a smoky yellow. The paper is much broken by the shrinkage of the boards, and large patches of it have been torn off in a dozen places. The walls and ceiling are handsomely decorated with wasps' mud nests and sooty-branched cobwebs. The bed is a dirty cotton mattress in an old-fashioned high-post bedstead. There are no sheets, and in fact nothing but a cotton-stuffed pillow and a calico spread. This establishment is the abode of a numerous and industrious colony of [bedbugs], to whom I nightly pay a heavy blood tribute. Beside the bed there is one cane-seat chair, a seven-by-ten looking-glass, and a three-foot-square and breast-high plain pine table, on which are a cracked wash-bowl and a handleless and noseless water-pitcher, to which I prevailed on Robert to add a cracked tumbler. In the window are six sound panes of glass, four cracked ones, and the remnants of five panes more. I suppose I should add also several very social and handsome mice, and a lively swarm of uncommonly large mosquitoes.

The house has three stories and a basement dining-room. The first and second floors have broad piazzas on each side of the house. The first floor has four rooms, and the second and third have five each. Robert says mine is the best on the upper floor. In the so-called drawing-room there are three old chairs, a rickety center-table, a sort of writing-desk, the wreck of a piano, and several pieces of carpet. In the dining-room are two twelve-foot plain pine tables, and twenty-three chairs of five different patterns. The table-spread of this noon was the same we had on the evening of my arrival, three days ago, and it was horribly filthy then. The dining-room itself is airy and clean. In the hall, and pasted to the wall, are a set of "rules for the hotel," twice as long and formidable as any I ever saw in any Northern house, whether first or fourth class.

The hotel grounds consist of a large yard, the gate of which is always open, and within which all the stray stock of the town has free ramble. At the bottom of the broad steps on the upper side of the house is a large mud-puddle, in which dogs and hogs alternately wallow, there being at least five of the former and nine of the latter running about. The dogs are gaunt and wolfish,—the hogs are half-grown. There is in the yard about everything one can name, except grass and cleanliness,—bits of wood and crockery, scraps of old iron, wisps of straw and fodder, old rags, broken bottles, sticks, stones, bones, hoofs, horns, nails, etc. The barber throws the sweepings of his shop on one side of the house, and the cook is equally free with her slops on the other side.

The "Missus" is the head of the house. She is tall and angular, with a complexion sallow to the last degree of sallowness, eyes in which there is neither life nor hope, hair which I am sure has not felt either comb or brush during my stay. Her dress is a greasy calico to which she sometimes adds an apron which isn't more repulsive only because it can't be. She is a type of women, thank God, without counterpart in the North. She goes about the house in a shuffling, shambling manner, with the cry "Robert—Robert—Robert," or "'Manda—'Manda—'Manda," always on her tongue. During meals she stands at the head of the table, and serves out the allowance of tea or coffee, and sugar and milk, with an unending string of such talk as this: "Robert, tend the hominy"; "Gal, get the gemman's cup and sasser"; "'Manda, mind the flies"; "Goodness gracious, nigger, why don't ye pass them biled eggs." She complains, in whining, listless fashion, to everybody, about the "niggers," telling how idle, shiftless, and ungrateful they are. She has a husband, who takes special pains to inform everybody that he hasn't anything to do with the hotel; and whose sole occupations, so far as I can see, are smoking, complaining about "the niggers," and doctoring a poor old blind, spavined horse.

The genius of the house is Robert, who is trim, pert, wide-awake; who picks out a Northern man with unerring instinct and is always ready and prompt to serve him; but who is forever out of the way, or very busy when that cry of "Robert— Ro-be-rt—R-o-b-e-r-t" shuffles up through the house. "*She* talk about the niggers,— bah!" he exclaims, as he goes about his work.

The table is wretched. The tea, eggs, and waffles are the only articles even passably good. Bread and biscuit are alike sour and leaden, and all the meats are swimming in strong fat. The cook is a large and raw-boned negro woman, who is aided by the "Missus," the boy Robert, and the girl 'Manda. I suppose Sarah cooks quite to the satisfaction of her mistress; but I doubt if it would be possible for any Northern girl, even with twenty years of training, to make of herself a cook so utterly bad as Sarah is.

The general management of the house, I scarcely need add, is hopelessly miserable. Everything is forever at sixes-and-sevens, and the knowledge of where anything was yesterday gives not the least indication of its present whereabouts. The establishment is unclean [and] shiftless. And the traveler's bill is three dollars and a half per day!

I have not drawn this picture except for a purpose. I hear, already, in this Southern trip, a great deal about the superior civilization of the South. This hotel is a part of its outgrowth. Orangeburg was a place of twenty-five hundred to three thousand inhabitants. It is the county seat. The place is midway between Charleston and the capital. Let any one consider what is the character of the only public house in any Northern town of the same size, and similarly situated, and then the quality of this boasted Southern civilization will be apparent. Nor can it be said that the war is responsible for the condition of things here, for the house was full from the beginning, and has not suffered any loss from either army. It could not receive a week's support in any community of any State from Maine to the Rocky Mountains. Yet here it lives on and on, year after year, a witness for Southern civilization. Let us call things by their right names,—then shall we say *Southern barbarism.*

{III}

The Situation with Respect to the Negro

ORANGEBURG C.H., SEPTEMBER 9, 1865

RECALLING how persistently the whites of this State have claimed, for twenty-five years, to be the negro's special friends, and seeing how these whites treat this poor black, one cannot help praying that he may be saved from his friends in future. Yet this cannot be. Talk never so eloquently as any one may of colonization or deportation, the inexorable fact remains, that the negro is in South Carolina, and must remain here till God pleases to call him away. The problem involved in his future must be met on the soil of which he is native; and any attempt to solve it elsewhere will be futile.

The work of the North, in respect to South Carolina, is twofold: the white man must be taught what the negro's rights are, and the negro must be taught to wait patiently and wisely for the full recognition of those rights.

The city negro and the country negro are as much unlike as two races. So, too, the city white man and the country white man differ much from each other. The latter, however, is just what he chooses to be, while the country negro is just what slavery and his late owners have made him. Tell me what you will derogatory of the country negro, and very likely I shall assent to most of the language you use. He is very often, and perhaps generally, idle, vicious, improvident, negligent, and unfit to care well for his interests. He is a hard, coarse, unlovely fact, and no amount of idealizing can make him otherwise. Yet he is worth quite as much as the average country white.

The negro is made by his master. I even doubt if he is, in many cases, morally responsible for his acts. With him there is no theft when he takes small property from the white; there is, of course, crime in the eye of the law, but there is none in the design or consciousness of the negro. Has not every day of his existence taught him that robbery is no crime? So, too, if this uncouth freedman, just from the plantation, falls into a passion and half kills somebody you will utterly fail in your effort to make him understand that he has committed a grave crime. Has not his whole life been witness of just such right and lawful outrage on humanity? This language may indicate a bad state of affairs; but it points out certain conditions with respect to the negro that must be taken into account by any one undertaking to deal with him as a freedman.

Everybody talks about the negro, at all hours of the day, and under all circumstances. One might in truth say—using the elegant language of opposition orators in Congress—that "the people have got nigger on the brain." Let conversation begin where it will, it ends with Sambo.

I scarcely talk with any white man who fails to tell me how anxious many of the negroes are to return to their old homes. In coming up from Charleston I heard of not less than eleven in this condition, and mention has been made to me here in Orangeburg of at least a score. The first curious circumstance is, that none of them are allowed to return; and the second is, that I can't find any of those desirous of returning. I have asked over a hundred negroes here and in Charleston if they wanted to go back and live with their old masters as slaves, or if they knew any negro who did desire to return to that condition, and I have yet to find one who hesitates an instant in answering "No."

They deserve better treatment than they get at our hands in Orangeburg; and I am told that what I see here is a forecast of what I shall see in all parts of the State. In the intent of Congress, the Freedmen's Bureau stands as the next friend of the blacks; practically, it appears to stand too often as their next enemy. That General Saxton is their good friend does not need to be asserted. Very likely the district commissioners under him are wise and humane men, and unquestionably the general regulations for the State are meant to secure justice to the freedmen.

The trouble arises from the fact that it is impossible for the State Commissioner or his chief deputies to personally know all, or even half, their various local agents. Take the case right in hand. Head-quarters for this district are thirty miles below here; and the ranking officer of the bureau has agents in at least forty different towns, the majority of whom are lieutenants from the volunteer forces of the army. They are detailed for this duty by the military commander of the post or the district. As the post garrisons are constantly changing, there may be a new agent of the bureau once a month in each town of the district; and the probabilities are that half the aggregate number on duty at any given time are wholly unfit for the work entrusted to them.

The acting agent here at present is a lieutenant from a New York regiment. He has been on duty several weeks. Yet he never has seen the district commissioner of the bureau. His duties are to examine, and approve or disapprove, all contracts between the planters and the negroes, and to hear and determine all cases of complaint or grievance arising between the negroes themselves, or between the whites and the negroes. He treats me courteously, but he has no sympathy with the poor and lowly; and his ideas of justice are [that] might makes right.

He doesn't really intend to outrage the rights of the negroes, but he has very little idea that they have any rights except such as the planters choose to give them. His position is a difficult one; and he brings to it a head muddled with liquor, a rough and coarse manner, a dictatorial and impatient temper, a most remarkable ability for cursing, and a hearty contempt for "the whole d——n pack o' niggers."

I found Charleston full of country negroes. Whites of all classes concur in saying that there is a general impression throughout the back districts that lands are to be given the freed people on the sea-coast; and this, I am told, renders them uneasy and unreliable as plantation hands. Whites also concur in saying that they will not work.

"I lost sixteen niggers," said a Charleston gentleman, "but I don't mind it, for they were always a nuisance, and you'll find them so in less than a year." I asked, as usual, what they are now doing. Two or three of the men went into the army, one of the women had gone North as a cook, another is chambermaid on a steamer, and he found three of the men at work on one wharf the other day. "But," said I, laughing, "I thought the free negro wouldn't work." "O well, this is only a temporary state of affairs, and they'll all be idle before winter; and I don't look for nothing else when cold weather comes but to have them all asking me to take them back; but I sha'n't do it. I wouldn't give ten cents apiece for them."

Many of the private soldiers on duty here tell me that the planters generally overreach the negroes on every possible occasion; and my observation tends to confirm this assertion. Coming up in the cars from Charleston I had for seatmate one of the delegates to the Convention which meets at Columbia next week. He was very courteous and agreeable, past middle age, and late the owner of twenty-two negroes. He was good enough to instruct me in respect to the character of the negro. "You Northern people are utterly mistaken in supposing anything can be done with these negroes in a free condition. They can't be governed except with the whip. Now on my plantation there wasn't much whipping, say once a fortnight; but the negroes knew they would be whipped if they didn't behave themselves, and the fear of the lash kept them in good order." He went on to explain what a good home they always had; laying stress on the fact that they never were obliged to think for themselves, but were always tenderly cared for, both in health and sickness; "and yet these niggers all left me the day after the Federals got into Charleston!"

Yesterday morning while I sat in the office of the agent of the Freedmen's Bureau there came in, with a score of other men, a planter living in this district, some sixteen miles from town. He had a woeful tale of an assault upon himself by one of his "niggers,"—"a boy who I broughten up, and who's allers had a good home down ter my place." The dreadful assault consisted in throwing a hatchet at the white man by one of a crowd of negroes who were having a dispute among themselves, and suddenly discovered, in the early evening, somebody sneaking along by the fence. The boy said it wasn't a hatchet, but a bit of brick; and added, that the man was so far away that no one could tell whether he was white or black, and that he didn't throw the brick till after he called out and told the man to go away. I followed the negro out after he had received his lecture from the officer, and had some talk with him. "D——n him," said he, referring to his employer, "he never done nufin all his d——n life but beat me and kick me and knock me down; an' I hopes I git eben with him some day."

Riding with an ex-Confederate major, we stopped at a house for water. The owner of the property, which was a very handsome one, was absent; and it was in charge of a dozen negroes, former slaves of the proprietor.

"Now here," said the late officer, "here is a place where the negroes always had the pleasantest sort of a home,—everything to eat and drink and wear, and a most kind master and mistress."

Pompey, aged about twelve, came to bring us the water.

"Pompey," said the Major, "Pompey, how do you like your freedom?"

He hung his head, and answered, "Dun know, mawssa."

"O, well, speak right out; don't be afraid; tell us just how it is now," said he again.

Whereupon Pompey: "Likes to be free man, sah; but we's all workin' on yer like we did afore."

"That's right, Pompey," said I; "keep on working; don't be a lazy boy."

"It won't do," said the Major; "he'll grow up idle and impudent and worthless, like all the rest."

"No, sah," answered Pompey, "I's free nigger now, and I's goin' to work."

There is much talk among the country people about a rising of the blacks. A planter who lives twelve miles to the west, told me that it was believed in his neighborhood that they had guns and pistols hid in the timber, and were organizing to use them. His ideas were not very clear about the matter; but he appeared to think they would make serious trouble after the crops are gathered. Another man, living in Union district, told the company, with evident pleasure, that they'd been able to keep control of the niggers up to his section till 'bout three weeks ago; he 'lowed thar'd bin some lickin', but no more'n was good fur the fellows. Now the Federals had come in, and the negroes were in a state of glad excitement, and everybody feared there would be bloody business right away.

A thing that much shocks me is the prevalent indifference to the negro's fate and life. Three fourths of the native whites consider him a nuisance, and would gladly be rid of his presence, even at the expense of his existence. And this in face of the fact that all the planters are complaining about the insufficiency of labor. Thus, in Charleston, a merchant told me, with relishing detail, that, soon after the order against wearing Confederate buttons, a negro soldier doing duty in the city halted a young man, informed him of the regulations, and told him that if he was seen on the street again wearing the obnoxious buttons, he would probably be arrested; whereupon the scion of the Charleston aristocracy whipped out a large knife, seized the negro by the beard, and cut his throat. The soldier died in about a week; but nothing had been done with the man who killed him. All the talk of men about the hotel indicates that it is held to be an evidence of smartness, rather than otherwise, to kill a freedman; and I have not found a man here who seems to believe that it is a sin against Divine law.

{ IV }

Scenes in the Track of Sherman's Army

COLUMBIA, SEPTEMBER 12, 1865

THE WAR was a long time in reaching South Carolina, but there was vengeance in its very breath when it did come,—wrath that blasted everything it touched. Columbia is in the heart of Destruction. You go north thirty-two miles, and find the end of one railroad; southeast thirty miles, and find the end of another; south forty-five miles, and find the end of a third; southwest fifty miles, and meet a fourth; and northwest twenty-nine miles, and find the end of still another. Sherman came in here, the papers used to say, to break up the railroad system of the seaboard States of the Confederacy. He did his work so thoroughly that half a dozen years will nothing more than begin to repair the damage.

The railway section of the route from Charleston lies mostly either in a pine barren or a pine swamp, though after passing Branchville we came into a more open and rolling country with occasional signs of life. Yet we could not anywhere after we left the immediate vicinity of the city, see much indication of either work or existence. The trim and handsome railway stations of the North, the little towns strung like beads on an iron string, are unknown here. In the whole seventy-seven miles there are but two towns that make any impression on the mind of a stranger, and even these are small and unimportant places. Elsewhere we stopped, as it appeared, whenever the train-men pleased,—the "station" sometimes existing only in the consciousness of the engineer and conductor.

I found the railroad in better condition than I supposed that I should. The rails are very much worn, but the roadbed is in fair order for nearly the entire distance. The freight-cars seemed in passably good repair; but the passenger-coaches were the most wretched I ever saw,—old, filthy, and rickety. On our train was one new feature,—a colored man and his wife, whose duty it was to wait on the passengers.

I came up from Orangeburg, forty-five miles, by "stage," an old spring-covered market-wagon, drawn by three jaded horses and driven by Sam, freedman, late slave,—of the race not able to take care of themselves, yet caring, week in and week out, for the horses and interests of his employer as faithfully and intelligently as any white man could. There were six of us passengers, and we paid ten dollars each passage-money. We left Orangeburg at four, P.M.; drove eight miles; supped by the roadside; drove all night; lunched at sunrise by a muddy brook; and reached Columbia and breakfast at eleven, A.M., thankful that we had not broken down at midnight, and had met only two or three minor accidents. Thirty-two miles of the forty-five lie in such heavy and deep sand that no team can travel faster than at a moderate walk. For the other thirteen miles the road is something better, though even there it is the exception and not the rule to trot your mules. The river here was formerly spanned by an elegant and expensive bridge, but the foolish Rebels burned it; and the crossing of the Congaree is now effected in a ferry, the style and management of which would disgrace any backwoods settlement of the West.

The "Shermanizing process," as an ex-Rebel colonel jocosely called it, has been complete everywhere. To say that the people hate that officer is to put a fact in very mild terms. They pronounce his spirit "infernal," "atrocious," "cowardly," "devilish," and would unquestionably use stronger terms if they were to be had. I have been told by dozens of men that he couldn't walk up the main street of Columbia in the daytime without being shot.

We rode over the road where the army marched. Now and then we found solitary chimneys, but, on the whole, comparatively few houses were burned, and some of those were fired, it is believed, by persons from the Rebel army or from the neighboring locality. The fences did not escape so well, and most of the planters have had these to build during the summer.

There is a great scarcity of stock of all kinds. What was left by the Rebel conscription officers was freely appropriated by Sherman's army, and the people really find considerable difficulty not less in living than in traveling. Milk, formerly an article much in use, can only be had now in limited quantities: even at the hotels we have more meals without than with it. There are more mules than horses; and the animals are all in ill condition and give evidence of severe overwork.

Columbia was doubtless once the gem of the State. It is as regularly laid out as a checker-board,—the squares being of uniform length and breadth and the streets of uniform width. What with its broad streets, beautiful shade-trees, handsome lawns, extensive gardens, and wealth of flowers, it must have been a delightful place of residence. No South Carolinian with whom I have spoken hesitates an instant in declaring that it was the most beautiful city on the continent; and they charge its destruction directly to General Sherman.

It is now a wilderness of ruins. Its heart is but a mass of blackened chimneys and crumbling walls. Two thirds of the buildings in the place were burned, including everything in the business portion. Not a store, office, or shop escaped; and for a distance of three-fourths of a mile on each of twelve streets there was not a building left. "They destroyed everything which the most infernal Yankee ingenuity could devise means to destroy," said one gentleman to me. The residence portion generally escaped conflagration, though houses were burned in all sections except the extreme northeastern. Every public building was destroyed, except the new and unfinished state-house. The poverty of this people is so deep that there is no probability that it can be finished, according to the original design, during this generation at least.

I find a commendable spirit of enterprise, though, of course, it is enterprise on a small scale, and the enterprise of stern necessity. The work of clearing away the ruins is going on, not rapidly or extensively, to be sure, but many small houses of the cheaper sort are going up. Yet this generation will not ever again see the beautiful city of a year ago. Old men and despondent men say it can never be rebuilt. "We shall have to give it up to the Yankees, I reckon," said one of two gentlemen conversing near me this morning. "Give it up!" said the other; "they've already moved in and taken possession without asking our leave."

Of course there is very little business doing yet. I judge that twenty thousand dollars would buy the whole stock of dry goods, groceries, clothing, &c. in store. The small change of the place is made in shinplasters, printed on most miserable paper; and issued by the various businessmen, "redeemable in United States currency when presented in sums of two dollars and upwards." "Greenbacks" and national currency notes pass without question in the city, but are looked upon with suspicion by the country people. "Having lost a great deal by one sort of paper, we propose to be careful now," they say. Occasionally one sees a State bank-note, but they pass for only from twenty-five to sixty or sixty-five cents on the dollar. There is none of the Confederate money in circulation; though I judge that considerable quantities of it are hoarded up in the belief that things will somehow take such a turn as to one day give it value.

The women who consider it essential to salvation to snub or insult Union officers and soldiers at every possible opportunity do not seem as numerous as they appeared to be in Charleston and indeed marriages between soldiers and women of the middle class are not uncommon; while I notice that several very elegant ladies do not seem at all averse to the attentions of the gentlemen of shoulder-straps. Can these things be, and not overcome the latent fire of Rebellion?

In coming up from Charleston I learned a great many things. One man insisted with much vehemence that cotton is king, and that a resolution on the part of the South not to sell any for a year would bring the North upon its knees. Another man was very confident that the North depends entirely upon the cotton trade for a living, and that a failure to get at least one million bales before spring will bring a tremendous financial crash.

Another gravely asserted that a state of anarchy prevails in the entire North; that the returned soldiers are plundering and butchering indiscriminately; and that there has recently been a most bloody riot in Boston.

Another, and a man of much apparent intelligence, informed me that the negroes have an organized military force in all sections of the State, and are almost certain to rise and massacre the whites about Christmas time.

A woman, evidently from the country districts, stated that there had been a rising of the negroes in Maryland; that a great many whites had been killed; and that some considerable portion of Baltimore and many of the plantations had been seized by the negroes.

And, finally, an elderly gentleman who represented himself as a cotton factor, declared that there would be a terrible civil war in the North within two years; that England would compel the repudiation of our National debt and the assumption of the Confederate debt.

The people of the central part of the State are poor, wretchedly poor; for the war not only swept away their stock and the material resources of their plantations, but also all money, stocks, and bonds, and generally left nothing that can be sold for money but cotton, and only a small proportion of the landholders have any of that. There is for most of them nothing but the beginning anew of life, on the strictest personal economy and a small amount of money borrowed in the city.

It would be a benefit of hundreds of millions of dollars if the North could be made to practice half the economy which poverty forces upon this people.

They are full of ignorance and prejudices, but they want peace and quiet, and seem not badly disposed toward the general government. Individuals there are who rant and rave and feed on fire as in the old days, but another war is a thing beyond the possibilities of time. So far as any fear of that is concerned we may treat this State as we please,—hold it as a conquered province or restore it at once to full communion in the sisterhood of States. The war spirit is gone, and no fury can re-enliven it.

The spirit of oppression still exists, however, and military authority cannot be withdrawn till the relation between employer and employed is put upon a better basis. On the one hand, the negro in the country districts must be made to understand that freedom does not mean idleness. On the other hand, the late master should specially be made to understand that the spirit of slavery must go to the grave with the thing itself. It will not be an easy work to teach either class its chief lesson. We must have patience,—patience, and faith that neither faints nor falters.

{ V }

Organization of the South Carolina Convention

COLUMBIA, SEPTEMBER 13, 1865

IN OBEDIENCE to the proclamation of Provisional Governor Perry, the delegates of the people of South Carolina assembled at noon today in State Convention for the purpose of repealing the ordinance of secession and remodeling the State Constitution. The Convention met in the Baptist Church, in which the Secession Convention of 1860 originally assembled; though that, after two sessions, adjourned to Charleston, where the ordinance of secession was passed. That Convention numbered 168 members. This has but 121,—that is, the proclamation fixes this as the number. In point of fact, however, the number present will not probably exceed 115; for it is known that three parishes held no elections, while Bishop Lynch, of Charleston, is in Europe, and Wade Hampton is not expected here. There were present today 101 delegates.

Five parishes are entirely unrepresented. There were two or three precincts in each of three districts where, so far as can be learned, there was no voting; but there is not even a pretence on the part of anybody that there was anywhere in the State any interference with the elections by the military. The Convention is the free choice of the people.

[Three] at least of the delegates have national reputation,—James L. Orr, late Federal representative, ex-Rebel colonel, and ex-Confederate senator; F. W. Pickens, late Federal representative, and the first Secession governor; and Samuel McGowan, late major-general in the Rebel army, and one of the bravest officers this State gave the Confederacy. One delegate, James Farrow, was four years a member of the Rebel Congress. Twelve others were delegates in the Secession Convention.

The people have cut loose from many of their old leaders, and others of that class have found their graves since the war began; but there are perhaps a score of delegates whose faces are more or less familiar to persons who have attended the sessions of the South Carolina General Assembly any time within a dozen or fifteen years. Of those who were officers in the Rebel army there are not less than twenty-five or thirty, including at least four generals and six colonels.

For the rest, three fourths of the delegates have titles,—captain, major, colonel, judge. It is the fashion of the South, as of the West, I suppose. There are a dozen young men, and about the same number of very old men; but otherwise they range mostly from forty-five to fifty-five years of age. It isn't by any means a prepossessing body. The average Southern head doesn't show near as much intellectual force and vigor as the average Northern head; and the beauty of the South is solely in the faces of its young women,—half of it at least in the faces of its mulatto and quadroon girls. A few of the delegates are clad wholly, and very many of them partly, in homespun. Many coats show Confederate buttons,—from the necessity of poverty rather than the choice of disloyalty, I judge. Many of the members are rough, ignorant country fellows, and the Convention will be managed by less than a score of delegates. The difference between the two classes of delegates—those who lead and those who are led—is much greater than could exist in any Northern body of the same numbers; not that the one class is any way superior to the best class of a Northern State, but that the other class is almost immeasurably inferior. Half these men are so deficient in capacity and knowledge that scarcely one of them could by any possibility get into a New England convention.

That, in the stress of war, South Carolina should implore to be made a colony of Great Britain does not now seem half so strange to me as it did nine months ago. The whole under-current of her society [is] set toward monarchical institutions. Everybody dreads popular elections; dozens of delegates have said to me that it isn't well to allow the people to elect their own rulers. Many of these delegates were elected, not because they represented the will of the parish or district, but because they represented the will of some great family. It was the English system reproduced here, with scarcely a variation. It was not a republican form of government; but, more than that, it was not, is not, and will not soon be, a republican community. Say the leaders,—men who, personally, are easy, agreeable, and abundant in courtesies to the stranger,—"it will not do to put power in the hands of the common people."

The delegates were called to order [and] Franklin J. Moses, of Sumter District, was made temporary chairman. The Convention at once proceeded to business.

The election of a permanent President was called; and [of five candidates], Hon. David L. Wardlaw, of Abbeville District, was declared elected. He is a small and kindly mannered gentleman, well along in years, and one of the judges of the Court of Sessions and Common Pleas. He has served many years in the General Assembly, and has often been elected speaker of the lower House. He was one of the Union men of the fall of 1860, accepted the decree of the State, was a delegate in the Secession Convention and chairman of the Committee on Revision of the Constitution. His home is in the northwestern part of the State. His remarks on taking his seat were very brief. He hoped the Convention would soon restore the State to the Union; and urged the delegates to do their duty in sincere and earnest spirit, that Peace and her blessings might once more abide in the whole land.

It seems that the fire-eaters are not yet all dead, for as soon as a committee had been appointed to wait on the Governor and tell him the Convention was ready for business, Mr. A. P. Aldrich, a delegate from the district of Barnwell, in the central part of the State, and in which there was a slave population of 17,400 to a white population of 12,000, offered the following resolution:

> "*Resolved,* That, under the present extraordinary circumstances, it is both wise and politic to accept the condition in which we are placed; to endure patiently the evils which we cannot avert or correct; and to await calmly the time and opportunity to effect our deliverance from unconstitutional rule."

In this resolution there is, of course, the very essence of Rebellion. More than one delegate saw the point, and a sharp running debate took place, in which the mover was opposed to four or five of the ablest men in the Convention.

Ex-Governor Pickens tersely said: "It doesn't become South Carolina to strut or bluster or threat or swagger; she points to her burned cities, her desolate plantations, her mourning hearths, her unnumbered graves, her widows and her orphans, her own torn and bleeding body,—this, she says, is the work of war; and she bids us bind up her wounds and pour in the oil of peace!"

Mr. Aldrich replied, that he was not satisfied with the condition of things; that there had always been in the country an unconstitutional Republican party and a constitutional Democratic party; that the South had always acted with the latter, and that her hope and salvation lies only in an immediate union with the Democratic party of the North; that the State is now ground under the iron heel of a military despotism, repugnant alike to her people and the spirit of the Constitution; that for his part, he would not submit without an indignant protest; that he hoped for the speedy overthrow of the party now in power; and that he meant just what the resolution says,—to be quiet till we are strong enough, through the aid of the Democratic party of the North, to get a constitutional government.

Mr. McGowan, of Abbeville District, late major-general in the Confederate service, and bearing the marks of several wounds, denounced the resolution in a brief speech, which brought hearty applause from the delegates and the galleries. "I protest with all the earnestness of my nature against this resolution. It is not true that South Carolina carries a dagger underneath her vestments; not true that she stands with obedient words on her lips and disloyal spirit in her heart. The work she begins today she begins in good faith. She was the first to secede, and she fought what she believed to be the good fight with all her energies of heart and head and hand and material resources. Whatever may have been charged against her, no one has ever dared charge her with double-dealing. She is so poor that she has lost everything, but honor. Pass this resolution, and you rob her of her honor, and bow in the dust the head of every one of her true sons. She has seen enough of war; in God's name I demand that she shall not be made to appear as if she still coveted fire and sword."

The Aldrich resolution [was] refused even the poor privilege of going to the printer or a committee.

COLUMBIA, SEPTEMBER 14, 1865

The Provisional Governor sent in his message to the Convention at noon. It was read by his son, who is one of the delegates, and its reading occupied about twenty-five minutes. What it has to say on the subjects of slavery and negro suffrage appears in the following paragraphs:

> "Under the war-making power, the military authorities of the United States have abolished slavery in all of the seceding States. The oath you have solemnly taken to 'abide by and faithfully support all laws and proclamations which have been made during the existing Rebellion, with refer-

ence to the emancipation of slaves,' requires you, in good faith, to abolish
slavery in your new or amended Constitution. The express terms on which
your pardons have issued stipulate that you shall never again own or em-
ploy slave labor. Moreover, it is impossible for South Carolina ever to regain
her civil rights and be restored to the Union till she voluntarily abolishes
slavery, and declares, by an organic law, that neither 'slavery nor involuntary servitude, except as a punishment for crime, whereof the party shall
have been duly convicted' shall ever again exist within the limits of the
State. Until this is done we shall be kept under military rule.

"The radical Republican party North are looking with great interest to
the action of the Southern States in reference to negro suffrage; and whilst
they admit that a man should be able to read and write and have a property qualification in order to vote, yet they contend that there should be
no distinction between voters on account of color. They forget that this is
a white man's government, and intended for white men only; and that the
Supreme Court of the United States has decided that the negro is not an
American citizen under the Federal Constitution. To extend universal suffrage to the 'freedmen' in their present ignorant and degraded condition
would be little less than folly and madness. It would be giving to the man
of wealth and large landed possessions in the State a most undue influence
in all elections. He would be enabled to march to the polls with his two or
three hundred 'freedmen' as employees, voting as he directed, and control
all elections. The poor white men in the election districts would have no influence, or their influence would be overpowered by one man of large
landed estate. That each and every State of the Union has the unquestioned
right of deciding for herself who shall exercise the right of suffrage is beyond all dispute. You will settle this grave question as the interest and honor
of the State demand."

{VI}

The Leaders of the Convention
and the Repeal of the Secession Ordinance

COLUMBIA, SEPTEMBER 16, 1865

I T IS THE reproach of South Carolina abroad that her Constitution is less popular and republican in its provisions than that of any other State in the Union,"
says Provisional Governor Perry in his message to the Convention. If the sea-coast
members could have their way this Constitution would scarcely be popularized
in the least. The Convention could easily have done what they desired in less than
four days. The upper-country members, however, have from the first said that no
one need look for an adjournment under two weeks, unless the coast delegates
gave them their way without much debate.

In fact there is as much difference of sentiment between the two classes of delegates as though one class came from this State and the other from Indiana. There
has been a conflict going on between the two sections of the State for thirty years,
which rages now with the more vigor because outside difficulties have compelled
unity of action for the past five years. It grows mainly out of what is called the
parish system of representation, whereby the legislation from the beginning of the
century has been controlled by the city of Charleston, and has been in the hands of
the members of the General Assembly from that city and county and three other
counties. Under that system, which originated soon after the settlement of the
State, and was endorsed in the formation of the original and all subsequent State
Constitutions, half a dozen counties on the sea-coast cast as many votes in the
Legislature as the balance of the State. In the early days of the State's existence,
when nearly all the wealth and population were in these counties, the system
worked no serious injustice; but of late years it has proved injurious to the interests
of the up-country, and has kept up an ever-increasing feud between the two sections. Originating chiefly in this cause, there are now a dozen different questions
of State policy in respect to which there is more or less bitterness of feeling between the two classes of delegates. Those from the up-country are determined that
a full and fair settlement shall now be had. "We have drawn the sword and thrown
away the scabbard," said one of them on the floor of the Convention. "I verily believe our people will fight on it," said another to me last evening.

The record of the first four days of the Convention proves that the delegates are generally well disposed toward the government. That they have fallen in love with President Johnson or with the Union party of the North, or with those whom everybody down here styles Yankees, no one even pretends. They are subdued Rebels, some of them are even conquered Rebels; but few are anything more. They have a very wholesome fear of the government, and a very wholesome respect for the power of the North. The whole crew of pestilent fellows does not number over a dozen. There are also about the same number who go to the other extreme, and are disgustingly servile and abject. With these exceptions, the delegates are generally frank, plainspoken men, owning that the South is beaten, desiring nothing so much as long years of peace, acquiescent in the overthrow of slavery, and mostly disposed to make the best they can of the freedman, but utterly without faith in his capacity to labor and take care of himself; anxious to be again in full fellowship in the Union, and ardently longing for the reopening of trade with the North.

The chief man in the Convention is Benjamin F. Perry, Provisional Governor of the State; not that he himself is on the list of delegates, but that his position, in the peculiar circumstances of the hour, makes his word and wish of very unusual significance. The executive office has been removed here for the time being; the rooms of the Governor at the hotel are full at all hours when the Convention is not in session; the Governor sometimes spends the whole day at the Convention; his son and private secretary is one of the delegates; it is an almost every-hour occurrence, in the debates, that the question is asked, "Is that view approved by the Provisional Governor?" or that the remark is made, "I think we had better consult the Governor first." He is a tall, large, straight man, who carries a gold-headed cane and wears gold-bowed spectacles. He looks like a man of power, and has an inoffensively self-satisfied appearance.

James L. Orr has a great deal to do with things, and is at the head of one of the eight standing committees,—that on the Executive Department of the Constitution. His public life is well known. He was considered one of the coolest-headed and soundest-hearted Union men in the State five years ago this summer; but, for all that, he was one of the leading members in the Secession Convention, and in the Rebel Senate during the whole existence of the Confederate government. Now he is one of the leading reconstructionists. Many of the delegates distrust him,—they say he changes from one side to the other too easily. Yet he has much influence in the body. He is over six feet in height, and of at least one hundred and ninety pounds weight. His face is florid and rubicund. He is ready and forcible in debate, and carries himself with a very democratic air.

Francis W. Pickens, ex-Governor of the "Independent State of South Carolina," as it was called at his inauguration, is a battered old wreck,—short and squarely built, with a large and squarish head, a broad and flat face, a small and insignificant nose, round and piggish eyes, and broad forehead. His voice is feeble, his manner colloquial, his air jaunty. He is third on Orr's committee, and is on his feet oftener than any other man. He eats his humble pie with some ostentation, and is solicitous that nothing shall be done to offend His Excellency the Provisional Governor, or His Excellency the President of the United States. His course and language are such as to call from delegates in private conversation frequent reference to the day when Fort Sumter surrendered, and to the speech he made on that occasion,— "The Independent State of South Carolina has humbled the flag that no nation on earth ever before humbled; it has been brought down in obedience to the behest of a sovereign State, on whose soil it shall never again be raised," &c.

A. P. Aldrich is the leader of the impracticable, unconquered element,—the men who are sullen or spiteful, the untamed fire-eaters. They number less than a dozen, though there are a dozen more who would like to follow his lead. He was a quartermaster in the Rebel army. "He'd feel differently if he'd met as many of your troops on the battle-field as I have," said one of the delegates, when I asked him about Mr. Aldrich. He is noticeable for his long and tumbled hair, and his long full whisker[s] and moustache. He is able and forcible in debate, and "a real good fellow," personally.

The first ordinance introduced into the Convention was the following:

> "We, the delegates of the people of the State of South Carolina, in General Convention met, do ordain, That the ordinance passed in Convention, December 20, 1860, withdrawing this State from the Federal Union, be, and the same hereby is, repealed."

This ordinance came from ex-Governor Pickens, on the first day of the session, and on the second day he called it up for immediate action, with the single remark that he thought it the first business for the Convention, in order that the country might see that South Carolina is in earnest in her profession of a desire to conform to the results of the war.

Rev. Dr. Boyce, President of the Baptist Theological Seminary at [Greenville], thought the ordinance insufficient in terms for the desired purpose; and at his suggestion it was sent to a special committee of three.

On the following clay, the third of the session, it was reported, by Governor Pickens, in this form:

"We, the people of the State of South Carolina, by our delegates in
Convention met, do ordain, That the ordinance adopted by us in
Convention on the twentieth day of December, in the year of our Lord one
thousand eight hundred and sixty, entitled, an 'Ordinance to dissolve the
union between the State of South Carolina and other States united with
her under the compact entitled "The Constitution of the United States of
America,"' is hereby repealed."

Immediately after the report was read, it was [passed] without debate[:] Yeas
105, Nays 3.

And so, on the 15th of September, 1865, the State of South Carolina, after nearly
five years of rebellious absence, in which she has very nigh destroyed herself, comes
home. There are no cheers or huzzas, no salvos of artillery and clanging of glad
bells, as when she set up the proud palmetto standard,—only suggestive silence.

The three nays were the delegates from Barnwell District. Mr. Aldrich explained, that, as the conquering party had carried on the war for four years on the
theory that the States were not out of the Union, he couldn't see any sense in repealing an ordinance of secession. His tone and manner were those of petty spite.

Immediately after the passage of this ordinance, there came to light the following very remarkable resolutions, which were introduced by William Wallace,
one of the delegates from this city:

"*Whereas,* By the fortunes of war, our former noble and beloved Chief
Magistrate, Jefferson Davis, is now languishing in prison, awaiting his trial
for treason; and

"*Whereas,* The fanatics of the North, not satisfied with the widespread ruin
and desolation which they have caused, are shrieking for his blood;—

"*Resolved,* That it is the paramount duty of South Carolina, who led the
way in our late struggle for independence, and for which struggle he is
now suffering, to use every lawful means in her power to avert the doom
which threatens him.

"*Resolved,* That to this end, a deputation of members of this body be sent to
the city of Washington, in behalf of the people of South Carolina, to ask of
His Excellency the President of the United States to extend to the
Honorable Jefferson Davis that clemency which he has shown to us, who
are equally the sharers of his guilt, if guilt there be, and which is accomplishing so much toward restoring the peace and harmony of the Union."

The fluttering began before the reading of these resolutions was finished, and several members were on their feet at once. Mr. Dudley got the floor, and quietly suggested that this was scarcely appropriate language for a body which had just returned the State to the Union, and was relying on the generosity of the North for full admission again into the sisterhood of States. Two or three other delegates made remarks to the same effect; and Mr. Wallace then accepted as a substitute a simple resolution appointing a committee to memorialize the President in favor of the pardon of Davis, Stephens, Magrath, and Trenholm.

During the four days of the Convention a large number of resolutions have been presented and referred to the appropriate committees. They are indicative of a disposition to make some sweeping and radical changes in the Constitution.

{ V I I }

Action of the Convention on the Slavery Question

COLUMBIA, SEPTEMBER 19, 1865

THERE were two things which, in a national point of view, it was essential that this Convention should do as soon as possible,—declare the abolition of slavery, and repeal the Ordinance of Secession. Ex-Governor Pickens saw this so clearly, that he introduced an ordinance, on the first day of the session, to accomplish both these things. I have already related how the Ordinance of Secession was repealed. The slavery question was settled today by the adoption of a clause for the Constitution.

There are two or three delegates who will not admit that slavery is overthrown, hoping, I judge, that the general government will one day be glad to settle the question by paying a certain compensation for the sake of quiet. There are two or three more who think the whole matter ought to be referred to the Legislature. The great body, however, were ready on the opening day of the session to take action upon it. Propositions embracing clauses for the new Constitution were therefore submitted by several members, as follows:

By ex-Governor Pickens: "The fortunes of war, together with the proclamations of the President of the United States and the generals in the field commanding, having decided that domestic slavery is abolished, therefore, under the circumstances, we acquiesce in said proclamations, and do hereby ordain implicit obedience to the Constitution of the United States and all laws made in pursuance thereof."

By William H. Perry, of Greenville District: "Slavery and involuntary servitude are hereby abolished in South Carolina, and shall not again exist in the State except as a punishment for crime whereof the party shall have been duly convicted."

These paragraphs show in what form the subject originally presented itself to the minds of such members as were specially interested in it. Five of seven delegates deemed it necessary to recite the manner in which the overthrow of slavery was accomplished. It seemed to an outsider like myself that there was no essential difference between these two propositions. The action of the Convention, however, was to prove that the happiness of a people, not to say the preservation of a State, may depend upon a nice observance of the distinction betwixt tweedledee and tweedledum.

The Committee on Amendments to the Constitution [proposed]: "Slavery having ceased to exist in this State, it shall not hereafter be permitted or reestablished."

First on the calendar, [though], was a report from the Committee on Ordinances, [which read]: "Slavery having actually been destroyed by the military force of the United States, it is hereby declared that slavery no longer exists in the State of South Carolina, and that all persons heretofore held as slaves are free; and it is further declared and ordained, that slavery shall not again be established in this State; provided, however, that the General Assembly may adjudge involuntary servitude as a punishment for crime whereof the party shall have been duly convicted."

Mr. L. W. R. Blair, a delegate from Kershaw District, a very tall and very homely man, with remarkably retreating forehead, an immense and immensely red nose, [and] no chin to speak of, whose misfortune it is to be ignorant of the fact that he lives in the nineteenth century, and also of the fact that there has been a great war, and who sublimely ignores all such things as emancipation proclamations, Congressional enactments, military orders, etc., gravely rose in the back part of the church and proposed the following as a substitute for the Ordinance Committee's report:

"Resolved, That the question of slavery and all questions connected therewith be referred to the Legislature of the State, whose duty it shall be to consult with the proper authorities of the United States, and learn the intention of the government in respect to the institution of slavery; and authority is hereby given to the Legislature to make laws applicable to colored persons alone, and shall enact such laws as are needful to prevent negroes and persons of color from engaging in any business or pursuit but such as involves manual labor, mining, road-making, agriculture, and the production of naval stores."

Mr. Blair was willing, he said, to give up slavery, but he was not willing to do it without some guaranties. He had great confidence in the President, but none in the party now in power in the North. That party was already clamoring for concessions which the South could never grant. Every true son of South Carolina would die rather than grant the right of suffrage to the negroes of the State. He was opposed to making a full surrender of slavery till the State had some guaranty that such surrender would bring full restoration of political rights to her people. Moreover, might it not hereafter appear that some pecuniary compensation would be adjudged as due to the South for the destruction of her slave property? He would not take any action till the whole subject had been considered in all its bearings, and the Legislature was the only body that could do that.

Mr. Dawkins, of Union District, chairman of the committee which made the report, said the committee had endeavored to choose language which would accomplish the end he believed all men desired, and would be as little distasteful as possible to the people of the State. The ordinance simply declared that slavery had been destroyed by the military force of the United States. Nothing was said as to the right of that force to thus act; and, on the other hand, there was nothing in the ordinance to preclude any man or the State from asking compensation. He was wholly opposed to the proposed amendment. It is impracticable. We shall have no Legislature till we declare slavery abolished. However it may displease any of us to admit it, we are at the mercy of the authorities at Washington. We have been beaten in the contest, and we can have no government but such as is agreeable to them. We are now under military rule. True, we have a provisional governor, but he is, after all, only a military governor with another name. I am glad that the military authorities are disposed to concede to us every possible advantage consistent with their views of public safety, and to see that there is a prospect of the speedy restoration to us of our civil rights. But I am confident that such restoration will only follow prompt and graceful acquiescence on our part in the action of the authorities on the slavery question.

Mr. Orr said he would accept the report of the committee. The election of Mr. Lincoln, five years ago, was taken by the people of the South as evidence that the people of the North were not disposed to allow them what they believed to be their rights. The State seceded. We went out to save slavery. Other States followed the example of South Carolina. The Confederacy was formed, and slavery was

made the corner-stone of the new government. The result was what any man ought
to have expected: it was not reasonable to suppose the North would allow a disrup-
tion of the Federal Union without war. The whole matter was referred to that tri-
bunal. It was decided against us. Shall we try the issue again? The institution of
slavery is hopelessly destroyed. Now the conqueror makes his terms,—abolish
slavery by your own enactment, declare that it shall never be re-established, treat
your freedpeople well, popularize your Constitution. Are these terms hard? Might
they not have been much harder? Are they not, on the whole, very liberal? We are
to retain nearly all our civil rights and most of our property other than slaves:
might we not have fared much worse? It may be hard in our judgment to concede
these terms; but what is it in their judgment? If we fail to do our duty according to
their judgment, what will be the consequence? Do we covet military rule as the
chief good? There have been states in which military governors made it their duty,
if not their pleasure, to break the spirit of the people: are we anxious for such authority over us? If we reject the boon now offered us,—and I tell you it is a boon for
a subjugated people to be allowed the restoration of most of their personal and
political rights,—if we reject this, what then? Let gentlemen consider. I refer you
to the speech of the Honorable Thaddeus Stevens, recently made. I know him as
a man of great ability, and as a leader among the radicals. He proposes to confiscate
the property of seventy thousand leading men in the South to pay the national
war debt; and if the radicals were in power, I don't doubt but that some such policy would prevail. We seem to forget where we stand; we forget that we made the
war and have been beaten; we forget that our conquerors have the right to dictate
terms to us. And I tell you, it is to the good favor of Andrew Johnson that our terms
are no worse,—nay, are so liberal. He is the dike between us and the waves of
Northern fanaticism. Let us be wise men. Let us strengthen his hands by graceful acquiescence in the results of the war. So shall we strengthen ourselves, and
soon bring again to our loved State the blessings of peace and civil rule.

Mr. Dunovant, of Edgefield District, denied that the war was on the question
of slavery. It was waged in the interests of State rights. We were whipped, and the
issue on that question is forever settled. But I deny the right of any one to dictate
to us in respect to matters not in issue in the war. I deny that slavery is abolished.
The relation of master and slave is disrupted, but that relation returns as soon as
you restore the civil authority. I will not admit that we are rightfully under military
rule; the President has no warrant in the Constitution for keeping a standing army
among us, and I will not submit my will to him in this matter. I don't mean to be
understood as opposing the abolition of slavery, but I think it is the business of

the Legislature and not of this Convention.

Mr. McGowan, of Abbeville District, said the Convention was called to declare the abolition of slavery. The war left us in the dust,—it put us at the mercy of the North. The conqueror had the right to prescribe the conditions of our restoration to civil and political rights. These conditions I accept in all fidelity, with one condition in return,—that we are hereafter to be left political masters in the State. We must be left free to legislate for all the people here, white or black, otherwise I would accept martyrdom before I would acquiesce in the demand made upon us respecting slavery.

The Blair substitute was tabled with only two or three dissenting voices.

A two hours' wrangle then ensued as to the phraseology which should be adopted to gain the desired end. The Convention was determined that it should appear in the Constitution that slavery was not abolished by the voluntary action of the State.

Judge Lesesne, of Charleston, would not stultify the State of South Carolina by leaving it possible for any one to suppose that, after four years of such devastating war as we have known, she did this thing of her own accord.

Mr. Dudley could see no necessity for attempting to say through what agency slavery had been lost. He thought there was no occasion to use language that might be offensive.

Colonel Rion said he did all he could for the South while the war lasted, and was now thoroughly whipped; yet he was not afraid to declare the historical fact that slavery had been destroyed by the Federal government.

Mr. Melton declared that the Constitution is not intended as a text-book on history.

General McGowan asked if there were ten men in the Convention who would favor the abolition of slavery as an independent proposition aside from the events of the last four years.

Mr. Dudley responded that there was need to remind the Convention that they were suppliants for mercy, though he believed that proper self-respect, aside from all other consideration, demanded that they should abstain from the use of needless words.

The Convention was determined, however, to have the so-called "historical fact," and finally, by a vote of 59 to 43, agreed upon the following language:

> "The slaves in South Carolina having been emancipated by the action of the United States authorities, neither slavery nor involuntary servi-

tude, except as a punishment for crime whereof the party shall have been duly convicted, shall ever be re-established in this State."

The occasion—the abolition of slavery in South Carolina—had lost its superficial interest, because of the senseless wrangle over a form of words. The fine audience of the early part of the day had wearied and gone away. Only the delegates and a few spectators whom nothing could disgust into forgetfulness of the import of the work in hand remained. The dull afternoon was fading into a dark and dreary evening.

Finally the vote on the main question—the passage of this clause as Sect. 11 of Article IX in the new Constitution—was called. The vote stood 98 Yeas and 8 Nays.

So the fact was accomplished, and South Carolina stepped into the ranks alongside Massachusetts,—joining hands with her to bear aloft the banner of freedom,—bowing to the logic of events rather than that of free speech,—convinced by cannon-balls rather than by arguments; yet, under the circumstances, turning from the things of slavery to the things of liberty with commendable grace.

At the gateway of the church, as I came out, I met an old negro woman,—neat, prim, deferential. "Well, Auntie," said I, "the Convention has just said there shall be no more slavery in South Carolina." "Is dat ar true, Massa?" "True as the Bible, Auntie." "Wall now tank de Lord fur dat ar. I's dun gone pray fur dat dese yer forty years. I's hope he come in my time; but 'pears like he idle by de way. Now he come, and I's ready fur my ole man in de hebens. Tank de Lord, tank de Lord!"

{VIII}

The Basis of Representation

COLUMBIA, SEPTEMBER 21, 1865

WHAT is the true basis of representation in a republican form of government? This is the profound question over which the Convention has today spent a session of about seven hours. Everybody expected a struggle when this matter was reached, for the first day's resolutions showed a very prevalent desire to at least discuss the subject. Yet that the negro could be brought into that discussion seemed never to enter the minds of even some of the oldest and ablest delegates; and his introduction into the assembly this afternoon was followed by scenes both ludicrous and humiliating.

The basis of representation in the Legislature of this State has always been unusual, not to say complex. In the House, half the members were apportioned on the
basis of white population, and the other half on the value of all property, slaves
included. In the Senate, the area occupied by the major part of the slave population
received not less than three times as great a representation as the same area mainly
occupied by white population.

The committee to which the legislative article of the Constitution was referred
reported in favor of retaining the old basis of representation in the House, and of
changing the system of representation in the Senate.

The debate today was upon that section fixing the basis of representation in
the House; but such range was given it that it embraced the whole question of the
true basis of republican representation.

Mr. James L. Orr advocated this basis of representation,—white population in
the House, and white population and taxation in the Senate.

Mr. Cadwallader Jones, of York, wanted the basis of representation in the
Senate to be property, and in the House white population.

Mr. Robert Dozier, of Georgetown, proposed that the basis for representation
in the House should be property, and all the inhabitants, white and black.

This proposition dragged the poor negro right in by the ears, and the discussion
upon the right and expediency of admitting the negro into the body politic as an
element of representation ran through five long hours. It was no proposition to
allow him to vote, or even to allow any one to vote in his name; but simply a proposition to allow ten thousand whites living in a district where there are twenty-five
thousand negroes, to send as many representatives to the General Assembly as are
sent by twenty-five thousand whites living in a district with only ten thousand negroes.

The discovery was soon made that it would ultimately give the control of the
House to the low-country. Sectional feeling was at once enlisted for or against it;
and some of the up-country members made furious speeches against it, while
some of the Charleston delegation endeavored to win votes by appealing to the
magnanimity of up-country friends.

The bearings of the amendment upon the question of Congressional representation were also of much interest. Mr. Dozier himself argued that as negroes are an
element in the Congressional representation, it would be inconsistent to exclude
them from the body politic as represented in the State Legislature. On what ground
can we ask Congress, said he, to allow us four representatives now, and probably
seven after the next census, when our present white population gives us but two,

if we deny the right of the negroes to be represented in our local government? This argument was used by a dozen or more delegates. On the other hand, it was argued that there is no connection between the two matters; that the apportionment of four representatives—two for whites and two for three fifths of the negroes—must stand till after the next census; and that then the whole population, black and white, must be counted in assigning the representation.

The just claim of the negro to representation was advocated by a few members, including three or four of the ablest delegates in the Convention. It was argued that he had heretofore been represented in both houses,—directly as property in the lower house, and indirectly through the parish system in the upper house; and that it would be unjust to now cut him off from all representation. On the other hand, it was held that if the negro be admitted into the body politic at all, he must be given a vote. "This is but the entering wedge of negro suffrage," said Colonel Rion, "and I oppose it as such." "Adopt this amendment," said General McGowan, "and you pass the political power of the State over into the hands of the negro." "This is a white man's government," echoed Dr. Boyce.

The Convention took a recess till this evening, during which the discussion among the eighty or ninety delegates at the hotel was kept up with even more intensity than on the floor of the church. As soon as the Convention came together after the recess, [it returned to the question].

Judge Edward Frost, of Charleston, an aged gentleman of high standing, [made] the only creditable speech of the whole debate. He said the chief error of the South had been that she was not favorably disposed toward discussion of questions affecting the welfare and relations of the negro; and he was very sorry to see such undue sensitiveness upon the subject in this debate. "The events of the last four or five years have settled a great many things, and one of the things thus settled is that South Carolina is not omnipotent. We cannot have our own way in everything. We assumed that we knew all there was to know about the negro; and that where the world differed from us in opinion, it was wrong. Events would seem to indicate that we were wrong in at least some very important particulars. The world insisted that the negro is a man, and we have been brought to that acknowledgment. The world now demands that we fix the political status of the negro; and we must consider the question, whether it does or does not please us so to do. The old relation of master and slave is abolished. What new relation shall be given to the negro? We cannot ignore him. We cannot give him suffrage,—he is not fit to exercise it; but if the community in which he lives has a representation on his account, he will be in one sense represented. Gentlemen talk about his ignorance, and plead that as a bar to his admission into the body politic in any form. He is ignorant; I grant you that; but how came he so? Did he ever have a chance to choose his station in life? Was it not an act of insubordination for him to ask instruction? We may as well admit it first as last,—slavery made him what he is. Ignorance is the natural and inevitable result of our former system of labor. Let us do the negro justice: he is mainly what we of the ruling class made him. In one sense, we still stand in the relation of master to him, as the educated and intelligent are always the masters of the ignorant and feebleminded. It is our duty to consider his condition and help him to become a better man. Take away his ignorance, and you take away some of the burdens and some of the dangers of society. If no higher considerations will move us, let us consult our own material interests, and give him a fair chance. Treat him as a free man, as an element of prosperity in the State, and you soon make him such an element. We cannot any more maintain the opinion of South Carolina against the world. The negro has civil rights, as we all have; political rights he will be slow to ask for, I think, if we treat him fairly. His natural temperament is such that he shuns responsibility. Fully and freely concede his rights as a man, and he will be willing you should make his laws. I have not known him to ask for suffrage except when influenced by bad or designing men. We must concede that the negro is a free man, having civil rights, having property rights, having the right to be represented in the body politic, and unquestionably destined at no very distant day to have political rights."

"Why, he's a Black Republican!" exclaimed a man who sat in the seat with me at the church, while Judge Frost spoke. "Well, he's the only one who has spoken," said I, in reply. "Yes, and d——n him, he's the only one here, I reckon," continued my seat-mate.

The pending amendment—originally offered by Mr. Dozier—went to the table by 75 to 24.

The basis of representation in the lower house of the General Assembly stands as it always has since the original Constitution was adopted,—white population and taxation.

{ I X }

The Great Contest between the Upper and Lower Sections of South Carolina

COLUMBIA, SEPTEMBER 23, 1865

THERE has long been strife between the two sections of the State locally known as the "up-country" and the "low-country." Just how it originated, and by what jealousies it has been fed, probably no one could satisfactorily explain to an outsider. A dozen gentlemen have volunteered to elucidate the whole matter for me, and having heard both parties, I am convinced that no one really comprehends it. That there is ill-blood is patent enough. "I hate the saints of New England in reference to national affairs, and I hate the saints of the low-country in State affairs," said one of the up-country men to me yesterday. The hostility of the one section to the other five years ago was scarcely less than the State hostility to the general government; and the up-country now charges the low-country with having brought on the war.

The opening day of the session of this Convention found the political power of the State where it always had been,—in the low-country. The second day's session made it apparent to everybody that the up-country had marshaled its forces for a struggle, and meant to take the reins of government into its own hands. The end of this, the tenth day's session, sees the low-country at the feet of the strong and innovating up-country.

The origin of the parish system of representation in the upper house of the General Assembly dates with the formation of the original Constitution. Theoretically the senatorial representation was one from each district. Practically this was the case only in the upper and back portions of the State. The sea-coast districts were divided into parishes, and each parish was entitled to a senator, even if it contained no more than one hundred voters. Therefore, as some of the districts were divided into several parishes, a few districts on the coast,—Charleston, Colleton, and Beaufort, for instance,—if they did not have an actual majority in the Senate, certainly were strong enough to control the vote of that body; and they did so control it, generally for their own benefit. This parish system has been an oppressive burden on the State, of which it seemed impossible to get rid; for it could not be reached except through an amendment to the Constitution, and a convention for that purpose could only be called by the Legislature; and legislatures so virtuous that they readily vote themselves and their constituents out of power are not numerous. A convention, therefore, called by other authority than the Legislature, and without restriction as to the questions upon which it should act, was to the up-country partial compensation for the overthrow of the Confederacy. The issue of the elections there was "death to the parishes."

The only hope for the parishes was that the Convention would limit itself to a narrow range of action. The quarrel between the two sections came to the surface on the question of appointing the standing committees. Few committees meant narrow range of work and a speedy adjournment; and of course that view was supported by the sea-coast members. Many committees meant a thorough revision of the Constitution, and that was what the up-country members wanted. The latter carried the day, after a good deal of skirmishing, getting eight committees.

On the fourth day, the three low-country members of the Committee on the Executive Department made a report, stating, "We are of the opinion that the Convention, not having been called according to the forms of the Constitution of the State, can only exercise such powers as are absolutely necessary to restore the State to the Union with a Constitution republican in its character; and that any fundamental change in the said Constitution is not within the exercise of such powers." This was signed by Messrs. Aldrich of Barnwell District, and Conner and Simonton of Charleston; but these names were not enough to secure the acquiescence of the Convention in the opinion, and the report went to the table.

On the seventh day, the parish system was brought out for trial, condemnation, and execution; and the work was thoroughly accomplished. The question came up indirectly, on a proposition to give the city of Charleston two senators instead of one, as recommended by the Legislative Committee. The debate was long and earnest, and called out the ablest men of the Convention. The merits and demerits of the parish system were discussed in all their length and breadth, and the amendment [allowing only one senator] was finally adopted by a vote of 78 to 30.

In this vote was the grand defeat of the low-country. It swept away the system which made South Carolina the leader in the Rebellion, and in a moment transferred the political power of the State from the conservative hands of the low-country to the progressive hands of the up-country. This fact is of grave importance. The parishes governed the State in the one sole interest of slavery; and though the up-country will not govern it just yet in the interest of freedom, the proportion of negroes in the low-country districts is very much larger than in the up-country districts. The inhabitants of the low-country are of direct foreign descent, with monarchical and aristocratic tendencies; those of the up-country came originally from the North, and have republican and democratic tendencies.

The people of the State are wretchedly poor; but on the evening of the day in which this great victory was gained, I heard, in the rooms of the leading up-country delegates, a lively and long-continued fire of champagne corks.

George D. Tilman, a man of immense frame and very considerable abilities, genial and off-hand, who has lived in South America and California, and now hails from Edgefield District, who has served six years in the State Legislature for honor, and two years in the State Penitentiary for manslaughter,—this man, who makes friends with everybody, and at whom the "gentlemen," so called, of the low-country, affect to sneer, is a genuine Red Republican in his disregard of what are called "ancient rights and privileges." Sitting with great blue-gray eyes that seem always half asleep, he is always alert and wide-awake; slouching along with a rolling gait, he is careful and earnest; utterly wanting in the power of oratory or rhetoric, he has made more points than any other member of the Convention, and has carried all of them but one. He is the leader of the up-country delegates. He has been from the first the restless and untiring and good-humored enemy of the parish system, or, to use his own phrase, "the Chinese conservatism of Charleston." His object has been, and still is, to cripple the power of the low-country in every possible way.

On the eighth day, the low-country attempted by strategy to recover what it had lost in a shoulder-to-shoulder contest. Power through control of the Senate had been taken away, but power might be regained through control of the House. Therefore the sea-coast delegates generally supported the scheme for including three fifths of the blacks as an element of population in establishing the basis of representation. There were various times during the day when it seemed as if the low-country would win the battle; but the final vote showed its strength to be relatively about the same as in the struggle on the parish representation. This was its last effort.

On the tenth day, Tilman smote the routed enemy once more; he called it "reaping the just fruits of victory." His blow came in the form of an amendment to the Constitution, providing that, after 1869, no district in the State shall have more than twelve representatives. This was aimed at the city of Charleston, which now has twenty. The low-country was exhausted, and the amendment was adopted after a brief debate by 61 to 43.

The up-country has won in every point it made. Hereafter it will be responsible for the legislation of the State. The first Legislature will be elected under the old system. Thenceforward the new Constitution will govern; under it South Carolina cannot be the haughty and exclusive creature she was in ante-Rebellion days.

{X}

Minor Work of the State Convention

COLUMBIA, SEPTEMBER 26, 1865

THE convention has about finished its labors. I have reported its action in regard to all the more important questions, and have now to speak of but three subjects,—first, the miscellaneous business; second, the attitude of the Convention toward the general government; third, its talk and action in respect to the freedmen.

The Convention can scarcely be said to have amended the old Constitution; it has, rather, been making a new one. The election of Presidential electors is taken from the Legislature and given to the people. The election of Governor is taken from the Legislature and given to the people; the term of office is changed from two years to four years; he is declared ineligible for two consecutive terms; and the fifteen hundred pounds sterling free-hold qualification is abolished. The questions involved in the action on this section have been much canvassed by the people, and there is a considerable body in the Convention strongly opposed to the change. It was, however, so well understood that this was one of the particulars in which the President required that a more republican form should be given the Constitution, that the section passed without a division.

The property qualification—a freehold of three hundred pounds sterling for State senator; a freehold of five hundred acres of land and ten negroes, or a real estate valued at one hundred and fifty pounds sterling, for State representative; and a freehold of fifty acres, or a town lot, for a voter—has been abolished. The first-mentioned charge prevailed by a vote of 59 to 47; the others were made without division.

The effort to provide that no man should vote unless he could read the Constitution was, of course, a failure. "It would disfranchise at least a quarter of the people," said one cautious delegate. "More than that," said another. "I have known a grand jury within the last ten years of which only one man could write his name," echoed a third.

The debate on the Aldrich resolution, on the Jeff Davis pardon-memorial ques-

tion, on the slavery clause of the Constitution, and on the Congressional-represen-
tation ordinance, showed very clearly the political standing of the delegates. They
have no special love for the Union, but war has taught them a hearty respect for
the United States. They talk very little and very mildly about State rights, but not
one of them was able to see that the secession ordinance should have been annulled
instead of repealed,—for does not a mere repeal amount to a practical reaffirmation
of the right to secede? However, the question never will be of special consequence
so far as this State is concerned; for the whole Confederacy, late and so-called,
could not coerce her into again taking up arms against the general government.

The temper of the Convention toward the negro is very far from being what
the friends of humanity desire. The delegates, generally speaking, are probably better disposed toward him than the majority of their constituents, for they represent
the best intelligence of their respective districts; but even their views, as a body,
are extremely narrow and supremely selfish, not to add of the most fancifully
fearful character.

Governor Perry began the hue and cry against the poor African in [his] message. True, he says slavery is gone, but he rails against the negro soldiers, actually
has the face to quote the Dred Scott decision against the negro's right to citizenship,
and indorses the absurd falsehood that "this is a white man's government, intended
for white men." This sort of talk can do no possible good to any living man, and
is productive of nothing but increased ill-feeling between the two classes of people
who now occupy the State, and must continue to occupy it during this generation
at least.

There has been a great deal of this white-man's-government talk, in face of the
fact that the negroes in the State number one third more than the whites, and the
fact that they have almost to a man desired the success of the Union in the war, and
the further fact that the whites of some sections are asking that soldiers may be
kept in the State to protect them.

Obnoxious and short-sighted as the Convention is in this regard, there is something still worse. "The negro is an animal whose character the North seems utterly unable to comprehend," said one of the sea-coast delegates. In that phrase
lies the key of the Convention's sentiment,—the negro is an animal; a higher sort
of animal, to be sure, than the dog or the horse, but, after all, an animal. Even so
taciturn a man as Mr. Chancellor Inglis felt it necessary to rise and gravely argue
that the negro is a human being, has the right of life and protection by the laws,
and must receive attention even from men who make Constitutions. The
Convention treats him like an animal whose presence is endured, but is no way

desirable. Individual men there are who sincerely sympathize with him in his anomalous and trying condition,—men who contemplate the labor question with as much grave anxiety as any man in the North; but these are the exception, not the rule, and they only serve to make more hideous the general average sentiment and political judgment.

Regarding negro evidence and negro suffrage: Mr. Mayor Macbeth, of Charleston, introduced the ordinance giving the negro the right to testify. "I consider it proper," said he, "that the Convention should act on this subject. It is not a question as to our opinion on the propriety of allowing him to thus give evidence, but a question of retaining military courts or permitting him to appear in our civil courts." No word for the inherent right of every man to be heard in his own defense, but simply a cold question of policy. Yet even this raised a storm. A bare majority allowed it to go to the Committee on the Judiciary Department, from which it finally came with a recommendation that it be passed, in the following form:

> "We, the people of the State of South Carolina, by our delegates in Convention met, do declare and ordain . . . that hereafter colored persons shall be permitted to testify in all the courts of this State, in all cases where the rights of person or of property of persons of that class are involved."

The report was received with a great deal of disfavor; and it was called up and ordered before the freedmen's code commission, which the Governor has been instructed to appoint, [since] only three delegates [were] prepared to vote at once for the ordinance.

"How long do you suppose the agitation of the question of negro suffrage can be staved off in the State?" said I to an up-country delegate of high standing. "Till the taking of the next census, I hope," he answered. "Do you really believe it can be kept down five years?" "Yes," was his final reply. That the Convention would show any favor to the question no one really expected. Even South Carolina, with all her desolation, doesn't yet fully comprehend that there has been a deluge. I did hope, however, that I should find half a dozen men at least in favor of giving suffrage to some negroes, as many more in favor of abolishing the barbaric color qualification, and still as many more ready to admit that suffrage would be the right of the negro as soon as he is able to use it understandingly. Vain hope! If there are six men who so much as admit that it will probably be right or politic to give suffrage to any negro of their State within ten years, four of them must be among the thirty or thirty-five whose views I have not personally learned.

A score of delegates have taken occasion to express themselves in very strong terms as forever opposed to negro suffrage in any form, no matter what the limitations. Mr. Dawkins said the freed people were clearly unfit to vote now, and he didn't think the Convention was called upon to express any opinion as to what they might be in the future. Mr. Orr would vote against giving them the ballot, but presumed the fanatics of the North would not be content till they had secured it for them. Mr. Dozier would accept negro suffrage when the moral and intellectual character of the negro has been so elevated that he is fit to take part in government. Mr. Inglis said negroes were no more qualified to vote now than children. Judge Frost said the negro was to be treated as a human being who had civil rights, and unquestionably would, at no very distant day, have political rights. Mr. Melton, of Chesterfield, said the idea that South Carolina might, within five years, admit negro suffrage, was not more startling than the idea would have been, in 1860, that she would within five years declare slavery abolished. With these six exceptions, no expression has been made indicating any degree of tolerance for the bare idea of negro suffrage.

The Convention adjourned *sine die* on the evening of September 27th, having held a session of thirteen days. On the last day of the session the Convention unanimously passed the following resolution:

> "*Resolved* by the delegates of the people of South Carolina in Convention assembled, That we indorse the administration of President Johnson, that we cordially approve the mode of pacification proposed by him, and that we will co-operate with him in the wise measures he has inaugurated for securing the peace and prosperity of the whole Union."

{ XI }

Summary of Four Weeks' Observations

CHESTER, SEPTEMBER 27, 1865

THE ATTITUDE of the people toward the general government is, on the whole, pretty good. I am convinced that even in South Carolina there was a large body of men who never favored Rebellion. State pride is what ruined South Carolina. Men went into Rebellion, not of original choice, but because the State did. These men said in the Convention to those who talked of conservatism in changes of the Constitution,—"O yes, if you'd had a little more conservatism five years ago, we shouldn't be where we are now."

It is already a question how the State got into Rebellion. "Disunion was born in the parishes," said an up-country delegate. "The political leaders carried us out," said one merchant to me. "The Rebellion came from the people," urged a man who had been a colonel in the Rebel army. "We went out to save slavery," argued Delegate Orr. "We went out for State rights," responded Delegate Dunovant. It is a good sign that the people are found thus differing. "I begin to wonder, after all," said the mayor of one of the back cities, "if there was any real occasion for us to go to war." "You never'll get us into another war till we know exactly what it is about," remarked a Columbia merchant.

There has been a great deal said about the existence of a sullen spirit in the State. I have not discovered much of it. The famous Aldrich resolution was an expression in that direction; but in a body of one hundred and ten members, it found but four supporters. I don't believe there are many Aldrich men in the State. The people have a prejudice against the Yankees, and they avow it without any hesitation. They exult in their war record. "We believed we were right," they say, "and we fought for our belief with every possible energy." Various sorts of pride abound, but any widespread sullenness or obstinacy in respect to the general government there is not, unless my observation is wholly at fault.

Some persons like to show why the Rebel defeat occurred. Delegate Youmans implies Davis was obstinate in keeping men in power whom the people would not trust; an up-country merchant with whom I traveled thought the negroes were not used as they ought to have been; a Charleston cotton-factor assured me the officials starved the army; a Columbia lady was confident victory went with us because we had the old banner, which the South might just as well have claimed; while an Orangeburg miss of eighteen or twenty said the Yankees had been deceitful and were able to fight a great deal better than the South ever supposed they could. The fact remains, that almost every man, woman, and child will readily own that the South is whipped. "We did the best we could in war, and were beaten; now we are going to do the best we can in peace," is the conclusion.

"Is there anything of defiance among the people?" some one asks. "Who is so mad as to talk of further war?" asks Delegate Inglis. "If the youngest of you lives to my age even, you will not see another musket shouldered in the South against the Union," observes venerable Delegate Huger, with the weight of his eighty years bending him toward the grave. "Whose voice could raise a regiment, nay, a company, in the whole State for further resistance?" exclaims Delegate McGowan.

There were a score of ex-Confederate officers in the Convention. "Doesn't that indicate a rebellious spirit?" may be queried. For my part, I wish every office in the State could be filled with ex-Confederate officers. It is the universal testimony of every officer of our own troops with whom I have conversed, as well as of every Northern man two months resident in the State, that the late Rebel soldiers are of better disposition toward the government, toward Northerners, toward progression, than any other class of citizens.

The delegates of the Convention have mostly united in asking Colonel James L. Orr to allow himself to be voted for as Governor. He replies that he does not desire the office, but will accept it if elected. That he will be elected I do not doubt. Mr. Orr never was very heartily in the Rebellion. The merit of his election will not, however, lie in his former relation to the war, but in his present views of State and National policy. He is the leader of the progressives, and is of far more liberal and sensible views, I think, than Governor Perry. When, four days ago, one of the Convention delegates, who mourns for the olden days, expressed his pride in the great men and the general hospitality of the State, Mr. Orr retorted that she never had anything else to be proud of; then burst into a passionate eulogy of the many-sided life of the North, and a scathing criticism of the narrow, inert, centralizing policy of South Carolina. "I am tired of South Carolina as she was," said he; "I covet for her the material prosperity of New England. I would have her acres teem with life and vigor and industry and intelligence, as do those of Massachusetts."

The white man and the negro do not understand each other, and consequently do not work together so harmoniously as they should. It would seem that, one party having work to do and the other needing work, there would be such community of interest as leads to unity of purpose and action; but the fact is, that each party distrusts the other, and therefrom results bickering and antagonism.

That there are many kind-hearted planters—men who made slavery in very truth a sort of patriarchal institution and who are now endeavoring in all sincerity to make the negro's situation not only tolerable, but comfortable—is as true as it is that there are many negroes who cling to the old places and the old customs, and are doing their work just as faithfully and unselfishly as ever. These men, on either side, are the exceptions.

The fault unquestionably, it appears to me, lies with the white man. He is of the ruling race, and might have established a different order of things if he had exercised good common sense in the beginning. That there are some planters who find the free negroes honest and faithful is positive proof that there might have been many more, and if many more, then without number.

Most of them began by assuming, however, that it was right to keep the negro in slavery just as long as possible, and by adding thereto the assumption that the free negro would not work. Military power has compelled the recognition of his freedom in every district, I believe, though in some of them not till within the last six weeks; but this almost universal belief that he will not work is doing a good deal to prove that he will not.

There is among the plantation negroes a widely spread idea that land is to be given them by the government, and this idea is at the bottom of much idleness and discontent. At Orangeburg and at Columbia, country negroes with whom I conversed asked me, "When is de land goin' fur to be dewided?" Some of them believe the land which they are to have is on the coast; others believe the plantations on which they have lived are to be divided among themselves. There is also a widely spread idea that the whites are to be driven out of the lower section of the State, and that the negroes are there to live by themselves. That so absurd ideas as these could exist I would not believe till I found them myself. Other absurd notions well known to prevail are, that freedom can only be found in the neighborhood of Charleston; that it is inseparable from the presence of the army, etc.

Some of these ideas, it was natural the negro should have,—they are born of his blind and passionate longing for liberty, born of his weary waiting in the house of bondage. Where the poor creature got the others, and most dangerous, I don't know. The whites charge the demoralization to the negro soldiers. However this may be, it is painfully certain that, next to teaching the whites that the negro is a free man and not an animal, the hardest work before the North now is to teach the negro what constitutes his freedom.

The negroes are drifting down toward the coast in great numbers. In the night of travel between Orangeburg and Columbia, we met scores of them trudging along with their whole earthly possession in a bundle on the head. Walking in the bright moonlight seventy or eighty rods ahead of the hack, I spoke with many. Whether talkative or taciturn, there was a firm foot and an unruffled voice for the coast. "What are you going to do there?" I asked,—only to get for my answer, "Dun know." It was the exodus of the negroes, going out ignorantly and mistakenly, yet seeking nothing less noble and worthy than freedom.

Some of the blacks are working along as heretofore, under private arrangements with their former masters; but in most cases there is a written contract between the employer and the employed,—one copy in the hands of the planter and the other at the Freedmen's Bureau office. I hear of very few cases in which the compensation is in money; in nearly all instances it is a part of the crop. The la-

borer's share ranges from one tenth to one half; on some small farms, where special privileges are given the negroes in the way of clothing, use of land, use of
team, use of time, the share may not be over one sixth to one tenth of the regular
crop; in the lower part of the State, where most of the labor is done by hand, and
where there are no special privileges, the share is from one third to one half; in
the upper part of the State, where horses or mules are more in use, the share is
from one fourth to one third. The contracts generally expire at New Year's.

It is beyond question that little work has been done in the State this season.
The free negro is the scapegoat on which the whites lay the burden of this wrong,
of course; but it seems to me that the disturbed condition of the country in the
early summer and through all the spring is extenuation enough.

It is, however, true that the lately freed negro has not generally been made to
comprehend that there are six laboring days in each week. The railroad companies complain that they can get but three or four days' work per week from the
blacks engaged in rebuilding the roads; and the contract officers of the Freedmen's
Bureau quite universally concur in the statement that five days make a plantation
negro's week for work. Contract officers have been called on to go out into the
country and convince the negroes that work must be done on Saturday as well as
on other days.

The indifference which so many of the people express as to the fate of the
negro is shocking and to the last degree revolting to me. He is to many of them
nothing but a troublesome animal; not a human being, with hopes and longings
and feelings, but a mere animal, valuable, but altogether unlovable. "I would shoot
one just as soon as I would a dog," said a man to me yesterday on the cars. And I
saw one shot at in Columbia as if he had been only a dog,—shot at from the door
of a store, and at midday! "If I can only git shet of 'em I don't care what becomes
of 'em," said one of my two stage companions in the ride from Columbia to
Winnsboro, speaking of the seventy negroes on his plantation.

There has been much talk that the planters are, now that the main work of the
season is over, turning the negroes adrift. It will not be easy to do this on any large
scale, nor can I believe that many employers will attempt it. Indifference most
heartless is one thing,—down right active cruelty is quite another. The one may
prevail; but, aside from all other considerations, fear of the military will prevent the
other. The facility with which the negro can bring his late master before the
provost-marshal is something not wholly unpleasant to see.

The whole labor system of the State is in an utterly demoralized condition.
How soon it can be thoroughly reorganized, and on just what basis that reorgan-

ization will take place, are questions of no easy answering. The labor question, and not reconstruction, is the main question among intelligent thinking men of the State. Scarcely one in a dozen of the best of them have any faith in the negro. "The experiment of free negro labor is bound to be a failure; and you of the North may as well prepare for it first as last," is substantially the language of hundreds. And thereafter follow questions of, "What shall then be done with the negro?" and, "Where shall we then get our labor?"

Look at the figures for a few districts. In Sumter there were, in 1860, of whites, 6,857, and of negroes, 17,012; in Fairfield, 6,373 whites, and 15,736 negroes; in Colleton, 9,255 whites, and 32,661 negroes; in Beaufort, 6,714 whites, and 33,339 negroes; and in Georgetown, 3,013 whites, and 18,292 negroes. Is it any wonder that the white population of these districts is nervously sensitive about the negro? The proportion of blacks is even greater now than these figures indicate; for war has taken out the whites and brought in the negroes to such an extent that one delegate told me there were in his parish but twenty-two voters and over two thousand negroes. What is to come of such a condition of affairs?

How will it regulate itself? Suppose you give suffrage to the negro in a State whose population now must be about one third white and two thirds negro? It is no question of punishment for those who have fought against the government; over that fleeting and insignificant matter is the great problem of the good of the two races, the advancement of humanity, and the democratic right of every man to a voice in choosing his rulers.

{XII}

The Great Military Prison of North Carolina

SALISBURY, SEPTEMBER 29, 1865

SALISBURY,—of hateful notoriety, of sharp and painful memory to a hundred thousand hearts! Salisbury,—cursed of men dying of cold and starvation, cursed of men driven mad by fiendish torture!

It is a comely enough little town, in a pleasant country, but one can never forget its slaughter-yard. You see its site from the car window as you come up from the south. Its southwestern corner came to within fifty feet of the railroad track. Its northwestern corner came up to the town line, and is scarcely eighty rods from the principal hotel.

The Salisbury military prison was established in the summer of 1863. At first, and for more than a year, it was occupied as a penitentiary for the confinement of what were called State prisoners,—Southern Union men, captured naval officers, deserters from the Union armies, and Northern men held on suspicion or as hostages. It was first used as a place of confinement for soldiers captured in battle in the fall of 1864. Previous to that time persons confined here were treated much better than at the majority of the Rebel prisons; but some time in the summer of that year Major John H. Gee, of Selma, Alabama, a coarse and brutal wretch, was made commandant; and his cruelties soon made the prison the terror of our army, and only less dreadful than Andersonville.

The prison proper was a brick building, forty by one hundred feet in size, and four stories in height, formerly a cotton factory. Connected with it were six small brick buildings,—formerly offices and tenement houses,—and a small frame hospital, large enough for no more than fifty or sixty beds. At a later day these buildings were enclosed in a yard of about six acres, and, after the fall of 1864, were entirely used for hospital purposes. The stockade wall was a stout board fence some twelve feet in height, on which sentinels were stationed fifty feet apart. Inside the wall was a ditch, varying in width from six to ten feet, and in depth from three to six feet.

In the spring and summer of 1864 respectable citizens were allowed to visit Northern men confined here, and the condition of the prisoners at that time was comparatively good. There were some genuine Union people resident in the town, and many more in the counties to the westward. These never wearied in good offices to the prisoners, and for a while they did much to mitigate the rigors of confinement. All this changed, however, when Gee became commandant, and particularly after the Rebels began to confine soldiers here.

In the fall and winter of 1864 not less than fourteen thousand men were herded within this small enclosure like sheep, tortured with infernal malignity, cheated of food when the storehouses half a mile away were bursting with rations, cheated of shelter when fifty or sixty thousand feet of lumber originally intended for this use was lying useless at the upper end of the town, cheated of fuel when magnificent forests were almost within rifle-shot! The poor wretches fought for bones like dogs. One boy went crazy, and ate nearly all the flesh from his arm below the elbow! To save themselves from storm and cold, they burrowed in the earth like wild animals; and the keeper went round of a morning and stirred up the mass in each hole to see how much of it had died during the night! The number of deaths ran as high as seventy-five per day; in one period of eight days, five hundred and

twenty-six were tumbled out for the dead-wagon; for three months the daily average was not less than forty. In the aggregate the Rebellion murdered here over
seven thousand men!

The prisoners, thanks to the tender mercies of their captors, came to the place
generally without shoes or blankets, rarely with overcoats, and often without
blouses. The buildings in the stockade were soon overflowing with the sick. For
those not admitted to the hospital there was very little shelter, though it is said by
negroes that the prisoners begged again and again for the privilege of going out
under guard to cut logs to use in building barracks. The winter of 1864–65 was
unusually severe in this latitude, and snow fell here to the depth of three inches on
several occasions between the 1st of November and the 1st of March.

It is beyond all question that the wretch Gee deliberately starved many of the
prisoners. Men who were Rebels during the war admit as much. I am told that the
commissary warehouses were full of provisions, which the commandant again and
again refused, in shockingly profane terms, to issue even to the poor creatures in
hospital. Much of the time only half-rations were allowed, and on more than one
occasion hundreds of men got nothing for forty-eight hours.

The sufferings of the prisoners were so great that efforts were constantly [being
made] to escape. That many of them did escape we all know. "Golly, I seed a-many
of 'em come down fru ole Mas'r's fiel' to Pete, hes cabin," said an aged negro man
whom I met yesterday. He lived thirty miles west of the town last winter, and had
been horsewhipped for feeding the Yankees. That the prisoners were sometimes
aided in escaping by officers of the prison is believed by not a few persons living
hereabouts.

"Does ye call dis yer hor'ble?" said a negro man whom I met this morning as I
walked over the stockade; "I calls it beautiful since Stoneman polished it up."
Indeed, flame and wrath did their work well. The walls of the old factory building stand intact, but roof and floors and windows are all gone. The small brick
buildings exist only as half a dozen irregular piles of rubbish. Some of the hundred great oak-trees within the stockade are already dead and others are dying.
The fence shows only a line of post-stumps and post-holes. There is satisfaction
in all this; yet signs remain of the dreary days of last winter. You find, in strolling
about, the broken bowl of an earthen pipe, the well-worn blade of a belt knife,
even the regulation button of a soldier's coat.

Treading at random over ground on which there is neither grass nor vegeta-
tion, you often find yourself on yielding soil. Here were the holes in which men
lived. They were filled by Stoneman's troops; but the filling of a few was done so

imperfectly that it is easy enough to see what they were. From three to five feet deep, irregularly circular in shape, from two to six feet in diameter on top, with sides so scooped under that the bottom diameter was generally half larger than the other,—this is what they were. In them lived all the negro and many of the white prisoners, for months. They were in the lower part of the stockade, and could scarcely have been dry even in the driest season of the year; while one shudders at the thought of what they were in the stormy months of winter and spring. It was in such mud-holes as these that Rebellion murdered our soldiers.

Night and morning the dead wagons came. "I saw'd three and four and five big wagons loaded of a mornin' right often," said the barber under whose hands I sat; "and they dragged 'em about by the legs and arms just like as if they'd been dead hogs; and none on 'em had much clothes on; and their hair was all full of red mud; and their heads swung over the sides of the wagon; and the fellers they'd crack a head with their whips, and say out loud, 'Lie still there, you d——d Yankee,' and then laugh; and they didn't take no more care on 'em than's if they'd been dead hogs."

Down the road where those poor bodies were hauled I walked to the place of their burial. There is a good view of the most pleasant part of the town, as you go, and full sight of hundreds of acres of heavy forests. It is a long slope to the southwest, a little muddy brook, a sharp ascent of forty or fifty feet, and there they were tumbled out into the trenches. "I heerd how 't was done," said an elderly white man who came along while I set on the fence,—"an' I cum over yer one Sun'ay to see was it so bad as the soldiers said 't was. 'T was a cold an' nasty evenin', sir, an' they jist caught 'em up, one man to the arms and one to the legs, an' slung 'em in from the wagon; an' some on 'em said one man wasn't dead, but they jist flung him in with the rest. I never cum yer no more, sir, till the Yankees got this yer fence built."

The cemetery is a quiet, retired, and lonesome spot, half a mile or so south of town. The enclosure is nearly square, and about an acre in extent. Around it is a neat, plain, high, and strong board fence, built by Stoneman's orders,—the oak posts having already done some service in the wall of the stockade. The ground slopes gently to the eastward; in the northeastern corner are two or three small oaks; in the southeastern some twenty or twenty-five small pines. The bodies were laid in thirteen long trenches. No headboards were used, no record was kept, and it is impossible to tell where any particular soldier lies. There are thirteen great graves. As the heartless Rebel guards filled them, so they must forever remain.

{ X I I I }

Affairs in Western North Carolina

GREENSBORO, SEPTEMBER 30, 1865

THERE were three of us in the stage from Columbia to Winnsboro on the evening of the 25th,—a North Carolina planter, and an ex-Rebel colonel, beside myself. The planter was a coarse, vulgar fellow, whose whole thought seemed to be given to an effort to outwit the officers of the Freedmen's Bureau, and "git shet" of some sixty negroes on his tobacco plantation. The colonel was a man of much travel, liberal culture, and good heart,—glad the war is over, anxious to hereafter live in peace, and fearful that the negroes of the State will see very sore times before spring. We made the thirty-two miles in eight hours, at an expense of nine dollars apiece.

The trip hither from Winnsboro is made by railway, one hundred and sixty-four miles, in sixteen hours, at a cost of twelve dollars, exclusive of meals. Sleeping cars are apparently an unknown thing on Southern railways, and bid fair to be so for some time to come. One can't help wondering frequently how it is possible for any one to be so stupidly opposed to comfort as are large numbers of Southern persons.

If sun and compass were both at fault, general observation would give ample assurance that I had moved northward. Much of the country through which one travels in Western North Carolina is suggestive of Pennsylvania, though occasionally there are oak openings like those of Minnesota and high plains like those of Iowa. Moreover, it abounds in small farms rather than in large plantations; and corn, not cotton, is the principal product. There are apple orchards and many peach-trees, some fences, and occasionally a comfortable and pleasantly situated farm-house. The ability of cooks for ruining eatables whilst preparing them for the table is also something less up here than in the low country, though they apparently labor to their utmost even in this State.

Winnsboro and Chester in South Carolina, and Charlotte and Salisbury and Greensboro in North Carolina, are five towns after one pattern. Each is a county town of three or four thousand inhabitants, and each has two hotels of such character that the chance traveler stopping at either wishes he had gone to the other. There is a main street, broad and dirty, about a mile in length, with a deep well and great pump in the middle of the carriage-way toward each end, and another

about half-way between; one narrow and dirty street on each side of the broad avenue; about a dozen narrow and dirty cross-streets. In each town the business is
mainly done on the principal street, and in each town the best private residences
are at either end of this principal street.

I begin to meet avowed Rebels. It is a mistake to suppose that this class of creatures is confined to South Carolina, even to suppose that it resides in that State
in any considerable numbers. There are half a dozen here to one there. Sherman
visited that State; his army swept through it like a demon of devastation and destruction. The pride and beauty thereof are laid in ruins. Yet that treatment was
what the haughty little State needed. Less fire would have spared more property,
but also more rebellion. More fire would have made more healthy spirit in this
State. The people in the western part scarcely know, so far as their material interests are concerned, that there has been a war.

In South Carolina every man was ready to take the oath; he made no professions of Unionism, but he owned that he had been fairly beaten, wanted peace
and privilege of trade, and would sincerely obey the government hereafter. Here
there is a great deal of talk about "our rights," complaint at the action of the government, and that spirit which still refuses to acquiesce. The manner of speech
there in regard to the "Yankees"—meaning all the people of the North—was
respectfully appreciative even when indicative of bitter personal hatred. With the
Rebel population of this section a "Yank" is spoken of in terms of contempt.

I was curious to see the Unionism of Western North Carolina of which we
heard so much during the war. Considerable of it, I am convinced, was less a love
for the Union than a personal hatred of those who went into the Rebellion. It was
not so much an uprising for the government as against a certain ruling class. This
is, of course, a general remark; for I find many intelligent men, whose Unionism
is of the judgment and affection, and whose speech on almost every phase of the
question at issue would do no discredit even to the radicalism of Massachusetts. Yet
a rebellion against the little tyranny of local politicians was unquestionably at the
foundation of much of the opposition to the Davis government.

For a man who wholly and passionately hates a Rebel,—hates him without
the least allowance for any extenuating circumstance,—give me one of these North
Carolina Unionists. At Charlotte I found one of them. He was something like sixty
years of age, but seemed vigorous as most men at forty. "There's six or seven
creeturs up in my deestric' as can't live there a gret while, now I tell ye," said he
when I asked him how the Union men and the late Rebels got along together;
"our deestric'll git shet of 'em putty soon. Ef they's fellers as can't taken a wink,

we'll jest haf ter giv' 'em a nod." And he brought his arms and head into position for sighting a gun.

"You don't mean that there'll be any shooting done," said I.

"Don't I, though?" he answered.

"Can't you let bygones be bygones, and all live in peace, and all turn in to improve the country and work on the farms?"

"What I tell ye is what me an' my neighbors'll stand to."

State the question to him as I would, he had only the one answer. The word "district" is unusual hereabouts, and I could get from him no definite idea of the extent of territory it included, though he said there was a matter of five hundred people lived there.

Since coming into the State I have heard from at least a score of men that there can be no fellowship with the ex-Rebel soldiers. I [often] inquired if the return of Rebel soldiers has been prevented by force or threats, or if there have been any outrages upon their persons or property. I found all men disinclined to converse upon the subject. A countryman from near Morgantown said a Rebel lieutenant was found dead near his house one morning three weeks ago, shot from behind through the head. An intelligent negro man from the section thirty miles back of Salisbury told one of the merchants of that town, in my hearing, that a certain Mr. Benson, formerly of that county, who had been in the Rebel army, was shot two weeks ago by some person unknown. Men of character tell me that the ex-Rebel soldiers, those who were in any sense leaders, will fare hard at the hands of the mountain Unionists.

On the other hand, an out-and-out unconquered Rebel who introduced himself to me at Salisbury said substantially that the Union men of the western portion of the State, whom he invariably called "nigger Yankees," are the "meanest set of men the sun ever saw"; didn't go into the army because they "are cowards and d——n fools," and "will have to lower their tail-feathers a good deal or get into trouble." So, too, an ex-Rebel captain, on the cars between the Catawba River and Charlotte, said to a gentleman sitting next me on the bench, that he didn't propose to allow any "stay-at-home cuss" to lord it over him. One of the officers on duty at district head-quarters at Salisbury told me that some of the returning Rebel soldiers were disposed to make trouble with the men who didn't go into the war, and particularly with the few who had been in our service.

The temper of a large number of men in this end of the State appears to be indicated by the remark of a man opposite whom I sat at dinner one day in Salisbury. His neighbor asked him for whom he would vote in the coming

Congressional election.

"I'll not vote again till I can do so without asking any d——d Yankee who I may vote for!"

Gentlemen assure me that in this section,—say the central part of the western half the State,—not more than one half, and some even say one third, of the legal voters appeared at the polls to vote for Convention delegates last week, for the reason that they knew that they could not vote for whom they pleased.

While there is no complaint of direct interference by the military, it is charged that certain men are not elected because it was understood that the commanding officer of the district would not allow any leading Rebel to serve. The Raleigh papers assert that many counties send so-called Union delegates, which, under a free election, would have sent men of an entirely different stamp. It would appear, therefore, that while the South Carolina Convention represented the actual sentiment of the people of that State, the North Carolina Convention will represent the sentiment of the class which calls itself the Union element. I can get no tangible evidence of interference or dictation, though it is asserted and reasserted that there was an "understanding" that some men would, and others would not, be allowed to serve as delegates.

The poor whites could be relied upon during the war because their instincts led them in a path parallel to that taken by the government. Now, however, say many of our officers in this section, they give us more trouble than the real Rebels,—those who voluntarily went into the Rebel army. They have very little judgment, and their instincts do not now lead them toward the ends the government is pursuing. Not a few of them claim that the farms of the leading Rebels should be apportioned out among those who fought Rebels. Unquestionably these North Carolina Unionists have suffered much from Rebels before the war as well as during the war. The root of the matter is, that they are making the readjustment just what they made the Rebellion,—a personal issue with another class of the people.

The best Unionism of [South Carolina] is more or less overgrown with the rank weed of State rights, but there are men here whose loyalty is as clean as that of Andrew Johnson. I have neither seen many nor heard of many; but that there are even a score whom any ordinary traveler can find, is a sign of the times full of encouragement. One of the Convention delegates from Rowan County is a man whom the Rebels had in prison for his Unionism. "The government has been a great deal more lenient towards us than we should have been toward the North under similar circumstances," said a Union man to me here this afternoon, thus repeating almost the very words of an ex-Rebel surgeon with whom I talked at Charlotte.

I saw today for the first time a man who would not take "greenbacks" in payment for property. He came in from the country with a load of wood, and actually hauled it out of town this evening because no one would pay him for it in gold. Much inquiry in South Carolina discovered only two or three localities in which there would be difficulty in traveling without gold; but one of our majors, whom duty has called through over a dozen of these western counties within the last six weeks, tells me that the localities in which paper money would be taken are the exception rather than the rule; and a surgeon of our army whose home is fifty miles back of this place, and who has been up on two weeks' leave, said to me this forenoon that he lost the opportunity to make several good trades while there, because he had only legal-tender money. The people say, he observes, that having lost so much by one sort of paper money, they don't propose to take any of the other sort at present.

The local police militia system is in full force through this section. "How does it work?" I asked of a lieutenant at Concord. "Hinders rather more than it helps," said he. I asked the same question of a smart negro man from the country back of Lexington, and he replied, "'Pears like it be ruther hard on de poor nigger." Yet, on the whole, I am satisfied that it has proved beneficial.

I saw one of the officers who organized the force in half a dozen counties. It is in companies of about seventy-five men, with officers approved or appointed by the district commander. Arms and ammunition are furnished by the government, the officers of the company being under bond for the proper use of the latter and the careful keeping and ultimate safe return of the former. The force is under control of the military, and receives its orders from the assistant provost-marshals. In organizing it, this captain said he endeavored to get the best men he could find,—men of property and mature years, whose interest it would be to preserve order and not oppress the negro.

Special cases there have been, I am sure, in which the negro was abused, even by members of this force. Thus in Concord, on the day of the election, a gang of rowdies from the country made a wholly unprovoked attack on the negroes with clubs and stones, and the militia was not only found worthless for the preservation of order, but some of its members actually joined in the brutal assault. Applejack and whiskey were at the bottom of the row, which resulted in the flight of the negroes, the serious but not dangerous injury of three or four of them, the calling out of a company of troops, the arrest of about forty whites, of whom about half were discharged, about a dozen released on bail, and six or seven are yet in confinement for a further hearing.

This case is, however, exceptional; and whilst the aggregate of reported cases in which individual negroes have been maltreated by individual members of the militia is much larger than one would like to find it, there is no question but that the force has done very much to keep down the antagonism between the ex-Rebels and the non-Rebels which is so dangerous to the ultimate good of the negro. With proper military authorities, and proper weeding out of the companies of militia, as the disposition of its members comes to light, I am satisfied that this local police force will become a strong influence on the right side, and be productive both of general good order and general protection to the negro.

{ XIV }

The North Carolina Freedmen's Convention

RALEIGH, OCTOBER 3, 1865

Have you been into both Conventions?" said I to an ex-Congressman from the North whom I met here this evening, referring to the Freedmen's Convention just closed, and the Constitutional Convention two days old.

"Yes, I've attended two sessions of each. I stopped down at the other hotel when I got here, and I took some pains to talk with a good many of the delegates to the Governor's Convention."

"Well, how do they talk about things in general and State affairs in particular?"

"There isn't loyalty enough in that whole house to hurt anything; and as for brains, they're pretty much all over at the African church."

Thus said the ex-Congressman, who has a national repute, and is not classed among the so-called "radicals."

In sober truth, the Freedmen's Convention was a body of which the negroes of any Southern State might well be proud, and which no Northern man could see without hearty respect. This Convention has done a good work, not alone for the Freedmen of this State, but for the Freedmen of the entire South.

The call came from a committee of three, appointed at a meeting held in Wilmington about a month ago:

"Let the leading men of each separate district issue a call for a meeting, that delegates may be chosen to express the sentiments of the Freedmen at Raleigh on the 29th of September, and let each county send as many delegates as it has representatives in the Legislature. Rally, old men, we want the counsel of your years and experience; rally, young men, we want your loyal presence, and need the ardor of youth to stimulate the timid; and may the spirit of our God come with the people to hallow all our sittings and wisely direct all our actions.

"A. H. GALLOWAY,
JOHN RANDOLPH, JR.,
GEORGE W. PRICE,
Committee."

The Convention met on Friday last, and terminated its labors today, after a four days' session. The sittings were held in the African church of this city. It is a plain, white, wooden building, with floor accommodations for about three hundred persons, and gallery accommodations for about one hundred more. Its floor is carpeted and its seats cushioned. The noticeable feature in it is a large and elegant and lifelike plaster-of-Paris bust of Mr. Lincoln, standing on a bracket, against a dark background in the farther end over the pulpit seat. Over the bust is a canvas, bordered with black, on which is neatly inscribed the last paragraph of Mr. Lincoln's last Message: "With malice toward none, with charity for all, with firmness in the right, as God gives us to see the right, let us strive on to finish the work we are in, to bind up the nation's wounds, to care for him who has borne the battle, and for his widow and orphan; to do all which may achieve and cherish a just and everlasting peace among ourselves and with all nations."

The call provided for one hundred and twenty-two delegates. On the assembling of such as appeared on Friday, it was found that but about half the counties in the State were represented. In some I presume the call has never been seen, for the newspapers entirely ignored it till within a few days of the time set for the Convention. Aside from this supposition, though, there was reason enough, in the cost of traveling and the condition of the freed people out of the towns, for the small attendance from the western section. "We should have counted it a decided success, if even only a quarter of the counties had been represented," said one of the leading delegates; "as it is, we think we have achieved a great victory."

Many of the delegates had regular credentials from the proper county officers, but others were certified only by local organizations, church societies, &c. The difficulty of the occasion was met by resolving the affair into a general mass Convention of those who had credentials of any sort from any organized body of freedmen. The aggregate of delegates was one hundred and seventeen, representing forty-two counties,—all sincere, earnest men, and most of them here in "the spirit of our God." The great majority of them were freedmen, not freemen, though some of them have hardly yet been given by their late masters a realization of the fact they are even freedmen.

The temper of the body was exceedingly good, and was in general accord with the speech of the permanent President,—Rev. John W. Hood of Newbern, of Northern birth, but of some years' residence in this State,—who, on taking the chair, spoke as follows:

"GENTLEMEN OF THE CONVENTION,—I hardly know how to express my thanks for the high honor you have conferred upon me; an honor I could scarcely have dreamed of enjoying, for I consider that there has never been and never will be a more important assembly than this now convened here. We have met to deliberate in a Christian spirit upon the best interests of our people,—holding up before God and men as our motto, 'Equal rights before the law,' yet understanding it to be wise and proper that, whether in doors or out of doors, we should bear ourselves respectfully toward all men. Let us avoid all harsh expressions toward anybody or about any line of policy. Let us keep constantly in mind that this State is our home, and that the white people are our neighbors and many of them our friends. We and the white people have got to live here together. Some people talk of emigration for the black race, some of expatriation, and some of colonization. I regard this as all nonsense. We have been living together for a hundred years or more, and we have got to live together still; and the best way is to harmonize our feelings as much as possible, and to treat all men respectfully. Respectability will always gain respect, not from ruffians, it is true, but from gentlemen; and I am convinced that the major part of the people of North Carolina are gentlemen and ladies. I do not mean one class alone, but the major part of the people, both white and black. That being the case, if we respect ourselves we shall be respected. I think the best way to prepare a people for the exercise of their rights is to put them in practice of those rights, and so I think the time has come when we should be given ours; but I am well aware that we shall not gain them all at once. Let us have faith, and patience, and moderation, yet assert always that we want three things,—first, the right to give evidence in the courts; second, the right to be represented in the jury-box; and third, the right to put votes in the ballot-box. Those rights we want, those rights we contend for, and these rights, under God, we must ultimately have."

The Convention was very much like the mass Convention of white folks, "only a little more so." There were parties, cliques, demagogues, ambitious men,—there was "log-rolling," "wire-pulling," and a general exhibition of most of the arts by which would-be leaders attempt to carry their ends against the will of the mass. It was pleasant to see, however, that the great body of the delegates not only had a pretty clear conception of what they wanted to do, but, as is not always the case with convention delegates, also of what they wanted not to do. The men who, by virtue of some education, some travel, and some association with Northern people, aspired to rule matters for their own interest and aggrandizement were very quietly shelved on the second day, and thereafter found that their power was gone. So, too, those of passionate nature and demagogical spirit, who undertook to uplift themselves on the breakers of angry epithet and inflammatory declamation were also put aside after the first day. That there were some droll scenes is, of course, true. Many of the delegates were like great noisy, ignorant children, and acted very much as such children do when they "play" convention. Others knew nothing of any meetings but the religious gatherings of their own people, and appeared to imagine that tears and shouts and sobs were as much in order here as in the prayer-meetings of the rural districts. The President's place was no office of mere honor, and the most diligent use of his powers would have been unequal to the task of keeping quiet and uniform good order.

Yet, when all these things are admitted, there is to be commended the sincere earnestness of the delegates as a body, the liberal spirit of their debates, the catholicity of their views of duty in the present emergency, the patient and cheerful tone of heart and head which prevailed, and the unfailing good-humor which bridged all chasms and overcame all difficulties. Their extra passion came only from extra zeal; their turbulence at times was merely the sudden flashing of warm good-will for their people; their unseemly drollery was but a manifestation of their natural disposition to enjoyment even under the most adverse circumstances.

Perhaps a dozen of the delegates were not native to this State; but, with few exceptions, those who took part in the debates or were in any way responsible for the action of the Convention, were not only North-Carolinians by birth, but slaves by growth,—men who have always lived and expect to continue living in the State. It is also worth remarking that it was really a Convention of colored men, not a colored men's Convention engineered by white men. It was even so strictly a Convention of the negroes of North Carolina, that there was some sensitive jealousy toward one or two delegates born in this State, but educated in the schools and under the influences of the North. "We meant it for a Convention of our own people," said one of the committee to me, "and these outsiders shall not control us." The deficiencies of the Convention will, of course, be charged to the negroes of the State: its excellences, in simple justice, also belong to them.

The leader of the body was Mr. John H. Harris of this city; a man of scarcely one eighth white blood; a former slave who did his daily task with other farm negroes and sat for hours, year in and year out, after that task was accomplished, in the fireplace, with a pine knot in one hand and a book in the other; who is, in the true sense, self-educated; an upholsterer by trade, and, latterly, a teacher by profession; a plain, patient, unassuming man, whose wise judgment, catholic views, genuine culture, and honest manhood, fit him to adorn any station in any society.

Others of the principal delegates were Mr. A. H. Galloway, of Fayetteville, of some service in our army, much association with Northern people, and of exceedingly radical and Jacobinical spirit; Mr. John P. Sampson, of Wilmington, a young man of ability, liberal education in Northern schools, and somewhat wordy radicalism; Mr. Isham Swett, barber, of Fayetteville, of rare dramatic talent, mature years, ready speech, moderate views; Mr. John R. Good, barber, of Newbern, of thoughtful heart and gray head and simple gentlemanhood; Mr. John Randolph, Jr., of Greensboro, carpenter by trade and teacher by profession, radical in desire, but conservative in action, longing for much but content to make haste slowly; Rev. George A. Rue, late chaplain of the Thirty-second United States Colored Troops, a pure African, of six years' ministerial service in Massachusetts, whom Northern favor has made neither foolish nor haughty.

Many unimportant matters were needlessly brought before the Convention, and there was much talk on trivial affairs, and a deal of wordy debate in respect to some legitimate business. Yet even all this was not without its value; for it brought out many facts and opinions of general use to the delegates as individuals, and served to help them to closer fellowship and more unity of sentiment in respect to the future. On the whole, the Convention did its work with commendable directness; and there were a number of speeches, and one or two somewhat lengthy debates, that would have been creditable to any white man's convention, with even picked delegates.

The chief resolution declares that it is not the policy of the colored people to flock to the cities, and urges them to remain at their old homes and at their old employments, unless good reasons exist for changing; advises them to live soberly and honestly, work faithfully and industriously, save money and buy a few acres of land as soon as possible; build themselves houses, and sacredly observe the marriage relation; avoid quarrels, and cultivate friendly relations with the white people; help each other, and educate themselves and their children.

Other resolutions which were adopted express reverence for the memory of "those heroes, John Brown, Robert G. Shaw," numerous others of less note, "and last and greatest, Abraham Lincoln"; hail with satisfaction the passage of the Constitutional amendment, the organization of the Freedmen's Bureau, the establishment of schools for the education of seventy-five thousand colored children, the admission of John S. Rock to the bar of the Supreme Court, the issuing of the Emancipation Proclamation, and the recognition of Hayti and Liberia; thank the good people of the North for their aid so freely extended to the freedmen in a thousand ways; thank that portion of the Republican party led by Messrs. Chase, Greeley, Sumner, and others, for its efforts to secure to the colored man his rights through Congressional action; and declare that any colored man who will not do for another colored man what he would for a white man under similar circumstances is unworthy of respect.

A considerable part of one afternoon was given to debate upon a resolution which advised colored teachers for colored children and colored preachers for colored congregations. The argument for its passage was, that it would tend to stimulate education among the young men and women; that against it was, that it would serve to set up another wall between blacks and whites. Several delegates favored the general policy enunciated in the resolution, but opposed its passage, on the ground that some of the more ignorant of their people would look upon it as a recommendation not to send their children to the schools established by the Freedmen's Bureau and the Aid Societies of the North. This argument carried the day, and the resolution was tabled.

The chief thing done by the Convention, however, was to adopt an address for presentation to the State Convention which met yesterday, and to the Legislature which meets in November. How this address should be prepared was a subject of anxious consideration. The real good sense of the Convention showed itself in the hearty unanimity with which it adopted the following very noteworthy paper:

"To the Constitutional Convention of North Carolina and the Legislature to assemble thereafter:—

"Assembled as delegates from different portions of the State of North Carolina, and representing a large body of the colored population, we most respectfully and humbly beg leave to present to you, and through you to the people of the State, something of our situation and our wants as a people.

"Earnestly disclaiming all wish to forestall your action or to dictate in the solemn and important duties which have been intrusted to you at this most critical period, and confiding in your justice, wisdom, and patriotism to guard the interests of all classes, and more particularly of that class which, being more helpless, will most need your just and kind consideration, we but exercise the right guaranteed to the humblest citizen in thus petitioning.

"It is with reverent and grateful acknowledgment of the Divine power and interposition, that we accept the precious boon of freedom, resulting, as it has, from a prolonged and sanguinary struggle between two great powers; and finally decreed as it has been by the national will, we look forward with confidence to see the decree ratified by the whole people of this State.

"Though it was impossible for us to be indifferent spectators of such a struggle, you will do us the justice to admit that we have remained throughout obedient and passive, acting such part only as has been assigned us, and calmly waiting upon Providence. Our brethren have fought on the side of the Union, while we have been obliged to serve in the camp, to build fortifications, and raise subsistence for the Confederate army. Do you blame us that we have, meantime, prayed for the freedom of our race?

"Just emerging from bondage, under which our race has groaned for two hundred and fifty years, and suffering from its consequent degradation, we are fully conscious that we possess no power to control legislation in our behalf, and that we must depend wholly upon moral appeal to the hearts and consciences of the people of our State.

"Born upon the same soil, and brought up in an intimacy of relationship unknown to any other state of society, we have formed attachments for the white race which must be as enduring as life, and we can conceive of no reason that our God-bestowed freedom should now sever the kindly ties which have so long united us.

"We are fully conscious that we cannot long expect the presence of government agents, or of the troops, to secure us against evil treatment from unreasonable prejudice and unjust men. Yet we have no desire to look abroad for protection and sympathy. We know we must find both at home and among the people of our own State, and merit them by our industry, sobriety, and respectful demeanor, or suffer long and grievous evils.

"We acknowledge with gratitude that there are those among former slave masters who have promptly conceded our freedom, and have manifested a just and humane disposition towards their former slaves. We think no such persons, or very few at least, have lost their working-hands by desertion.

"At the same time, it must be known to you that many planters have either kept the freedman in doubt, have wholly denied his freedom, or have grudgingly conceded it, and while doing so have expelled his family from the plantations which they perhaps cleared and enriched by their toil through long and weary years. Some have withheld a just compensation, or have awarded such pay as would not support the laborer and his family. Others have driven their hands away without any pay at all, or even a share of the crops they have raised. Women with families of children, whose husbands have been sold, have died, or have wrongfully deserted them, have in some cases been driven away from the homes where, under slavery, they have spent a lifetime of hard service. Is it just or Christian thus to thrust out upon the cold world helpless families to perish? These grosser forms of evil we believe will correct themselves under wise and humane legislation; but we do most respectfully urge that some suitable measures may be adopted to prevent unscrupulous and avaricious employers from the practice of these and other similar acts of injustice towards our people.

"Our first and engrossing concern in our new relation is, how we may provide shelter and an honorable subsistence for ourselves and families. You will say, work; but without your just and considerate aid, how shall we secure adequate compensation for our labor? If the friendly relations which we so much desire shall prevail, must there not be mutual co-operation? As our longer degradation cannot add to your comfort, make us more obedient as servants, or more useful as citizens, will you not aid us by wise and just legislation to elevate ourselves?

"We desire education for our children, that they may be made useful in all the relations of life. We most earnestly desire to have the disabilities under which we formerly labored removed, and to have all the oppressive laws which make unjust discriminations on account of race or color wiped from the statutes of the State. We invoke your protection for the sanctity of our family relations. Is this asking too much? We most respectfully and earnestly pray that some provision may be made for the care of the great number of orphan children and the helpless and infirm, who, by the new order of affairs, will be thrown upon the world without protection; also that you will favor, by some timely and wise measures, the re-union of families which have long been broken up by war or by the operations of slavery.

"Though associated with many memories of suffering, as well as of enjoyment, we have always loved our homes, and dreaded, as the worst of evils, a forcible separation from them. Now that freedom and a new career are before us, we love this land and people more than ever before. Here we have toiled and suffered; our parents, wives, and children are buried here; and in this land we will remain, unless forcibly driven away.

"Finally, praying for such encouragement to our industry as the proper regulation of the hours of labor and the providing of the means of protection against rapacious and cruel employers, and for the collection of just claims, we commit our cause into your hands, invoking Heaven's choicest blessings upon your deliberations and upon the State.

"J. H. HARRIS,

JOHN R. GOOD,

GEORGE A. RUE,

ISHAM SWETT,

J. RANDOLPH, JR.,

Committee."

This address, in which the action of the Convention finally crystallized, I regard as one of the most remarkable documents that the time has brought forth. When I consider the untutored condition and manifold discouragements of this people, the sudden revolution in their social and political relations, all that they have suffered, all that they have cause to fear, and all that they hope for, the wisdom and propriety of their action challenges admiration. This is their first political act; and I do not see how they could have presented their claims with more dignity, with a more just appreciation of the state of affairs, or in a manner which should appeal more forcibly either to the reason or the sentiment of those whom they address.

Scarcely a quarter of these late delegates to this, the first negro convention in a Southern State, can read and write. Some of them have hardly yet been allowed to realize that slavery has been overthrown,—were obliged to leave their homes in the night, are asking safe-conduct papers from the military authorities, and will even then quietly return home in the night. They are dressed in the very cheapest of homespun, are awed by the very atmosphere of a city, speak a language that no Northern white man can understand. To them, as to all men, by travel and association there has come enlargement of view, enlargement of desire and aspiration, a new sense of freedom, and a new purpose to labor for their rights. To them and to all others there has also come, I am convinced, a new sense of the responsibilities of manhood, and a new sense of the manner in which they must meet these responsibilities. They have not forgotten God in their labors; who shall doubt that He will bless this work of theirs?

{ X V }

The Organization and Personnel of the North Carolina State Convention

RALEIGH, OCTOBER 5, 1865

T H E State Convention met at noon on Monday, the 2d instant. The delegates begin their work as though they expected to be here three or four weeks. In South Carolina, where the whole Constitution was to be remodeled, but nine [eight?] committees were appointed, while here thirteen have been already ordered, and the Committee on a Division of Business has not yet concluded its labors.

The Convention is composed of one hundred and twenty delegates, all of whom are present but three, detained at home by sickness. Of the number there are six of Governor Holden's eight provisional judges, five of his eight provisional solicitors, and two members of his personal military staff.

The sessions of the Convention are held in the hall of the lower house of the Legislature,—in the north end of the State Capitol. The room much needs cleaning and painting. Its only ornament is a full-length copy of Stuart's Washington, which hangs at the right of the Speaker's chair, and has been retouched by a daubing artist, I judge. The sessions of the Secession Convention of May, 1861, were also held in this hall.

In point of average ability, I think the delegates here rank above those in the South Carolina Convention; though in that body were half a dozen men whose standing is equaled by not more than one or two delegates in this. In that, however, were a great many fifth-rate or sixth-rate men; while here the majority are second-rate or third-rate men as compared with those. There half a dozen men controlled the action of the whole body in respect to most questions; here there are a score or more who deem their opinions of some special importance.

The President [of the Convention] is Honorable E. G. Reade, of Person County. He is a tall, slim man, with iron-gray hair, whiskers, and moustache; is quiet, easy, precise; has a thin face and a particularly thin nose, and wears kid gloves during the sessions of the Convention. He is regarded as one of the best jurists in the State, was a Whig and an opponent of secession and State rights, and is now provisional judge of the eighth circuit by appointment of the Governor.

After the delegates had presented their credentials, they were called forward in groups, and sworn to "support the Constitution of the United States."

The Governor's message came in on the second day. He takes it for granted that the Convention will recognize the abolition of slavery, provide that it shall not be re-established, and submit the amended Constitution to a vote of the people. He says:

> "North Carolina attempted, in May, 1861, to separate herself from the Federal Union. This attempt involved her, with other slaveholding States, in a protracted and disastrous war, the result of which was a vast expenditure of blood and treasure on her part, and the practical abolition of domestic slavery. She entered the Rebellion a slaveholding State, and emerged from it a non-slaveholding State. In other respects, so far as her existence as a State and her rights as a State are concerned, she has undergone no change.
>
> "Allow me to congratulate you, gentlemen, upon the favorable circumstances which surround you, while engaged in this great work of restoring the State to her former and natural position. It is my firm belief that the policy of the President in this respect, which is as broad, as liberal, and as just as the Constitution itself, will be approved by the great body of the people of the United States; and that the period is not distant, if we are true to ourselves, and properly regardful of the reasonable expectations of our friends in other States, when our senators and representatives will resume their seats in Congress, and when our State will enjoy, in common with the other States, the protection of just laws under the Constitution of our fathers."

I find that I, in common with many other persons of the North, was entirely wrong in supposing that the Whig party and the Democratic party, as distinct political organizations, died at least ten years ago. In North Carolina, I discover, with amazement, that the old parties are both alive, and neither of them a whit less pugilistic than it was twenty years ago. To be an "old line Whig" is to be a perfect gentleman, while to be an "old line Democrat" is to be a vulgar fellow outside the pale of good society; or, on the other hand, to be an "old line Democrat" is to be a man of good sense and sound opinions, while to be an "old line Whig" is to be a conceited fool and bloated aristocrat.

This old party spirit is the foundation-stone of this North Carolina Constitutional Convention. Delegates talk of the Whig party and of the Democratic party, even during grave and serious debates on the most important questions. It is the Democratic party, one class affirms, that made secession a possible thing, and brought the State to the verge of ruin. It is the Whig party, the other class retorts, that was half disloyal to the State, and caused disaster by its coldness in behalf of the war. These things are publicly spoken on the floor of the Convention, while in private conversation half the delegates have no measuring-rule for a man but the fact that he is either a Whig or a Democrat, and no judgment for a measure but that it originates with one of these parties.

Of the one hundred and seventeen delegates in this body, I judge that there are about eight or nine who, in the winter of 1860–61, really believed in the constitutional right of a State to secede; about twenty more who desired North Carolina to secede, and didn't trouble themselves to settle the question whether she had a right to do so; and about a dozen more who wanted her to go out, but recognized that it would be an act of rebellion for her to do so; leaving seventy-five or eighty who were not believers either in secession or revolution. Of these, I judge, about twenty-five quietly acquiesced in the work of the Secession Convention; about forty submitted to Confederate rule, but were always its avowed enemies; and about eight or ten stubbornly refused to acknowledge any allegiance to the Rebel government. This, I believe, may be taken as a fair statement of the record of the delegates. The progress and result of the war, however, changed the views of many of those who originally favored rebellion or secession; and of the whole number, not more than the odd seventeen were, I judge, known as "Secessionists" at the close of hostilities. Of these seventeen, I doubt if more than half a dozen are to any extent believers in the State-rights doctrine, and Judge Manly, of the Supreme Court, is the only one who has avowed his belief publicly in that dogma.

Nine of the delegates in this body were members of the Secession Convention. Of this nine, four held positions, civil or military, under the Rebel government; and two are now provisional judges.

B. F. Moore, of this city, is not only one of the ablest men in the Convention, but also in the State. His standing is indicated by the fact that he was put at the head of the committee appointed to prepare business for the Convention. He is a clear-headed and comprehensive lawyer, of short and stocky person, round face, rosy complexion, white hair, clean-shaven chin, and, though carrying at least sixty-five years, stands as straight and square as a boy of twenty. Intellectually he is tough and pugnacious; politically he is a Whig, and an uncompromising opponent both of Secession and Rebellion.

"Uncle Nat Boyden," though not one of the ablest men, should be set down as one of the leaders of the Convention. He lives at Salisbury, and must be near seventy years of age. His hatred of Secessionists and "the infernal heresy of secession," as he terms it, is something charming to see. He is at the head of the Committee on the Ordinance of Secession. In appearance he is one of the cleanly, precise gentlemen of the old school: in manner he is blunt and courteous. He is of slight and bent figure, and has a delicate and scholarly face, noticeable for its small chin and exceedingly high, full, and broad forehead. His plain, hard, practical good sense, rather than any particular ability or acumen, gives him a good deal of power among the average men of the Convention; and he stood next to Mr. Reade in the informal ballot for the Presidency.

M. E. Manly, of Craven County, is perhaps the leading Calhoun man of the State, as he is the only member of the Convention who has courage and frankness enough to openly avow his belief in the doctrine of State rights. "I still believe in that doctrine, as expounded by Mr. Calhoun," said he, this afternoon, "and still hold that it is necessary, to save us from centralization and secure to us our rights under the Constitution." Mr. Manly is a tall, spare man of about fifty-three, I judge, with a noticeably long, thin face, much cut up with fine wrinkles. Forget everything else about him you might, but, having seen him even but once, you never could forget his eyes,—small, steely, restless, incisive, half-closed, set far back under jutting frontals,—eyes that at first glance seem to see nothing, but that see everything. Mr. Manly is a poor speaker, a very able jurist, and was one of the secession leaders, and a judge under the Rebel government.

{ XVI }

Debate and Action in Respect to the Ordinance of Secession

RALEIGH, OCTOBER 7, 1865

THE Convention has been five days in session, and has done but one thing. That thing, however, it did in the most thorough manner.

When Mr. Boyden was announced as chairman of the Committee on the Ordinance of Secession, everybody understood that the Secessionists would get no favor from that committee. There was little surprise, therefore, when he reported the following:

> "Be it declared and ordained by the delegates of the good people of the State of North Carolina in Convention assembled, . . . That the ordinance of the Convention of the State of North Carolina, ratified on the 21st day of November, 1789, which adopted and ratified the Constitution of the United States, and all acts and parts of acts of the General Assembly ratifying the same, are now and at all times since the adoption and ratification thereof have been, in full force and effect, notwithstanding the supposed ordinance of the 20th day of May, 1861, declaring that the same be repealed, rescinded, and abrogated; and the said supposed ordinance is now, and at all times hath been, null and void."

When this came in, Judge Manly said its phraseology was very objectionable to him, and hoped he might have time to prepare an amendment. When it came up yesterday, Mr. D. D. Ferrebee, of Camden County, announcing that he concurred with Judge Manly, offered the following as a substitute:

> "We, the delegates of the good people of the State of North Carolina, in Convention assembled, do declare and ordain, . . . That the ordinance of the Convention of the State of North Carolina, ratified on the 21st day of November, in the year 1789, which adopted and ratified the Constitution of the United States, is in full force and effect; and the ordinance of the late Convention of the State of the 20th day of May, in the year 1861, is hereby declared to be null, and the same is hereby repealed, rescinded, and abrogated."

Judge Manly argued that the language of the original was both unusual and unnecessary, and that it gravely reflected upon the able body which passed the ordinance of secession.

Thereupon the debate began, and the end was not reached till ten long hours had been consumed in talk. Twelve gentlemen advocated the original report, and eight favored the substitute. The difference between the two propositions lies in a single sentence,—the one simply repeals the ordinance of secession, while the other declares that ordinance to have been always null and void.

All that was said on the actual merits of the question in issue did not occupy more than two hours. Several sterling Union men, whose lips have been sealed for four or five years, took the opportunity to lash certain Secessionists and pound the dogma of secession; and what they had to say was by no means the least relishable part of the discussion, though it had no relevancy directly to the matter in hand.

Mr. Nathaniel Boyden, chairman of the committee, thought it of the utmost importance to declare that the secession ordinance had always been null and void, and that the ordinance of 1789 had always been in force. Before the passage of the ordinance of 1861 the State occupied her true position, and all her rights under the Constitution were granted to her. It is now of the greatest importance that we should affirm that we have always been entitled to those rights, and only deprived of them by illegal military force. I desire to put her in such position that no one in Congress can set up a denial of her equality when her representatives present themselves there. I want the secession ordinance buried so deep that even the Day of Resurrection can't find it. It becomes us now to make an end of the infernal heresy. If it be said that the phraseology is unusual, I answer, so is this assembly, so is the order under which we meet here, so is the history of the last four years, so was the action of that body which assembled here in May, 1861.

Colonel Ferrebee, a gentleman of fine figure, good looks, courteous manner, moderate abilities, and forty-five years, said he had always opposed secession, but had voted for it in the Convention of 1861, because he believed the situation of affairs at that time made it necessary for the State to withdraw from the Federal Union. She took a course which she may regret, but of which she has no cause to be ashamed. And I maintain that the ordinance of the committee casts a stigma upon every son of North Carolina who took up arms in her defense, and is an insult to every member of the Convention of 1861. I am as tired of the war and as anxious to return to the Union as anybody. Why not go back with kindly feelings? We can all vote for the substitute which I have proposed. Why not accept it, and have harmonious action? Whether the principle of secession is true or not, thirty thousand North Carolina soldiers are in their graves in attestation of the validity of the ordinance of May 20, 1861.

Mr. John B. Odom, of Northampton County, said the war has taught us that the government of the United States is something more than a rope of sand,—it has given the lie to despots who say that republicanism has no inherent life. I have no fear that any faction will ever again attempt a dissolution of the Union; but secession has wellnigh ruined the country. It is odious to me, and I care not how strong the language in which I express my detestation of it. The leaders of the Rebellion were men who wanted to steal from us the freedom of the ballot-box. Since the war began they've made me swallow many a bitter pill; now I want them to take this dose without the least sweetening.

Mr. John Pool, of Bertie County, a prominent candidate for United States senator, said he believed the action of the Convention to be of the utmost importance. The State is in the Union or out of it. If in the Union, then she has the high powers and privileges belonging to the States under the Constitution. If she is out of the Union, she is a conquered province. It is no small matter which of the two propositions presented is accepted. Shall we admit that we are a conquered province? We do that if we accept the proposed substitute. There are those in the States never in rebellion, who affirm that the rights of the conqueror are over us. Shall we furnish them with arguments in support of that doctrine? Not so. The act of the Convention of 1861 was revolutionary,—the ordinance of secession has always been null. It is the old question of the right of secession, on which I cannot compromise.

Colonel Ferrebee interrupted, and said that both ordinances declared the act of secession null.

Mr. Pool answered, not so. One says it *is* null: the other says it *was* null. Of course, it is null now: the result of the war has made it so; but I demand that you shall say it always was null. This isn't a mere question of language, but a question of principle; and I warn gentlemen not to overlook this fact. I am proud as any one can be of the valor and patriotism and devotion of the sons of North Carolina, who battled for what their leaders taught them was right. If there is a stigma on any one, it is on us and not on them.

Colonel Ferrebee asked if the Convention of 1861 did not obey the voice of the people in passing the secession ordinance.

Mr. Pool answered that he did not now believe, and never had believed, that a majority of the people of the State ever favored secession or revolution.

Mr. Edward Conigland, of Halifax County, thought it useless to declare that North Carolina never favored secession. She would go down to posterity as having been for it almost unanimously.

Mr. D. F. Caldwell, of Guilford County, said he had been mobbed, inhumanly assaulted, rotten-egged, shot at repeatedly, dragged into the army, and forced into double duty continually, because he was an avowed Union man; and he admitted that he couldn't have much sympathy for the fine scruples of gentlemen who desired such tenderness of treatment for the Secession Convention.

Judge E. J. Warren, of Beaufort County,—a man forty years old, of medium size, having a dark skin, dark brown hair and whiskers, long nose, projecting chin, large, deeply sunken and sluggish brown eyes, and serious, half-sad cast of countenance,—said secession is an abominable heresy. I was in the Convention of 1861, and voted for the act which makes it necessary for us to come here. I denied then, as I deny now, that any State has a Constitutional right to secede. A people may always attempt a revolution, and this the dominant party in North Carolina had already well begun before that Convention met. The passage of the original ordinance reported today from your committee will only be an act of pure justice to those of us who were forced into voting for the so-called secession ordinance. Talk to me of courtesy to that body! To whom did they show courtesy? If we are called discourteous, we demand why courtesy should be shown to a body which would listen neither to age nor wisdom, but, with hot-headed haste, passed an ordinance tearing the State away from the Union within two hours after assembling, and then resolved itself into a mob amid the firing of cannon and the ringing of bells! And they tell us we shall insult the brave soldiers of our State if we agree to the committee's report! I tell them, and I tell the country, that a large majority of those who bore aloft the standard of North Carolina in this pitiful conflict—carried it with rare honor to themselves, but with shame to the judgment of their political leaders—have their opinions expressed in the language of this original ordinance, not in the lying terms of the substitute!

Mr. Boyden said he had very recently been North, and while in Washington called on the President, the Secretary of State, the Attorney-General, the acting Secretary of War, and other officers of the government. I alluded to reports regarding the loyalty of our people; and I assured these officers that the citizens of our State are entirely cured of any love they ever had for secession, and would in all respects demean themselves as sincere and loyal men. The language I have heard during this debate, the bitter opposition that this ordinance has encountered, has convinced me that I was wrong in my assurances to the President and his

associates. The correspondents have comprehended the spirit of some of our people more clearly than I did. Yet I am satisfied that the great body of them will sanc-
tion our passage of the original ordinance. However the leaders may talk, I don't believe you can ever get the masses into another fight with the general government.
Still, this debate has convinced me that it is necessary for us to declare that the
ordinance of secession never had any binding effect whatever. It was an act of
open rebellion, and of course falls with the end of the Rebellion; but I want a positive declaration that no body of men ever had a right to pass such an act. As we
knock at the door of the old homestead, let us present this ordinance. It will give
assurance that neither principalities, nor powers, nor life, nor death, nor any other
thing, shall hereafter separate us from the sisterhood of States.

The secession heresy died hard, but the Convention was determined to kill it.
Finally, when an hour and a half beyond the usual time of adjournment had passed,
when the second day of the contest fell low in the west, and the shafts of sunset lay
silvery and horizontal in the somber chamber, Colonel Ferrebee grounded arms
and gave up the battle.

The substitute was rejected by Yeas 94, Nays 19.

It was late in the day, and everybody was tired. "Let's put the ordinance on its
passage tonight," cried Settle. Nobody objected, and the President stood up and
demanded in a loud and measured voice, "Shall the ordinance pass?" There was a
strong and exultant "Aye," the clear and emphatic "No" of Howard and McCoy,
the suggestive silence of Manly and Ferrebee,—and then the President's word of
announcement, "The ordinance is passed."

Thus did the State set her heel on the head of the viper of secession; and thus
was the mild sovereignty of the old banner reaffirmed and re-established, never
more to be defied or denied in North Carolina.

{XVII}

Action in Regard to Slavery and the Freedmen

RALEIGH, OCTOBER 11, 1865

THE curse of North Carolina is [that] the best men in the Convention stand unblushingly in their places and repeat, one after another: "I believe in the white man only. I believe that this country was made for white men only. I believe this is the white man's government, and no negro should have any part in it." Thus they justify their individual action, and the collective action of their constituents.

The action of the Convention on the slavery question, was, however, as prompt, decisive, and radical as any man could desire. The clause for the new Constitution is substantially in the words of the ordinance of 1787, and is as follows:

> "Slavery and involuntary servitude, otherwise than for crimes, whereof the parties shall have been duly convicted, shall be and hereby are forever prohibited within the State."

In South Carolina a long time was spent in determining the phraseology of the slavery clause. Exceeding sensitiveness was manifested in regard to the matter by many gentlemen, three or four of whom even went so far as to say that they would not vote for it at all unless it recited the "historical fact" that the abolition was by the United States authorities. That a question of this sort would be raised here was certain, but that it would find less than a dozen supporters was unexpected.

Mr. John B. Odom proposed: "The institution of slavery having been destroyed in North Carolina, it is hereby declared that slavery and involuntary servitude," etc. He very briefly said that he fully accepted the terms of the President for restoration to political rights, and would cheerfully vote for the prohibition of slavery, but he thought it advisable to declare the historical fact about the matter.

Mr. Settle favored the language of the report, as being plain, simple, and direct. If it were necessary to insert the historical fact, let the mover go on and recite that slavery was killed by secession, which a majority of the people of the State always opposed; that it might have been partially retained if the Davis government had not been obstinate; and that it received its death-thrust when the Confederate government adopted the policy of taking negroes into the army.

Mr. Bedford Brown also wanted the clause to stand as it came from the committee, pure and simple; he wanted it to appear that the people of North Carolina now, wiser for the result of the late war, of their own free choice abolish and forever prohibit slavery.

Probably these arguments would have proved sufficient to kill the amendment; but its little show of vitality vanished in an instant when a member moved to insert in it after the words "North Carolina," the words, "by the Secessionists." This palpable hit caused an explosion of laughter, which carried it to the table with only six or eight opposing voices.

Colonel Thomas J. Faison, of Sampson County, a Rebel of the most virulent and malignant type, proposed to strike the word "forever" from the ordinance, "so as to let the next generation," he explained, "do what it pleases about the matter." Half a dozen delegates were on their feet demanding the yeas and nays; and poor Faison, dumbfounded at the storm he had unwittingly raised, withdrew his amendment, and followed that action by withdrawing himself in confusion from the chamber.

This closed the debate, which had not occupied over fifteen minutes. It was twenty minutes before noon on the 7th instant. One hundred and nine delegates answered to their names on the call of the roll. William Baker, of Ashe County, plumply responded "No"; but every other name in the list was against him, and he changed his vote before it was announced.

And so, by a unanimous vote of her delegates in Convention assembled, the State of North Carolina, acting under the force of necessity, declared slavery abolished and forever prohibited within her limits.

The question of negro suffrage does not come before the Convention; yet three or four delegates have [shown] their standing. "I am unalterably opposed to negro suffrage," said one delegate; "the negro was not intended to use a ballot." "I am opposed to negro suffrage, because this is a white man's government," said another. It is all of that sort,—no one takes cognizance of the fact that there has been a deluge, nor of the other fact that the whole superstructure of Southern society rests on the back of the negro.

There is in the Convention, as in some sections of the State, a good deal of talk I do not understand. Said one delegate: "It is uncharitable and unkind to feel any resentment toward the negro for anything that happened during the war; it is not his fault that he was made free; he was faithful and obedient to the end." Said another: "The negro had no agency in establishing his freedom, and we must not condemn him for that which he made no effort to produce." As if it were a sin to be free! Or, as if in getting freedom the negro had got a great evil!

Of course colonization finds favor, and finds it in some unexpected quarters.

General Alfred Dockery, venerable of years and venerated for his public and private character, is its leading advocate. "The blacks have ceased to be producers, and the whites cannot support them," he argued; "therefore it would be better for both races that they be separated." Mr. Caldwell, of Greensboro, wanted an equal distribution of the negroes to all parts of the country; "and when that is done, North Carolina will do as much for the negro as Connecticut does." It was pleasant to find in the *Progress* newspaper of this city, the editor of which is a Southerner and a former slaveholder, the following vigorous editorial paragraph concerning this miserable colonization business:

> "If there is any one Christian duty more binding upon the Southern people than any other, it is the duty to take hold of this unfortunate race and educate, Christianize, and elevate them. If they are now licentious, ignorant, vicious, lewd, and generally depraved, it is the result of slavery, and of itself is sufficient argument against the institution; and it should be the pride of those who are responsible for their present condition, and who have grown rich and prospered on their labor, to treat them with justice and kindness. The mob may throw up their hats and sing hosannas to those political leaders who advocate running the negroes away and oppressing them now; but right, honesty, and justice will finally triumph, and the verdict of a virtuous, Christian people will bring them to shame. When the blacks could be put upon the block and sold like other merchandise, and parents and children, husbands and wives, separated like cattle, the poorest non-slaveholder had no objection to their remaining here, and no one felt, not even the poor whites, who were kept poor and degraded by the 'institution,' that they were in the way; but now that, in the order of Providence, they have been lifted from the degradation of slavery, and a prospect of moral and intellectual improvement is opened up to them, the mob cries, 'Away with them!' And, to our shame be it said, the mob finds leaders among those who claim to be foremost in their devotion to the Union."

The address of the Freedmen's Convention was sent in, courteously received, and referred to a special committee of five, of which one of the ablest lawyers of the State, is chairman. That committee had the subject under consideration for four or five days, and then made the following report, which the Convention at once adopted:

> "The subject-matter of the address and petition could be more appropri-

ately acted on by the Legislature than by this Convention; but the importance of the subject, and the necessity for careful and considerate action, are so great that it may be proper for the Convention to take some initiatory steps towards its adjustment.

"The former relations of master and slave having ceased in North Carolina, new and mutual rights and duties have supervened, which require corresponding legislation. A large class of the population, ignorant and poor, has been released from the stringent restraints of its late social and political position and from its dependence upon the individual obligations of another class for its support, government, and protection; and it now becomes the duty of the State to assume their charge, and enact such laws as right and justice may require, and as may be most conducive to the general welfare.

"The abolition of slavery has been adopted in good faith, and with full determination that it shall not again exist in the State, either in form or substance; but the consequences of its former existence will inevitably affect the state of society for years to come. In consequence of his late condition as a slave, the freedman is ignorant of the operations of civil government, improvident of the future, careless of the restraints of public opinion, and without any real appreciation of the duties and obligations imposed by the change in his relations to society. It is the interest of the white race, if he is to reside among us, to improve and elevate him by the enactment of such laws, conceived in a spirit of fairness and liberality, as will encourage him to seek his true welfare in honest industry and the faithful discharge of the duties of his life. His intelligence and social condition must depend upon his industry and virtue.

"Prejudices of a social character will probably forever exist. They are not confined to this State, nor to those States or countries where the institution of African slavery has been recognized, but have pervaded every society where the two races have been brought in contact. However unjust such prejudices may be deemed in theory, wisdom and prudence require that they should be so far recognized and respected by legislators as to avoid rash attempts at measures that might serve only to inflame and strengthen them. Although we cannot hope for the entire correction of many of the evils under which we now labor, yet time will materially modify them, and much may be safely trusted to its silent but effective operation. Hasty and inconsiderate action should be avoided; and above all things, should the delicate questions evolved from the new relations among us be kept from the arena of party politics.

"There are, at present, in North Carolina, some real bonds of attachment between the two races. Families have been brought up and nurtured together under our former domestic relations,—faithful servants have gained the esteem and confidence of their former masters, and possess and reciprocate tender feelings of affection from those whose infancy they have watched, and in the pleasures and sports of whose childhood they have participated. Their services and sympathy in affliction are remembered, and the dearest memories of the dead are associated and shared with them. From such ties, and from the common feelings of interest, justice, and humanity, more is to be hoped for their improvement and welfare than from the assertion of impracticable claims for social and political rights or from the aid of those whose interference is likely to be regarded with jealousy and met with resentment. We deplore the premature introduction of any schemes that may disturb the operations of these kindly feelings, or inflame the inherent social prejudice that exists against the colored race. The necessary legislation should be conceived in a spirit of perfect fairness and justice, and in full and unreserved conformity to existing relations; but it should be suited to the actual condition of the parties, and be aimed rather to their material and moral welfare, and to the general peace and prosperity of the State, than to any theoretical scheme of social and political equality.

"The committee therefore recommends that the Provisional Governor of the State be requested to appoint and constitute a commission of three gentlemen, eminent for legal ability, to propose and submit to the consideration of the Legislature at its next session a system of laws upon the subject of freedmen, and to designate such laws or parts of laws now in force as should be repealed in order to conform the statutes of the State to the ordinance of this Convention abolishing the institution of slavery."

Neither the Convention as a body, nor any delegate as an individual, was wise enough to see that there must be no laws for white men, no laws for black men, but only laws for all men alike.

In the Freedmen's Convention, something was one day said about the ignorance of the negro, and one of the members repeated the remark of an ex-Rebel, to the effect that "the nigger has no business to talk of his 'rights under the

Constitution,' for he don't know what the word means." "It may be," said Mr. Isham Sweat,* barber at Fayetteville, with a passionate burst of eloquence,—"it may be that we are so ignorant we don't know what the word 'Constitution' means; but none of us are so ignorant that we don't know what the principle of justice means!" Is the North less wise than this negro barber who stands and pleads for his people?

{XVIII}

The War-Debt Question and the Minor Work of the Convention

RALEIGH, OCTOBER 14, 1865

WHILE traveling in the western part of the State, I was often told that the Convention would of course be strongly Union, because the Rebel element did not vote,—shielding itself behind the assertion that the "authorities," either military or provisional, would not allow Southern men to run as delegates. Conversation with the officers on duty here, and with the members and hangers-on of the Convention, has convinced me that [these reports] are substantially true.

If "hatred of Secession" and "love of the Union" were synonymous phrases, there would be cause for sincere rejoicing in the position of affairs here. "We'll get these d——d Secesh on the record good and strong," said a delegate to me. They boast of their soldiers, but they very rarely indorse the cause for which those soldiers fought. They are prolific in assertion that the "geographical position" of the State forced her into an alliance with the Confederacy; and they are at much pains to convince strangers that, whatever it may be necessary to do with respect to other States, North Carolina should at once be restored to her old position in the government. If this something that calls itself Unionism had for even one of its component parts a broad love of impartial justice, there might be reason for un-troubled hope of the future. As it is, it will be a sad thing if the President pins his faith to everything in North Carolina that throws stones at Secession and boasts of its Unionism.

There is, on the part of many delegates, an extreme nervousness on the subject of the Congressional representation. "I think we ought to take up the ordinance re-districting the State as soon as possible," says Colonel Love, "so that gentlemen

---

*Editor's note: Andrews spells this name "Swett" earlier.

who are likely to be sent to Congress may have full time for preparation." "It is of the utmost importance," says Mr. Boyden, "that you declare the secession ordinance null and void, now and always, so that no just claim may be set up for refusing admission to our representatives in Congress." "It is a part of the public policy of the State that our Congressional delegation should be in Washington on the first day of the session," says Mr. Moore, who would like to have it appear that he speaks for Governor Holden. "They must demand, and insist upon having, all the rights and privileges now given to the members from Massachusetts or any other State," responds another.

The ordinance redistricting the State was therefore, at the proper time, taken up and promptly passed.

The "basis of representation" question with respect to the lower house of the Legislature, which excited so much debate at Columbia, could get attention from but one delegate here, who was allowed to make a speech of an hour's length in favor of making that basis the white population of the State. It remains as heretofore, i.e. "Federal population,—that is, all free persons and three fifths of all other persons."

The attendance on the daily sessions of the Convention has been very meagre. I doubt if one hundred persons of the resident population have, from first to last, looked into the chamber. I have only to add, further, that the ordinance declaring secession null and void, and that prohibiting slavery, are to be submitted to a vote of the people of the State.

For my final judgment with regard to the Convention, I say that a conquered Rebel will, to my thinking, be much more easily converted into a good citizen than most of these North Carolina Unionists.

POSTSCRIPT

When I left Raleigh, it was generally understood that the Convention would not take any decisive action in respect to the war-debt question. There was an extreme sensitiveness in regard to the matter. The secession ordinance had been emphatically declared null and void from the beginning; but I believe the debt incurred in the endeavor to support that ordinance would have been assumed, had it been possible to get a vote upon the direct proposition! It was comparatively easy to repudiate an act which the result of the war had already repudiated; but the debt was a question of pocket instead of principle, and very many of the so-called Union leaders were unable to see its illegality.

On the sixth day, Mr. Settle introduced an ordinance providing for the payment of all just debts of the State, and also declaring that no part of the Rebel war debt should be paid.

On the eighth day the Finance Committee recommend[ed] that no action be taken by the Convention on the war-debt question.

On the fourteenth day it was agreed that the Convention should adjourn *sine die* on the evening of the following day. Nothing had been done about the war debt, and everybody understood that nothing would be done. There were, to be sure, a dozen or more delegates anxious to settle the questions connected therewith; but, on the other hand, there was a strong party, including several of those who were foremost in the effort to annul the secession ordinance, which openly favored the assumption of that debt, and another large party which chose only to be known as opposed to any action in regard thereto. The pressure of the lobby was very strong.

On the fifteenth day, during the debate on [a] local ordinance, the Provisional Governor announced that he had received from the President the following telegram:

"WASHINGTON, October 18, 1865.

"W. W. HOLDEN, *Provisional Governor:*

"Every dollar of the debt created to aid the Rebellion against the United States should be repudiated finally and forever. The great mass of the people should not be taxed to pay a debt to aid in carrying on a Rebellion to which they in fact, if left to themselves, were opposed. Let those who have given their means for the obligations of the States look for payment to that power they tried to establish in violation of law, Constitution, and the will of the people. They must meet their fate. It is their misfortune, and cannot be recognized by the people of any State professing themselves loyal to the government of the United States, and in the Union.

"ANDREW JOHNSON"

The scene which followed the reading of this Presidential message was extraordinary. The score of faithful Union men applauded it, and one excited delegate exclaimed, "Hurrah for Andy Johnson!" Then silence fell upon the house, and every man looked to his neighbor for guidance. Mr. Conigland, of Halifax County, was the first to speak[:] "My conscience is my own, and I shall allow no earthly government to control my thoughts or form my opinions."

On the sixteenth and last day the contest was renewed, and continued for four hours. Great indignation was manifested at the turn which affairs had taken.

During the day numerous amendments to the Settle ordinance were offered and urged, but none of them were accepted. Finally, Mr. Moore of Raleigh, chairman of the Business Committee, and therefore virtually the leader of the Convention, again proposed, not withstanding the advice of the President, to leave the whole matter to the people. This proposition was only defeated by four majority, the vote being 46 to 50.

The evening session showed that this was the final effort of the assumptionists. They made no more motions for amendment, and the Settle ordinance was passed by a weak *viva voce* vote,—only a few voices being heard in the negative, though about a dozen delegates afterward signed a protest against the action of the Convention. The ordinance as passed is as follows:

> "*Be it declared and ordained by the Delegates of the State of North Carolina in Convention assembled,* . . . That all debts and obligations created or incurred by the State in aid of the Rebellion, directly or indirectly, are void; and no General Assembly of this State shall have power to assume or provide for the payment of the same, or any portion thereof; nor shall any General Assembly of this State have power to assume or provide for the payment of any portion of the debts or obligations created and incurred, directly or indirectly, by the late so-called Confederate States or by its agents, or under its authority."

{XIX}

Affairs in Central North Carolina

GOLDSBORO, OCTOBER 16, 1865

A FAYETTEVILLE merchant whom I met told me that he should have no hope of the future if the Black Republicans carried the day in the forthcoming Northern elections. He considered it essential that they should be overthrown now and forever. They forced the South into the war, and the South would hardly believe the North wished peace unless they were beaten at the ballot-box.

I asked him if it seemed necessary that the North should consult the will of the South in respect to its own State officers.

Well, he thought it was the duty of the North to show that she really desired the South to come back into the Union, and he was certain that the election to office of men avowedly hostile to the South would not indicate any such desire.

But, I said, what would you have? What general policy does it appear to you we of the North should adopt?

He wouldn't dictate, he answered; but the North ought to rise above passion and elect conservative men.

Two gentlemen of this town favored me with their views at some length last evening in regard to the duty of the South and the duty of the nation in the present emergency. They were clearly of the opinion that the Southern representatives should be admitted to their seats at the assembling of Congress; that the President should revoke the twenty thousand dollar clause in his amnesty proclamation; and that the South should be relieved for at least five years from the payment of any national taxes. They thought it very cruel in the North to doubt the word of the South when she said, on her honor, that she accepted the results of the war, and would in good faith abide by them, and hinted that the South might wish she had not so readily given up the position she could have taken at the close of the war.

I asked the landlord of my hotel if there were many Northern men in this section of the State. "Not many," he said, "outside the large towns."

"Is there any feeling of hostility to them that would make it dangerous for them to try to live here?"

"O no, they can live in Goldsboro well enough, and we should like to have a hundred on 'em come in here at once."

"But how about living in the country?"

"Well, there are some towns where they could live; but the planters don't like 'em very well, I reckon."

I asked him if the leading men of the various counties couldn't see that it would be for the interest of the State to encourage the influx of Northern spirit and labor and capital.

Yes, he thought all the best men saw that, and he didn't know as there was any trouble about such men. But the common classes was another thing, and they weren't fond of the Yankees. He believed any Northern man would get along well enough if 't was knowed that he was befriended by the best men in his neighborhood, however.

There can be no lower class of people than the North Carolina "clay-eaters,"— this being the local name for the poor whites. I have looked into [their] cabins, and have made inquiries concerning them. The average negroes are superior in force and intellect to the great majority of these clay-eaters. Many of them—all of those not married—must be called vagabonds. They are generally without fixed home and without definite occupation. They are always thinly clad, their habitations are mere hovels, they are entirely uneducated, and many of them are hardly above beasts in their habits. Very few families have fifty dollars' worth of property of any kind. The men live most of the time in the woods, and generally keep one or two dogs and own a cheap rifle. The women are slatternly and utterly without any idea of decency or propriety; they cultivate a little corn, and sometimes a little patch of cow-peas, collards, or sweet potatoes. The whole class is bigoted and superstitious to the last degree; they generally believe in evil spirits, but rarely in a Divine Father. They are lazy and thriftless, mostly choose to live by begging or pilfering, and are more unreliable as farm hands than the worst of the negroes.

I find here as everywhere the complaint that the free negro will not work. There seems considerable demand for labor, yet, strange as it may seem, the people are warm colonizationists. They talk much about importing white labor, which, of course, they can't get till they put it on such footing as it commands in the North. The idea of everybody is that labor must be kept out of good society; and so I hear much assertion to the effect that German laborers can be imported who will work for about ten or twelve dollars per month, and occupy the cabins which the negroes have vacated.

The fact, if not the name, of slavery remains in many of these central counties. An officer in our army, for twelve years a resident of the State, tells me that many of the people hope some system of peonage or apprenticeship will be established as soon as the State gets full control of her affairs; and an officer of the Freedmen's Bureau says that in some counties, negroes are whipped almost as much now as ever.

"The war," says the *Raleigh Sentinel* in a late issue, "has settled that African slavery shall no longer exist in the United States, and we accept it as a fixed fact; but the principle whether African slavery is right or wrong, whether it is best, wisest for both races, that the slaves should be free, or whether it is just and right to the former slaveholders that they shall be free, or whether the slaves are of right entitled to be free, these are still open questions."

A Johnston County man told in my hearing, and with a great deal of gusto, how he managed his negroes. He couldn't whip them, he said, because they'd sneak off to the provost marshal and complain of him. "But I'll be d——d if I don't get even with the cusses when they try to ride ahead; I jest tell 'em I'm in for a fight, and then I go into 'em for about ten minutes; they understand it, an' come down on thar knees right sudden." He told this with plain indications that he considered himself smart in thus retaining the essential feature of slavery.

A Moore County man whom I met at Raleigh had much to say of the marital relations of the negroes. He believed two thirds of the men would abandon their wives whenever the notion took them, and he doubted if one woman in six was true to her husband. He had no idea that any law could be made to reach this people in this regard, and expected their condition in respect to virtue would be worse hereafter than when they were slaves. He told me a story of a negro who came to him, said he had two wives in Wilmington, but wanted to be married to a third for the war or so long as the Yankees held that city. This seemed to him such conclusive evidence of the negro's unfitness for freedom, that I was glad to be able to match his story with one from the adjoining county of Harnett, to the effect that a white man, having a wife in Virginia, had applied to a magistrate to be married to another woman for forty days, and had tendered a bushel of sweet potatoes in payment for the job.

There is much hostility to the Freedmen's Bureau,—more hereabouts than I found in the western part of the State. The people claim that it "interferes with the regular operations of labor." I get this phrase from several different persons: just what it means is more than I can tell. I judge, however, from all I hear, that the farmers and small planters are disposed to retain their old relations to the negroes, and that the Bureau is acting as the black man's next friend.

Not a few persons seem to me to be trying to find a pretext for a general onslaught upon the negroes. They charge that the blacks are pretty generally organizing, and in many of the lower counties are drilling semi-weekly. I am not able to satisfy myself that there is any truth in these charges. That the negroes hold weekly meetings in some neighborhoods many of the delegates in the Freedmen's Convention told me; but they assured me that they were always of a social or religious character, and I have neither seen nor heard anything that causes me to doubt their word. Most of the blacks seem to me unusually well informed as to the situation so far as it affects their race, and exceedingly anxious to bear themselves with propriety and decorum before all men.

As I have already said, there are the usual complaints about the idleness of the negroes. Some of them have, to be sure, left their old homes; but I estimate that the number who have wandered away does not exceed one tenth of the aggregate. The others are, for the most part, quietly at work on the plantations and farms. "From our experience and observation," says the editor of the *Progress*, of Raleigh, a native, and a former slaveholder, "we believe that by treating the blacks justly, and paying them promptly, more will be produced, by good management, under the free-labor system than was under the old slave system."

{ XX }

Summary of Three Weeks' Observations
in North Carolina

WILMINGTON, OCTOBER 17, 1865

SPINDLING of legs, round of shoulders, sunken of chest, lank of body, stooping of posture, narrow of face, retreating of forehead, thin of nose, small of
chin, large of mouth,—this is the native North-Carolinian as one sees him outside the cities and large towns. There is insipidity in his face, indecision in his
step, and inefficiency in his whole bearing. His house has two rooms and a loft,
and is meanly furnished,—one, and possibly two, beds, three or four chairs, half a
dozen stools, a cheap pine table, an old spinning-wheel, a water-bucket and drinking gourd, two tin washbasins, half a dozen tin platters, a few cooking utensils,
and a dozen odd pieces of crockery. Paint and whitewash and wall-paper and win-
dow-curtains are to him needless luxuries. His wife is leaner, more round-shoul-
dered, more sunken of chest, and more pinched of face than her husband. He
"chaws" and she "dips." The children of these two are large-eyed, tow-headed,
urchins, alike ignorant of the decencies and the possibilities of life. In this house
there is often neither book nor newspaper; and, what is infinitely worse, no longing for either. The day begins at sunrise and ends at dark; its duties are alike devoid
of dignity and mental or moral compensation. The man has a small farm, and once
owned six or eight negroes. How the family now lives, the propping hands of the
negroes being taken away, is a mystery, even if one remembers the simple cheap-
ness of mere animal life.

I am not speaking either of the white resident of the cities or of the "poor
white," but of the common inhabitant of the country,—the man who pays a tax
and votes, but never runs for office; who was a private in the Rebel army, but never
anything more; who hates the Yankees as a matter of course, but has no personal
ill-will toward them; who believes in the Divine right of slavery, but is positive
that a free negro cannot be made to work. He is hospitable enough in words and
manner, but expects you to pay extravagantly in greenbacks or liberally in silver for
a seat at his table and the use of his odd bed. His larder is lean, and his cookery is
in the last degree wretched. He tenders "applejack," as an evidence of good-will,
and wonders how a man can live who don't drink it at least half a dozen times a
day. He likes to talk, and rarely has any work that prevents him from hanging on

the fence to chat with the chance traveler; but his conversation runs in an everlasting circle round the negro, with an occasional pause for the relation of personal adventures in the war. He receives two or three letters per year, perhaps, and wonders why a man should take a daily newspaper. He troubles himself very little about schools or education, but likes to go to meeting, and thinks himself well informed as to matters of theology. He believes the "abolishioners" brought on the war; but he doesn't love Jeff Davis or Governor Vance. He "allers dun hansumly by his niggers," and thinks them the "most ongratefullest creeturs on the face of the yerth."

If you say that half the men and nearly all the women are very pale, you strike at the matter, but fail to hit it. Their whiteness of skin is the whiteness of ordinary tallow. Unquestionably soap and water would improve the appearance, but I doubt if they would give any bloom to the cheek. The skin seems utterly without vitality[;] it has a pitiful and repulsive death-in-life appearance. I am told the climate is in fault, but my judgment says the root of the matter is in the diet of the people. The range of eatables is exceedingly narrow, and swine's flesh constitutes at least half the food of all classes outside the towns and cities; while the consumption of grease—of fat in one form or another—would astonish even an Arctic explorer. The whole economy of life seems radically wrong, and there is no inherent energy which promises reformation.

The amount of tobacco consumed by the people is beyond all calculation. At least seven tenths of all persons above the age of twelve use it in some form. Nearly every man and boy smokes or chews, and very many of them do both, while the country women chew and smoke to some extent, and women of most classes "dip." To see a man take his quid of tobacco from his mouth and put it in his hat when he goes to breakfast is by no means uncommon. I have even seen men lay it under the edge of their plate at dinner; and one of the leading delegates in the Convention held an immense quid between the thumb and finger of the hand with which he abundantly gesticulated during a ten-minutes speech! Could nastiness go further? And do not these things mark the civilization of a people? In South Carolina, though seeing all classes, I did not once observe a white woman "dipping" snuff; but in this State I have seen scores,—"dipping" in the porches of their own houses, on the streets, and twice in the public parlors of hotels. If barbaric life has a filthier and more disgusting custom than this, may I be excused from seeing it.

The labor system of the State is not so badly disorganized as that of South Carolina, but it is thoroughly demoralized. One sees here more white men in trades there almost given up to negroes, but he also sees negroes in trades here from which they are excluded there. The number of grown men, middle-aged men, who have no ostensible business but lounging and whiskey-drinking, is much greater in this State than in that. It is the complaint of papers in all sections of the State, that there never before were so many idle men,—vagrants, consumers, non-producers, non-taxpayers. The chief pity of the matter, however, is, that they seem to have no desire for work. "And who makes so much fuss about the negroes not working as these very white drones who hug the street-corners, lounge about dram-shops, and trust to chance for food and raiment?" asks one of the Raleigh papers, very pertinently. "We trust our law-makers will do all in their power," adds another journal, "to compel the freedmen to work for an honest living; but we consider it equally incumbent on them to take steps to reduce the amount of vagrancy among the whites." These extracts are not from papers edited by Northern or outside men, but the two writers are men who have always lived in the State. The columns of the Wilmington and Newbern papers, edited by newcomers, bear witness to the same state of facts.

It probably never will be settled whether the State did or did not want to go out of the Union in May, 1861. That she did not in December, 1860, nor in February, 1861, is clear enough from the votes cast in those months; but the condition of affairs had greatly changed by the following May. I am everywhere urged to believe that "geographical necessity" forced her out. While many seem anxious that the stranger should believe the State did not voluntarily secede, there are others who insist that it was her matured will to go out in that fatal May. "If she did not believe in the constitutional right of secession, she at least believed the time had come for a revolution," said a gentleman to me here last evening.

Much of the "Unionism" of the State is mere personal bitterness toward Jeff Davis, or Governor Vance, or some less noted secession leader. The *Progress* is quite right when it remarks that "there must be a great change of heart in North Carolina before Andrew Johnson, as a candidate for the Presidency, can carry it against any prominent leader of the Rebellion who may oppose him"; and also quite right again when it says that "the work of restoration in our State has been damaged by attempts to conciliate men who deserve nothing but stripes."

The action of the Convention in respect to the secession ordinance and the war debt pointedly marks the outlines of the situation. Over thirty delegates declared by a solemn vote that the ordinance never had any force whatever, and then turned squarely about and put themselves on record in favor of assuming the debt made in trying to sustain that pretended ordinance! In other words, a large number of gentlemen who consider themselves insulted if called by any other name than "Unionist" desire the State to pay her share of the expense of the war for breaking up the Union. There is startling proof that words are very cheap, and that Unionism in name is one thing, and Unionism in fact quite another.

The average sentiment of the State is very far from being up to that of the Convention. That there will be further resistance to the government is not possible. I do not forget that Delegate Phillips declared in debate that "if the North and South ever again come into the position they occupied in 1860–61, blood will be again spilled"; nor do I forget that another delegate said he knew men of position who declared themselves "ready for further trial of the present issue, if England and France would recognize the confederacy"; yet against these signs of the hour I set the declaration of Uncle Nat Boyden, "Neither principalities, nor powers, nor things present, nor things to come, nor life, nor death, nor any other creature, shall hereafter separate us from the sisterhood of States!" We need to help the Union men of the State. The average sentiment of her people may be brought up to the best sentiment of the Convention, [if] we make haste slowly in the work of reconstruction.

The condition of the negro is in some respects worse and in others better than in South Carolina. He is in such minority here that he cannot enforce his natural rights so easily as he does there; but, on the other hand, because of that same fact, the essential natural rights are generally more readily granted to him here than there. The cold [prejudice] of this people, however, stands immovably in his way, and gives him little chance. It is greatly to his credit that he has not been seized by such discontent as prevails below. In the extreme western part of the State he got uneasy and drifted over the line and off toward Charleston; and in the eastern part he must needs go down to Newbern and Wilmington to find freedom. Elsewhere, however, with local exceptions, he is staying on the old place, and working at the old tasks; and I am convinced that, in the main, he has not given serious cause of complaint.

"The chief ambition of a wench seems to be to wear a veil and carry a parasol," said a ladylike-appearing woman at the hotel in Salisbury. The mistress of the hotel in Charlotte complained that "the nasty niggers must have a parasol when they ha'n't got no shoes." One of two misses, who passed me on the street one day in Raleigh was scolding because her girl had stolen her veil, and she added, finally, "She got so crazy for it that ma had to get her one." An officer of the Freedmen's Bureau told me the wearing of black veils by the young negro women had given great offence to the young white women, and that there was a time earlier in the season when the latter would not wear them at all. This matter of veils and parasols is of serious import to the bitter, spiteful women whose passionate hearts nursed the Rebellion. I have heard so much about it, that I am not at liberty to suppose it a mere matter of local or temporary grievance.

"The nigger is crazy to ride,—to own an old mule and an old cart, and to be seen driving through the streets," said an ex-Rebel colonel to me at Charlotte. And it seems to give grave offence to the gentry of the State that the negro likes riding better than walking, that he will insist on buying a poor old mule and a poor old cart and going into business for himself! In this grief is indirect proof that Sambo appreciates the situation, and is anxious to be at work for himself as soon as possible.

To his average good disposition is due the fact that in many counties slavery still exists as a fact even if abolished as a name. The State is so large and sparsely settled, and means of communicating with some sections are so unfavorable, that even the Freedmen's Bureau has not yet found all the counties. When one of the delegates to the Constitutional Convention chuckles over the fact that some of his constituents don't yet know that slavery is abolished, he furnishes proof unquestionable as to the actual situation.

"What my people wants first," said an intelligent colored man to me at Salisbury, "is de right to be free." He compassed the whole case in few words. In other States, where their number in proportion to the number of whites is greater than it is here, or where the revolution made by the war has been deeper, they assume and hold this first right, to be free; but here, in many counties, even this primary right is yet denied them. Some of the delegates to the Freedmen's Convention were obliged to sneak off from home in the night, and expected punishment on their return. The negro is no model of virtue, and he delights in laziness and the excitement of the city; but, on the whole, I think he is bearing himself very well in North Carolina,—with credit to himself and to his friends.

So far as I can learn, the intelligent colored men are pleading very little as yet for the right of suffrage, but very much for the right to testify in the courts. "We can live without a vote, but not without the right to speak for ourselves" said one of them to me at Greensboro,—anticipating the sentiment of the lame barber here who observed, as he brushed my hair this morning, and emphasized his words with a thump of my head for which he made a hundred apologies, "To be sure, sah, we wants to vote, but, sah, de great matter is to git into de witness-box." One of the leading lawyers of the western part of the State, a former District Attorney and member of the Legislature, told a friend of mine that he knows no prominent member of the bar who does not favor the admission to the courts of negro evidence. The distance between these leading men and the common people is very great; and the latter are far from being willing to allow the negro to be heard in court in his own behalf.

"We are too poor to educate our own children now," said Delegate Settle; "and much as I wish for the education of the negro, his help will have to come from the North at present." It is something to get a desire that the negro shall be educated,— and Mr. Settle is one of those who want him colonized. The North took Mr. Settle at his spirit before he uttered his word, and this year has in operation, in various parts of the State, about fifty schools, under charge of about sixty teachers, and embracing nearly five thousand different pupils. Most of these teachers are ladies, not a few of whom are from Massachusetts. The State Superintendent reports a good degree of progress, and the most indifferent inquiry anywhere among the negroes develops a living and grasping interest.

The labor system, as I have already said, is in better order than in South Carolina. The negroes are not, however, any better paid than there. Where they work for a share of the crop they get from one fourth to one third. Many of them, though, are working for regular wages,—six to eight dollars per month with board, and nine to twelve dollars without board. The planters and farmers rather pride themselves on the liberality of these wages; but they are, of course, utterly insufficient for anything more than bare support. There is less complaint here than below that the negro fails to observe his contract. The local county police does much to keep down disorder, and doubtless is something of a terror to negroes of vicious tendencies who would like to desert their work.

Yet it cannot be denied that there are conflicts between employers and employed, and some careful and observant officers tell me they are increasing because of the injustice of some masters who strive to keep up the old authority of slave days. "It is generally known that the prejudice and bitterness is increasing between the whites and the blacks," says one Raleigh paper; and "clashings between the races are unfortunately becoming more and more frequent," responds another. The real question of the hour is neither one of suffrage nor one of giving testimony, but one of establishing the true relations of employer and employed. The true course is luminously indicated by another paper of the State: "If the employers, and especially the late slaveowners, will treat the blacks kindly and justly, these troubles that now annoy us will soon pass away." Will the white man be wise? For the negro, strong in his longing for freedom, gropes blindly and passionately, and will not be cheated of what the earth, and the very heavens themselves, assure him is his right.

{XXI}

The Great Military Prison of South Carolina

WITHIN THE STOCKADE, FLORENCE, OCTOBER 19, 1865

I WRITE in my note-book, on my knee, sitting on a block of wood, in one of the hut houses built by the hands of those who served the cause of Union and Liberty in the prisons of secession and slavery,—write to the accompaniment of glaring lightning and crashing thunder and driving rain. Will these mud walls shelter me through the storm of this hot afternoon? I cannot forget that they have sheltered men who periled vastly more than ease and comfort; and as I look through the hole that they called a "door," and see the acres of such barbaric but sanctified habitations, I lift reverent heart of thanksgiving to Him who gave us the victory, and blessed the struggle and suffering of that great army through whom we have national unity and the assured promise of universal freedom.

Florence is a point at which three railroads center, rather than a town. There is a hotel, and a church, and a machine-shop, and two so-called stores, and three bar-rooms, and twenty-five or thirty residences, and a great pine forest. There is a long, broad street; at one end of which is the hotel,—a somewhat pretentious two-story wood building, with a wide and lofty piazza in front, and an ungainly tower in the center. At the farther end of the street are the stores and the machine-shop. Midway are the apothecary's, and the hospital, and a vacant law office. Back of this street, in the pines, are the dwellings which constitute the town. The three railroads have a common starting-point just in front of the hotel. Passengers from Wilmington to Charleston reach here about seven in the evening, and leave about three in the morning, after paying two dollars each for supper and lodging of a passably good character. The town is a railroad eating-house, with sleeping-rooms attached.

Situated at the intersection of the great cross-line of railroad with the great coast-line, about one hundred miles from either Wilmington or Charleston, and about seventy-five miles from either the coast or Columbia, it was peculiarly adapted for the location and safety of a prison.

The stockade is about a mile and a half north east from the hotel, about a third of a mile from the railroad, and near the center of a great opening in the pine forest, which is locally known as "the old field." The field is a sandy, rolling, fenceless, irregularly-shaped tract of five hundred acres, more or less, which probably at some time formed the tillable portion of two or three plantations mostly given up to turpentine and rosin making. The stockade is about thirty-five rods wide north and south, and some seventy rods long east and west; containing, perhaps, fifteen or sixteen acres. Through the middle of this enclosure, from north to south, flows a little stream of water, five or six feet in width and four or five inches in depth. It is a swiftly running stream, and the water has a not unpleasant taste. From either end the prison-pen slopes off to this brook,—making five or six acres of low, marshy ground, lying principally east of the stream, full of sink-holes and stagnant waters and miasmatic odors and malarial influences,—the breeding-place of agues and fevers and typhoids and rheumatic complaints,—the rank and pestiferous home of disease and death.

Everything remains as the Rebels left it when they evacuated Florence,—remains almost as it was when these hillsides swarmed with our soldier prisoners. On the east and on the west, outside the stockade, twenty rods or so distant from the walls, are the long lines of earthworks reaching away to the timber on either side, and far down in front of these again are the numerous rifle-pits commanding the advance for nearly a hundred rods. The main entrance to the stockade was at the northwestern corner. Near this corner were the log-houses of the guard. The barracks stand almost as they did when last occupied. Just north of this entrance is a handsome little grove of a dozen trees, among which yet remain the benches and stools of the officers of the guard. Fifty feet in front of the middle of the western wall was the flag-staff whence floated the banner of treason and slavery. Its stump only remains, and loyal and disloyal alike cut chips of memento therefrom. Across the pestilential quagmire, beyond the northeastern corner, is another deserted village of log-houses,—houses of the guard for the rear of the prison-pen, not one of which has been touched. In the southeastern corner of the pen was the rear entrance—thence the prisoners went to fetch wood, a dozen cords of which yet lie piled only five or six rods away.

The walls of the stockade are sixteen feet high, built of unhewn logs some nine or ten inches in diameter, set deeply in the ground. This solid wall of oak and pine logs is unbroken, except by the gate openings and the quagmire,—the marshy ground necessitating the substitution of a stout board fence for the wall of logs. Outside the wall is, of course, a wide and deep ditch, the earth from which is thrown against the logs and forms a narrow path about three or four feet below their tops, whereon the guard walked and overlooked this prison-pen, and from whence fiends in human shape shot half-crazed boys who straggled over this deadline, which runs just behind the hut within which I sit. A ditch could not be dug through the quagmire, and so there are picket platforms built on the fence there,—one, noticeably, on each side over the brook.

Inside the stockade, in the northwestern corner, near the main entrance, was the hospital,—seven log-houses, each some forty feet long and twenty feet wide. These the guard partially burned when they left. The Rebels attempted to burn the stockade wall by firing piles of wood thrown against it on the inside, but the fire refused its work and only scorched the logs at seventy-five or a hundred points of the long line; and the half-burned sticks of wood and the little bundles of pitch-pine remain in their places to show how the most destructive of the elements enlisted in the service of the Union, and saved this prison-pen as an eloquent token of the cost of liberty.

Does any man, horrified by the stories told concerning it, believe that the infamous "dead-line" was a myth? It is about twenty feet inside the stockade walls. Part of the way it is marked by a light pole laid in crotches; elsewhere it is only marked by the line which distinguishes trodden from untrodden ground,—of earth rank with grass and of earth bare of grass. Just back of this hut, in the northeastern quarter, there is only this line of grass and no-grass. Doubtless this was the best of the Southern prison-pens; but even here, if current report among such of the townspeople as can be induced to speak at all of the stockade is true, the guards indulged in that very pleasant and exceedingly humorous amusement which consisted in tossing pieces of meat or bread into the stockade, between the wall and dead-line, in order to get a shot at some Yankee boy who was so hungry as to thoughtlessly rush for it. If they serve who stand and wait, did not these also serve who died between the wall and the dead-line?

Here is the city of the living dead. On these ten or eleven acres there were at least 2,500 houses,—perhaps 3,000 would be a more correct figure; and not less than three fourths of them are nearly as good as they were on the day of their sudden evacuation, and in hundreds of them are memorials of that life of want and woe which 13,000 men knew here, and from which 4,000 passed out through the door of the dead-house to the slope way yonder by the timber, and laid themselves down in long rows for the final sleep and for the glorious reward due unselfish souls.

In the construction of these habitations there is almost infinite variety on a common, general plan. This one in which I sit, and through which the driving storm begins to beat, furnishes that general plan, with very little elaboration or decoration. Come in and see it. Do you find the door low and narrow, and have you a horror of this squat roof and these smoky walls and this earth floor? Yet here lived three or four men, for many weeks, doubtless, and, perhaps, for many months!

The hut is six and a half feet long, four feet and three inches wide, and about five feet high in the center. A hole of fifteen inches depth was dug; at either end of it was set a forked stick; in these two forks was laid a ridge-pole. The wall of our house is the side of the hole; the roof is the slope of sticks or slabs of wood resting on the ridge-pole and at the edge of the hole. This is the general plan. The huts smaller than this are more numerous than those larger.

The back end is made of sticks driven into the ground, against which earth has been thrown. The front end is built with more care. Half of it is of mud brick, and the door and the little chimney at the corner occupy the other half. The door is simply a hole; the chimney is seemingly built up of little bricks, and gives a tiny fireplace of about fifteen inches square. The roof was first covered with pine brush and then with six or eight inches of earth.

Perhaps a hundred of the huts are entirely above ground. Possibly a score are so high that an ordinary man can stand straight in them. But then there are a thousand built over holes three feet deep, a thousand not more than four feet high in the ridge, a thousand not more than four feet square, some hundreds that show only such height above ground as a well-filled grave. Do you deem it awful that men should live in such habitations as these? Yet they were palaces beside the burrows of Salisbury. The thousands of tiny bricks used here were made from the reddish earth of the hillside west of the brook. The graded flat, extending back sixty or seventy feet from the stream, suggests a parade-ground; but it was only the bed on which these little bricks were sun-baked. In the use of the brick there was sometimes a great deal of skill and ingenuity displayed. One sees with pleasure a score or two of chimneys that are models of architectural beauty; one finds not a few fireplaces that are constructed with elaborate improvements. So, too, a few of the huts have doors curiously braided or woven of splinters. There is, indeed, over in the southwestern corner, one whole house above ground, woven, walls and roof, like a basket. These things, though, are exceptional; generally there was only so much as would answer the baldest utilitarianism.

I saw with gladness that there was plenty of wood. Some of it, as I have already said, is still piled in a long rank just outside the stockade. There is an abundance, also, scattered all about the enclosure, particularly east of the brook. Look into a hundred huts, and you shall see wood ready cut for the little fireplace in seventy-five of them surely. In a few cases it even yet lies nicely piled against the chimney on the outside.

They were Yankee boys, the inhabitants of this city. Here is a great pine knot fashioned into a barber's chair, for which many a man would be glad to bid a hundred dollars at a Sanitary Fair. It is nothing but a rough bit of log, but its purpose is evident enough. They pitched quoits sometimes; for over in the southeastern corner is even now the little post at which they aimed, with an old horseshoe lying near. So, too, they seem to have indulged in cricket in the sweet spring days when General Sherman and his forces were in the State above, for I found one wicket in its place. Did they indulge in games at bows and arrows? for I picked up what was clearly an arrow. That they played checkers is certain, for just down the hill a little is a hut in which is a rude checkerboard, and in the corner near the fireplace I tumbled out half a dozen of their pieces,—four round, and two square, cut from pine splinters. I guess they also played cards, for in one hut I picked up the ten of clubs, the five spot and the queen of hearts, and the ace and the jack of spades. You see life came to a sudden pause here,—there was no time for blotting out all the marks of this daily existence; and, walk where you will, you stumble against something that suggests it was but yesterday these prison-boys found liberty.

The occupant of one house was a German. Here is a scrap from some German newspaper, a leaf from a German Testament,—parts of the second and third chapters of Second Corinthians,—and a bit of German manuscript, probably a letter.

In another hut I found an old tin plate, part of an iron fork, the blade of a table-knife, and the bowl of a clay pipe. An Irishman lived here; he wrote his name on one of the posts, "Mic O'Lary"; and I have half a leaf from his Prayer-Book: "O Lord God, I would not only pray for myself, but for all men. Bless my relatives and friends wherever they are. Bless, too, my enemies, and may they become my friends. May universal peace soon prevail." So the simple heart lifted sublime prayer in the night-time, and consecrated his tent with the balm of forgiveness.

In this adjoining cabin must have lived a boy direct from one of the New England States. It is six months since he last passed through the door, yet everything is as orderly and neat as if arranged but an hour ago. His wood is carefully piled in the corner next to the fireplace, his stool is sound and strong, his seat against the wall has not fallen down, the bowl of his brierwood pipe is sweet and clean. He was saving and thoughtful: here is the spring of a pocket-knife laid away against a possible need; carefully in the pine-bush covering of his roof is a little roll of blue army cloth for patches; on a string, tied in the corner, are strung three buttons. He read somebody's History of English Literature, for here is a leaf from the book, pages 229 and 230; he kept the roll of his mess, I judge, for here is a page, wet and dingy, from his diary, on which are a dozen names.

In still another hut I find a rude pipe-bowl, dug out of a sassafras-root, and a wooden spoon large enough for a giant. The boy was at home, too, to the tract distributor, for here is No. 80—"Do you know the Way?"—"published by a South Carolina Colportage Board."

In the house with a door at each end,—and there is but one such house,—I found the rarest treasure of the morning. It was tucked into the thatching, and concealed by a scrap of red woollen cloth. It is a daguerreotype, with the cases half worn away by long shuffling in the knapsack, and the whole tied together with a bit of black thread. It is apparently the picture of mother and two sisters. A good-looking, sober-faced woman of forty-five, wearing black bonnet and veil and cape and dress, and holding a dark parasol; a young lady of nineteen or twenty, wearing a hat trimmed with black, a light spring or fall dress, and a gray cloth sack, and holding a fan; and, between and behind the two, a sweet-faced miss of large and loving eyes, who stands in such position that the only article of dress visible is a black silk cape.

A quarter of a mile away from the entrance-gate are the eight long rows of mounds, to which so much of this life finally came. 2,352, that is the highest number of the graves; but there are many score unnumbered, and the negroes say the men were often buried at random in the old field. "Chucked 'em in like muttons," said an intelligent negro carpenter, who was often in trouble for trying to feed and help the boys in blue. The half-acre of ground occupied by these known and numbered graves is not enclosed, and vagrant cows wander at will over the low mounds. Of course the Rebels kept a record of this potter's field, else why the numbered graves? But that has not been, and probably never will be, found.

The storm has passed by, and the sun, now almost in its setting, suffuses the low west with a flood of golden glory. I have spent the entire day in the stockade. The little accessories of its prison life remain as I have drawn them; its body and substance are told in the fact that from one third to one fourth of the prisoners brought here are lying yonder in the sandy hill-slope.

{XXII}

Life and Labor in the South Carolina Low-Country

CHARLESTON, OCTOBER 21, 1865

LET no man come into the Carolinas this fall or winter for a so-called pleasure-trip. Since the first week in September I have traveled over most of the stage and railway routes in the two States; and I assure you that, though I may have found some profit, I have not found very much pleasure.

The railroads are worn out, and there is not a single line in either State that should not be relaid with new iron at the earliest possible day. Half the freight cars are fit for a few months more service, but the other half and all the passenger coaches were ready months ago for condemnation; though I suppose they must be used another half-year at least, because the various companies are unable to buy new stock. The engines seem generally in rather worse order than the cars, and a careful inspection of almost any one of them is calculated to vividly impress the traveler with the uncertainty of life. That delays and accidents are numerous follows as a matter of course. It must be said, however, that the accidents do not very frequently result in loss of life or serious injury of person. The average rate of railway speed is about nine miles per hour in South Carolina, and about eleven miles per hour in North Carolina. The cost of travel is about seven and a half cents per mile; on one road it is only six cents, and on another it is about eleven cents.

The late election passed off without any serious disturbance. With respect to Governor, the vote of Charleston stands,—James L. Orr, 785; Wade Hampton, 661. The city elected two senators and twenty representatives for the Legislature. The delegation italicizes the fact that the people are disposed to break away from the old leaders and take up new men. Judge Lesesne, who has been senator for a number of years, is defeated by a heavy majority, though he is an estimable gentleman of much influence in State affairs. With three or four exceptions, the representatives are without legislative experience. They were mostly nominated by the "Workingmen's Association," and of course there is considerable disgust at the result among the so-called aristocracy of the city. In respect to the matter of Unionism, it is only to be said that some of them were Union men from the beginning to the end, some were original Secessionists, and some were men who took sides as little as possible. In a word, the result is only significant as marking the triumph of the common people against the upper classes.

The city election takes place in less than a fortnight. As yet very little has been said about it, "but I expect this d——d 'Workingmen's Association' will carry the day," complained one gentleman with whom I spoke.

At Florence I found a most intelligent negro carpenter who lived three miles out of town, but came in every day to his work. He had been traveling through the district lately,—in connection with the league, I judged. "What is the real cause of trouble between the plantation negroes and their employers?" said I. "Well, sah," he answered, "there's a many masters as wants to git de colored peoples away, ye see; an' dey's got de contrac's, an' dey can't do it, ye see, lawful; so dey 'buses dem, an' jerks 'em up by de two fums, an' don't give 'em de bacon, an' calls on 'em to do work in de night time an' Sun'ay, till de colored people dey gits oneasy an' goes off."

In the cars, between the Santee and this city, I asked a man who was loudly complaining about his "niggers" if the planters generally gave their hands full allowance of bacon this fall. "Many of 'em don't give out any at all," said he, somewhat snappishly. So, too, while we lunched at the river, I asked of a countryman who got on at Kingstree, "I suppose now you give your negroes better meat than this?" alluding to some on the table. "Havn't guv 'em any at all fur nigh on two months." "How's that?" said I; "I don't see how you get much work out of them unless you give them meat." He answered that there wasn't much in the country, and that the contracts didn't bind them to give the negroes meat.

A man who got on the cars at Marion "'lowed" he had been in jail for "whippin' a nigger,—bin in fifteen days, sir; was there ever such a d——d outrage!" he exclaimed. No one disputing him, he went on to say, "But I larnt a trick wuth two o' his'n," alluding, I suppose, to the officer who sent him to jail. "I jest strings 'em up by the thumbs for 'bout half an hour, an' then they are d——d glad to go to work."

I infer from all I saw and heard while in the northeastern section, that the negroes at work in the pines are more generally contented than those on plantations anywhere in the State. There is more variety in the turpentine and rosin business than in cotton-growing; and though the work may be harder for one or two days in any given week, there are other days in which there is but little to do.

The negro's situation in the other districts of the so-called low-country is not so good as in those already named. From Georgetown there are many complaints that he is turbulent and "rebellious," and these are made the pretext for treating him with much severity. A gentleman from the town of that name tells me of a case in which a negro was cruelly beaten over the head and shoulders with a large club for insisting that an examination of his contract would show that he was under no obligation to perform certain work required of him. In the upper part of Charleston District the planters are quietly holding meetings at which they pass resolutions not to sell land to negroes, and not to hire negroes unless they can show a "consent-paper" from their former owner. In Beaufort District they not only refuse to sell land to negroes, but also refuse to rent it to them; and many black men have been told that they would be shot if they leased land and undertook to work for themselves. From Colleton District there are complaints that our own soldiers are being used as negro-drivers; and an old man from near St. George's showed me what he claimed was the wound of a bayonet, inflicted upon him by a soldier because he would not obey his orders in regard to the performance of a certain piece of work.

I have no hesitation in saying that the negro troops ought at once to be removed from the interior and put in garrison on the coast. I believe that the two Massachusetts regiments, and perhaps one New York regiment, have done their duty well, creditably to the States they represent, and honorably to the flag they bear; but, generally, the black regiments are wretchedly officered, and unless discipline is well kept up the presence of the negro soldiery is sadly demoralizing to the resident negroes. These have troubles enough without bearing those brought upon them by soldiers of their own race who are ruled by rude and rough and lawless white officers.

All these low-country districts are filled with negroes from the up-country,— not with negroes raised there, but with those taken up there during the war. Many of them have drifted down here in search of freedom, but a large proportion have, after the summer's work, been turned away from the plantations, and sent hither to live by begging or stealing. The cruelty of the old planters in this regard is shocking, and the tales told of the conduct of some of them would be past belief if they were not well authenticated.

The better class of planters in the districts hereabouts very much fear serious difficulty before spring with these homeless and wandering negroes. Hunger will lead, they say, to theft, and theft will lead to organizations of white men for protection of property; and these organizations will lead to conflicts between the negroes and the lower class of whites, in which the negroes will be worsted. That such an issue of the present condition of affairs is possible, I can very easily see; that it is probable, I do not incline to believe; that the majority of the large planters will seek to prevent it, I am quite certain.

If a "war of the races" is brought on in South Carolina it can have but one result, unless the United States troops are made a third party to it. "We 'ns smart nuff t' hold 'r own," said a scowling but intelligent negro to me at Orangeburg. And they are. Moreover, the whites of all these low-country districts know that fact, too.

Immigration is held to be the panacea for all present evils and troubles. One of the representatives elect from this city will make strong efforts to secure legislative action at the coming session of the General Assembly in favor of a bill granting State aid to foreign immigrants. The Yankee is not wanted here, except by the enlightened few; but Germans who will consent to take a secondary position will be welcomed. Yet even they, with their liberal and democratic ideas, are likely to encounter serious opposition.

General Howard [is in this city, acting under] the following order:

"WAR DEPARTMENT ADJUTANT-GENERAL'S OFFICE,
"WASHINGTON, October 9, 1865.

"*General Order*, No. 145.

"Whereas, certain tracts of land situated on the coast of South Carolina, Georgia, and Florida, at the time for the most part vacant, were set apart, by Major-General W. T. Sherman's Special Field Order, No. 15, for the benefit of refugees and freedmen that had been congregated by the operations of war, or had been left to take care of themselves by their former owners; and, whereas, an expectation was thereby created that they would be able to retain possession of said lands; and, whereas, a large number of the former owners are earnestly soliciting the restoration of the same, and promising to absorb the labor and care for the freedmen: It is ordered, that Major-General Howard, Commissioner of the Bureau of Refugees, Freedmen, and Abandoned Lands, proceed to the several above-named States, and endeavor to effect an arrangement mutually satisfactory to the freedmen and the land-owners.

"By order of the President of the United States.

"E. D. TOWNSEND,
Assistant Adjutant-General."

The publication of this order has produced considerable excitement and anticipative satisfaction among the rebellious portion of this community, and much anxiety among the friends of the freedmen. That the original intention of government in setting apart the Sea Islands was to either give or sell them to the freedmen I sincerely believe. That the negroes were allowed to receive the impression that this was the purpose of the government is beyond all question. That General

Saxton colonized them in vast numbers on those islands, with this understanding
on his part and theirs, is matter of record. If the faith of the nation was ever impliedly pledged to anything, it was to the assurance that the colored people should
have a home there,—as witness the famous order of General Sherman, approved
by the Secretary of War, and practically indorsed for nearly nine months by all
branches of the government:

"HEAD-QUARTERS MILITARY DIVISION OF THE MISSISSIPPI,
IN THE FIELD, SAVANNAH, GA., January 16, 1865.
"Special Field Order, No. 15.

"I. The islands from Charleston, south, the abandoned rice-fields along
the rivers for thirty miles back from the sea, and the country bordering the
St. John's River, Florida, are reserved and set apart for the settlement of
the negroes now made free by the acts of war and the proclamation of the
President of the United States.

"II. At Beaufort, Hilton Head, Savannah, Fernandina, St. Augustine,
and Jacksonville the blacks may remain in their chosen or accustomed vo-
cations; but on the islands and in the settlements hereafter to be established no white person whatever, unless military officers and soldiers detailed for duty, will be permitted to reside; and the sole and exclusive
management of affairs will be left to the freed people themselves, subject
only to the United States military authority and the acts of Congress. By
the laws of war, and orders of the President of the United States, the negro
is free, and must be dealt with as such. He cannot be subjected to conscription or forced military service, save by the written orders of the highest
military authority of the Department, under such regulations as the
President or Congress may prescribe. Domestic servants, blacksmiths, carpenters, and other mechanics will be free to select their own work and residence, but the young and able-bodied negroes must be encouraged to en-
list as soldiers in the service of the United States, to contribute their share
toward maintaining their freedom and securing their rights as citizens of
the United States.

"III. Whenever three respectable negroes, heads of families, shall desire to settle on land, and shall have selected for that purpose an island or
a locality clearly defined, within the limits above designated, the Inspector
of Settlements and Plantations will himself, or by such subordinate officer as he may appoint, give them a license to settle such island or district,

and afford them such assistance as he can to enable them to establish a peaceable agricultural settlement. The three parties named will subdivide the land, under the supervision of the Inspector, among themselves and such other as may choose to settle near them, so that each family shall have a plot of not more than (40) forty acres of tillable ground, and when it borders on some water channel, with not more than eight hundred feet of water front, in the possession of which land the military authorities will afford them protection until such time as they can protect themselves, or until Congress shall regulate their title.

"IV. Whenever a negro has enlisted in the military service of the United States, he may locate his family in any one of the settlements at pleasure, and acquire a homestead, and all other rights and privileges of a settler, as though present in person.

"By order of Major-General W. T. Sherman.

"L. M. Dayton,

Assistant Adjutant-General."

If this order means anything, it means that the government intended to give the negroes "an expectation that they would be able to retain possession of said lands"; and if the President's order of the 9th does not break the implied national pledge, then everybody in Charleston fails to comprehend its spirit and purpose.

The ex-Rebel owners of the islands are quite ready to make promises, which one in five may perhaps keep. Yet I talked with one this forenoon who doesn't believe a free negro will work, who expects to have control of his land by Christmas or New Year's, and who is already devising ways to get rid of the negroes upon it. In a word, the interpretation of the order is, that [General Howard] is to make the best terms he can for the freedmen, and then surrender the islands to their former owners.

Three days ago General Howard went down to Edisto Island in company with a representative of the old owners thereof. They were met at a church by over two thousand freedmen, and a long and painfully interesting meeting was held. To say that the negroes were overwhelmed with sorrow and dissatisfaction is to state a fact in sober phrase. General Howard explained to them with careful and sympathetic words what he believed to be the wishes of the President, and asked them to appoint a committee to consider the terms proposed by the planters. This they did; and while the committee were in consultation, the assembly sang several of the most touching and mournful of the negro songs, and were addressed in broken and tearful words by some of their own preachers. The scarcely concealed spirit of all was that the government had deceived them, and it required the most earnest efforts of General Howard and his associates to keep this spirit from finding stormy outbreak. They say that they will not, under any circumstances, work with overseers as heretofore, which is what the planters propose. Some few of them seemed willing to work for fair wages, but the great body were anxious to rent or buy the lands, to which the planters will not consent.

General Howard has represented the difficulties of the case to the President in strong terms. I am sure he will do his hard task with all possible consideration for the interests of the freedmen. He has issued some orders, the main features of which are, that the agents of the bureau on the several islands are to constitute boards of supervisors representing the government, the planters, and the freedmen; and that no lands occupied by negroes are to be restored till the planters engage to give the freedmen all the crops of this year, secure them in their homes, and pay them fair wages for the work of the coming year.

I have no idea this bargain will or can be carried out, because, first, the planters will not agree to their part of it; and, second, the negroes will not give up the islands on such terms. The South Carolinians are reasonably well disposed toward the government, because they know the folly of further resistance to it; but their general hostility and antipathy to the negro is remarkable. The planters believe they ought to have their old estates, and they also believe the President means that they shall have them; and hence the "fair terms" which they propose are such as will neither satisfy the freedmen nor the friends of the freedmen. The negroes, on the other hand, almost universally believe that the islands have been given to them, and they are not likely to relinquish that belief. They long ago lost all faith in their old masters. An attempt to force them from the islands at present, or to compel them to the acceptance of the terms proposed by the planters, will overthrow their faith in the government, and then there will be—bloodshed.

{XXIII}

Life and Labor in the South Carolina Up-Country

BLACKVILLE, OCTOBER 23, 1865

THE trip from Charleston to Augusta is not one that can be recommended as agreeable to make. There are four routes by which you may travel, and no one in Charleston, so far as I could find, can tell which a traveler had better take. The air-line distance between the two points is about one hundred and ten miles. The routes are as follows: first, one hundred miles by sea, ninety miles by railroad, and forty-six miles by stage; second, one hundred and ten miles by railroad and forty-five miles by stage; third, ninety-four miles by railroad and fifty-one miles by stage; fourth, eighty-five miles by railroad and fifty-six miles by stage. The expense of the trip is about the same on each route. I chose the last named.

Leaving Charleston early yesterday morning, I reached Branchville at eleven o'-clock,—sixty-three miles by rail. This morning we got off for Johnson's Turn-out. Our team is a span of horses, both poor, and one very aged. Our driver, the owner of the establishment, is a refugee from the sea-islands, of one of the great South Carolina families, whose different branches have so long intermarried that the present generation is neither shrewd nor intelligent. By twelve hours' continuous driving, over roads moderately good, we made thirty-two miles! and at half past eight this evening we were put out at a small house in the suburbs of Blackville.

All day we have traveled in the track of Sherman's army; and we come to our quarters tonight with the most profound admiration for the genius displayed by his troops in destroying railroads. To wind a bar of iron twice around a telegraph pole or a small tree seems to have been but mere pastime, and to fuse a dozen bars together at the center by an immense fire of ties appears to have been thought a happy joke. Our road has neither led us near many houses nor many ruins of houses; but of fences there are none worth mentioning, except such as have been built during the season.

One finds in this South Carolina up-country a strong feeling of favor toward Jeff Davis. Among the men to whom I spoke on the subject at Columbia and other points, at least two thirds were very confident that his release was advisable as a peace-offering to the South.

I had some conversation with a Fairfield man in regard to the matter, and what he said is substantially what a dozen other persons have said to me.

"Mr. Davis," he observed, "is a very pure man and a sincere Christian. He had little to do with bringing on the war, and your people can't afford to hang him."

"But is he not very unpopular with your own people?" I asked.

"Not with the people at large, sir. Some of our leaders don't like him, and just before the close of the war there was much denunciation of him in some of our newspapers. But I assure you they didn't reflect the sentiment of our people."

"I suppose you know," said I, "that we generally hold him deserving of death for treason."

"Yes, I reckon most of you would like to see him hang; but you would shock the whole civilized world if you hung him, sir."

"But suppose we judge that he must be hung to make treason odious, as the President says?"

"I think Andy Johnson never will hang him. He is a Southern man, and he loves the South better than he does the North."

He said the President had been more lenient toward the South than any one could have hoped he would be. The order against wearing the Confederate button is neither so generally obeyed nor so vigorously enforced up this way as in the low-country. I notice it not only on old garments, but on coats made within a month; and whereas it appears to be elsewhere worn usually because of the poverty of the people, men sport it here as the badge of allegiance to the South. In some towns where the order in respect to it has been carried into effect, the young men accomplish their purpose of spite by ostentatiously wearing coats on which there are no buttons.

While in Lexington District I called on a planter who was exceedingly anxious to learn what the government was going to do about paying for the slaves.

I told him I didn't know as anything was to be done.

"I 'low the gov'ment won't take away all our niggers fur nothin'."

I answered that I had no idea a single dollar would ever be given as compensation.

"But the Cons'tution makes niggers prop'ty, and gov'ment is bound to pay for 'em."

I explained to him at some length what had been from time to time done by the authorities in respect to slavery and the freedmen, and repeated the expression of my belief that no action would ever be had even looking to the payment of money as compensation for emancipation.

Well, Congress had paid for niggers in Washington, he knew, and he thought 't would be a d——n shame if it didn't pay for 'em in South Carolina. If everybody was to be plundered in that way, he didn't know as he cared to come back into the Union.

The military arm was slow in making itself felt in the South Carolina up-country generally, and, [as a] consequence, the negroes were held in actual slavery much longer than in the low-country. It was impossible but that such a state of facts should produce discontent and anxiety among them, and collisions between the two races are of much more frequent occurrence than in the lower part of the State. Speaking in general terms, the whites are not so well disposed toward practical recognition of the negro's freedom as are those of the other section, nor are the negroes so generally disposed to remain quietly on the plantations where they have been living.

This district, Barnwell, has gained an unenviable notoriety throughout the State for the cruelty with which its negro population is treated. If half the stories are true that I hear, the resident agent of the Freedmen's Bureau is not only unfit for his place, but is deserving of court-martial. I learn of many outrages upon the negroes; and to knock one of them down with a club, or tie one of them up and horsewhip him, seems to be regarded as only a pleasant pastime. One of the men employed about the stables here cut off a negro boy's ear last week with one blow of a whip, and tells of the act as though it were a good joke. In the lower section of the district, as a planter tells me, there is a regular patrol-and-pass system, such as prevailed in the days of slavery. There is, I judge, much lawlessness on the part of the negroes. How much of it is induced by their treatment I am unable to say. I have the statement from several parties that the blacks have organized a band of about one hundred persons, which goes up and down the district for the purpose of robbery. One gentleman assures me that the band is led by a white man.

The district above this, Edgefield, has also an undesirable name. At Columbia I heard two delegates speaking of affairs therein. They admitted that "many negroes" had been beaten to death during the summer, and said the planters were very slow in discovering what emancipation meant. Among the negroes whom I met at Orangeburg was one from Edgefield, who showed me a back not yet healed from a severe whipping given him in August.

In Greenville District, which is the home of Governor Perry, there is, I believe, from what I can learn, a band of so-called "regulators," who, on a small scale, are assuming to govern the negroes.

In Anderson District, which is the home of Governor Orr, a case has just occurred, of which I learned the particulars from head-quarters at Charleston. On the night of the 8th, three soldiers of a Maine regiment, who were guarding some government cotton which a treasury agent was shipping down the river, were brutally murdered,—shot from behind, as is the custom of the country. There is not the least complaint that they were in any way specially obnoxious or had been guilty of any wrong deed. They were simply killed because they were Yankees. Investigations already made lead to the conclusion that at least a score of persons were engaged in the murder, only three or four of whom have been arrested. A negro who was supposed to have communicated some information to the authorities in respect to the matter has also been murdered; and anonymous letters have been circulated in which it is distinctly announced that any one will be killed who aids in bringing the murderers to punishment.

In Newberry District a case has recently occurred in which the negroes took justice into their own hands. It appears that in a car which was standing on the track were three or four women and two Rebel soldiers,—one of them a Texan. A negro sergeant had occasion to enter the car, and was roughly ordered out by the Texan. He responded to the effect that he knew his business and should mind it. The two Rebel soldiers thereupon seized him and undertook to thrust him out. He resisted, and the Texan stabbed him, inflicting what was supposed to be a mortal wound. In an hour the two Rebels were caught by the negro soldiers of the regiment to which the sergeant belonged; and in three hours more the Texan had been tried by drum-head court-martial, shot, and buried. The other Confederate escaped while they were taking him up for trial, and will not be retaken.

I find very few negroes willing to make contracts for the coming year. Many appear to have a notion that they can live more easily and comfortably by job work. A considerable number are anxious to become landholders, by lease or by time purchases. Large numbers are "waitin' fur Janawry," hoping that some change for the better will occur at that time. The great body of the freedmen have worked during this season for wholly inadequate wages, and seem, under the circumstances, to have worked with reasonable faithfulness.

{XXIV}

Social Characteristics of the South-Carolinians

AIKEN, OCTOBER 24, 1865

THE importance of soap and water as elements in civilization have been much ignored or overlooked. I am satisfied that if the people of this State, with all their belongings and surroundings, could be thoroughly washed at least once a week, a year would show a very material advance toward civilization. I do not now speak of inward or mental foulness, though doubtless a weekly cleansing in this regard would be beneficial; but I am convinced that he would be a great public benefactor who could prevail upon the common people of South Carolina to make good use of soap and water. Thrift and tidiness are handmaids of cleanliness; and if it were possible to bring the latter into the homes of the poorer classes of this State, I make no doubt that the next generation would find here the material prosperity of Massachusetts.

I am too much a traveler to be upset by even a wide departure from the average cleanliness of New England housewives, and I very readily make allowance for difference of custom; but, after all this, I cannot help remarking what general negligence and slovenliness there is in the houses of the poorer and so-called lower class of inhabitants, and how easily people accommodate themselves to conditions that could not exist a week in any Northern community.

Personal cleanliness is much more general than household cleanliness, whence I conclude that there is something radically rotten in the labor system of the State. It would seem that negroes are natural slovens, or that the relation of master and slave has ruined them in this regard. It would also seem that master and mistress have either not cared, or have been unable, to insist upon the right and proper thing in this respect.

Any thoughtful traveler will notice that the aggregate number of white men in the State of ages ranging from twenty-five to forty-five is comparatively small; and he cannot help remarking with pain and sorrow that the majority of them are idlers or semi-vagabonds. I don't forget that the whole labor system of the State is thoroughly demoralized and disorganized; and the sad thing is, not that so many men are out of regular business, but that so many are using no endeavor to get into business. I have talked with hundreds who have done nothing since the war closed, and don't intend doing anything before next spring at best.

"I saw a very painful thing the other day," said an intelligent gentleman to me at Columbia one evening; "it was the only son of one of our first families driving an express-wagon. His father was killed in the war, your government has taken the house and grounds, and he is actually supporting his mother and sister by driving a hack!"

"Is labor honorable?" I asked.

"Well, but you see we are not accustomed to manual labor: it has always been counted degrading, and it is really humiliating that Henry should drive a hack!"

"Better that than starvation?" I queried.

"O, well, of course; but then his friends would gladly have helped him along till he could find something less degrading than hack-driving."

I judge, from various conversations I have had with young men, that no considerable number are likely, just at present, to pain their friends by engaging in any useful employment. Lads of sixteen to twenty are plenty enough at all loafing-places, and their talk is not at all encouraging to one hopeful of the future.

The negro, bad as his condition is, seems to me to accommodate himself more easily than the white to the change of situation. He doesn't like plantation work, and moves, day by day, in a great wave of life, toward the sea-coast. He can't tell you why he is going toward Charleston. It is vagabondism with some; it is a blind instinct for freedom and proximity to the Yankee with others. Just how all these negroes who have deserted the plantation manage to live no one can tell; but live in some way, and without very much stealing, they do. Half a dollar will start a whole family in trade, and a negro woman in Columbia, to whom that amount had been given, was next day selling corn-cake and peaches on a corner near the post-office, where I found her on every succeeding day of my stay. I asked a middle-aged colored man who had a little stand under a large tree near the church in which the Convention met, how all the negroes who had quit the plantations managed to get along. "Dun know, sah, but 'pears like dey got 'long somehow."

I should say that the real question at issue in the South is, not "What shall be done with the negro?" but "What shall be done with the white?" It is both absurd and wicked to charge that the negroes, as a class, are not at work. Their vitality is at least thirty or forty percent greater than that of the average whites. They can support their cheap lives with very little labor, and the niggardly short-sightedness of the planters prevents them from becoming landholders: why should they concern themselves to do much work? Of course the whites are forever complaining. They demand that all labor shall be, as heretofore, in the hands of the blacks; and all ease and profit, as heretofore, in the hands of themselves.

If the nation allows the whites to work out the problem of the future in their own way, the negro's condition in three years will be as bad as it was before the war. All that force and spirit and energy which made them such bitter enemies of the government is now turned into a channel for the overwhelming of the blacks. The viciousness that could not overturn the nation is now mainly engaged in the effort to retain the substance of slavery.

There is, of course, another side to this labor question. White men don't know how to work, and the organization of society has been such that in many cases this is their misfortune rather than their fault. Take the useful occupations of mason, carpenter, blacksmith, by which so many men at the North find support, comfort, and even opulence,—more than half the blacksmiths, most of the brick-masons, and nearly all the hundred or more carpenters that I have seen were colored men. The few white men one meets who seem anxious to go into business really don't know what to do. The resources of tact, handicraft, and intelligence at the command of a Northern man are not at their command. They will get a wood contract, or will establish a line of hauling-wagons, or open a store. "Going into trade" seems a very common resort; and as a consequence, small shops are exceedingly numerous, and are daily increasing.

Really, the promise of the morrow is not wholly encouraging. Existence has supported itself so long on the shoulder of the slave that it has few resources of its own; and numbers of men who would be at something by which the lease on life and comfort could be held, sit idly by without either ability or energy. The whole organization of society was unsound, and the whole burden of its disease falls upon the men of this generation: the few have inherent energy enough to make for themselves a place in the ranks of labor; but the many wait, half listlessly and half hopefully, for time to bring them victory over necessity.

The strictest economy in personal expenditure is everywhere a pressing necessity. The people are very poor. Three fourths of the property which they had at the beginning of the war is gone. Their slovenly method of living is neither pleasant to see nor agreeable to share, but it would be worth hundreds of millions of dollars if the same degree of economy could be made to prevail throughout the country. Not that this meager and narrow life is in itself a good thing, but that the salvation of a people lies in days of forethought and a considerate expenditure of the gains of business.

South Carolina is just now an excellent place of residence for one who is forced to the wearing of old clothes. Any possible style of garment is in full fashion; and a week's travel in the interior will give anybody the sight of coats, for instance, in styles enough to drive a tailor crazy. Southern homespun is doubtless a serviceable cloth, but it is very rarely a handsome one. How garments made from it at a Broadway house might look is an open question; in garments made after the scant patterns of the back-country there is neither comfort to the wearer nor satisfaction to the beholder. Yet one cannot help rejoicing at seeing how proud some of the people are of this same ill-looking homespun. It is in special cases the mark of Southern allegiance, but it is at least the sign and token of native industry. Possibly the negroes spun and wove it, but mechanical skill in any class is one of the elements of a prosperous future.

Education never was general in the State, and for the last two or three years it has been almost entirely neglected. The ignorance of the great body of the whites will astonish any observer conversant with the middle classes of the North. Travel where you will, and that sure indication of modern civilization, the school-house, is not to be found. Outside half a dozen of the larger towns I have not seen a dozen in over six hundred miles of travel. A few persons express the hope that the Legislature will do something to set the College once more at work; but, generally speaking, the indifference of the masses to the whole subject of education is as startling as it is painful.

The negroes, on the other hand, though in a very ignorant manner, are much interested in the matter. They all seem anxious to learn to read,—many of them appearing to have a notion that thereby will come honor and happiness. Schools for their benefit have already been established at some of the principal points, and the intent of the Freedmen's Bureau is that there shall be at least one in each district before spring. The disposition of the whites toward the negro schools is not good, and in many localities the teachers would be subject to insult, and probably to outrage, but for the presence of the military.

The language of the common people of the State is a curious mixture of English and African. There is so little communication between the various sections that the speech of the northern part is in many particulars quite unlike that of the southern part. The language of the negroes is even more marked than that of the lower classes of the whites, and their isolation is such that each district of the State has a dialect of its own. To show how speech is corrupted, I may mention that I have met many negroes whose jargon was so utterly unintelligible that I could scarcely comprehend the ideas they tried to convey.

The negroes almost invariably drop the final g in words of two or more syllables that end in ing, as comin' for coming, meetin' for meeting, &c. They also drop the final d in words of all syllables, as an' for and, fin' for find, aroun' for around, &c.

The final *t* is usually, but not always dropped, as *fas'* for *fast, mos'* for *most*; though by a change of vowel it is sometimes retained, as *fut* for *foot, fust* for *first,* &c. The *f* in *of* is, I believe, always dropped, as *o' corn* for *of corn,* and *o' my cabin* for *of my cabin.* For the letter thus dropped *b* is sometimes substituted, as *chil' ob Pete* for *child of Peter, ob life* for *of life,* &c.

Exceptions to this general rule in regard to final letters are numerous: thus *going* becomes *gwine,* child becomes *chile* or *cheel, set* becomes *sette,* &c.

The letters *w* and *v* are frequently interchanged: thus *very* becomes *werry,* and *well* becomes *vell,* &c. On the other hand, *ve* is often changed into *b,* as *forgib* for *forgive, lib* for *live,* &c. The letters *th* are never heard; their place in short words is filled by *d,* as *de* for *the, dis* for *this, dat* for *that;* while in longer words the *h* is lost and the *t* retained, as *tree* for *three, trow* for *throw, tings* for *things,* &c.

From dropping letters the way is short to dropping syllables, and *gentleman* becomes *gen'l'man,* little becomes *leel, government* becomes *gov'ment, plantation* becomes *plan'shun, tobacco* becomes *bacca,* &c.

From a change of syllables the way is short to a change of words, and *us* becomes *we, she* becomes *her,* and *he* becomes *him;* thus *all of us* is *all we, she runs* is *her runs, he has got a whip* is *him's got whip.*

By a still more curious trick of words the pronoun *them* is used in the objective for any gender or number, but undergoes, among the low-country negroes especially, such a change itself as to be hardly recognizable. Tell me the meaning of the unique word *shum?* Yet it is in very common use among the negroes of this class, and is their corruption of the words *see them.*

The term applied by the negroes to their owners or employers is not, as generally printed, *massa* or *mass'r.* They use the long *a,* and the word is really, out of the cities, *mawssa,* and sometimes even *mawrssa,* though this last pronunciation is rarely heard.

The terms *cousin* and *brother* are in common use among the negroes, and seem to be expressive of equality. The older and more trusted blacks of a plantation never speak of a field hand as cousin; but the field-hands designate each other as Bro' Bob, Bro' John, Co'n Sally, Co' Pete, &c.

Of words whose pronunciation is without rule, so far as I can discover, take the following instances: *shut* is *shet, such* is *sich, drove* is *druv, catch* is *ketch, there* is *thar, car* is *kear, steady* is *studdy, another* is *nudder, hear* is *hare, sure* is *sho, both* is *boff.*

The particle *da* is curiously used; thus, for *John is coming,* we have *John da come;* for *he runs in the road,* we have *he da run.*

The salutation *how do you do* is never anything more than *how-dy,* and with the lower class of negroes is simply *huddy*. The words *dun gone* are in very common use, as, "He's dun gone to town," "All we gang o' nigger dun gone an' lef um." The word *both* is not generally used, the phrase *all-two* taking its place.

The language of the lower classes of the whites is so much like that of the negroes that it is difficult to say where the English ends and the African begins. Very many of the strange words and phrases which I have mentioned as in use among the negroes I have also heard among the back-country whites. There are other instances, however, of a corruption of language in which the negroes have no part.

A South-Carolinian never *thinks* or *guesses*, but *'lows* or *reckons*. He *ha'n't got no use for a Yankee nohow*, and thinks him a *no-'count fellow*, or a *low-down triflin' cuss*, of whom he would like to *git shet*; and he will *feel obligated* to you if you will help him out of his *ill-fortunate* situation; and, *dog-gone-you*, as you are not an *ill-conditioned* man, and as he has *refugeed* from the Yankees, he will take a little whiskey with you *dry so*.

{XXV}

First Glimpses of Georgia

MILLEDGEVILLE, OCTOBER 26, 1865

THE distance from Aiken to Augusta is twenty miles, and it is made by railroad in two hours and a half, at an expense of two dollars, on the narrow, pine-board, backless seats of a tolerably clean car.

Augusta is considered by many persons the handsomest city in the South, and I have often been told that I would find its general appearance much like that of a Northern city. It certainly is a pleasant place, and there are not many finer streets than the long, wide avenue on which most of its business is done; and yet in respect of beauty the city has no advantage over Raleigh, and cannot be compared with the Columbia that existed a year ago. That anybody should have fancied it had the appearance of a Northern city seems to me very remarkable. Everything about it, from the piazzaed cottages on its back streets to the great hotel in which it domiciles its guests, from the broad-doored cigar-shop on the corner to the dry-goods palace in its principal block, is distinctively Southern; and he certainly must have had a dull eye for local characteristics who could ever have found here any striking resemblance to either Portland or Worcester or Syracuse or Detroit or Dubuque.

The air-line distance from Augusta to Milledgeville is about eighty-five miles. There are three routes, and no one to tell the traveler which is the most expeditious, comfortable, or inexpensive. Being once here, I don't wonder everybody in Augusta is professedly so ignorant concerning the various routes; for the truth is, come by which you will you wish you had taken some other.

I chose [one] of the three routes, and fifty miles of railroad travel brought me, at 10 A.M., to Camak, a lively railroad station of three private residences, a vacant store, and a deserted law-office.

In going up and down its busy streets I met a matronly and neatly dressed negro woman to whom I touched my hat, and an elderly and somewhat pompous white man of whom I asked my prospects for getting a dinner. He could guv me dinner up yon at his house, he said, when noon cum on. So I went there, and got a dinner of stewed beef, boiled sweet potatoes, hoe-cake, and buttermilk. Not being quite sure that I was an invited guest, I was a little embarrassed by the question of compensation. I found, however, on broaching the matter, that the old gentleman had no difficulty in charging me a dollar.

The gentlemen whom I met on the cars did not appear to believe that any honest jury in the country would, on trial, find Davis or Lee or any other Southern leader guilty of treason.

"Treason is a crime unknown to the genius of our institutions, sir," said one gentleman, in a lofty way; "and no act can be treason if it is sustained by any considerable body of the people."

"We were all for the war," responded a Convention delegate; "I was opposed to secession, but I couldn't do any other way than follow the State; and what I did we all did; and if you try Mr. Davis you must try all of us, sir."

"Mr. Davis was always a fourth-rate man," observed the judge; "and the government would give him more prominence than he deserves if it tried him for treason."

"He ought to be hung," answered the colonel, "but not for treason. He was the marplot of our revolution; his obstinacy ruined our cause, and he deserves hanging for that if for anything, though I've no idea he will ever be harmed."

Several of us fell into a chat about the various generals of the two armies. Lee they all considered the greatest man of the age. Grant they didn't call much of a soldier; but one of them said he "told a d——d deal of truth" when he wrote that the South had recruited from the cradle and the grave. Sherman, one more observed, "is a child of hell; he couldn't be a gentleman if he would, and I'm d——d if I believe he would if he could." Howard seemed a clever man and a good officer, but "is soft on the nigger." Sheridan is "a lucky cuss." Of their own officers they said Joe Johnston was loved like a brother. Bragg is "an old ass who ought to be hung for blundering."

At Camak three or four of us had some conversation about the freedmen. They will not work, I was told, and near Augusta they have taken forcible possession of several plantations and will not allow any white persons thereon. One delegate said a negro woman living ten miles above Augusta was nearly horsewhipped to death last week by her master; and another had heard that a negro man on a plantation some miles below the city was recently shot for claiming his freedom.

The gentlemen pretty generally agreed that Andrew Johnson had disappointed the South, being less harsh than it was expected he would be. Two men thought he was figuring for the Southern vote in 1868, and one of them believed the South and the Democratic party could elect him.

After five hours waiting we took the cars for Maysville, and made our thirteen miles in an hour and a half, to find one small hack waiting to carry ten of us to Sparta, twelve miles distant. We managed it, however, the five elderly gentlemen taking the inside. They were all Convention delegates,—a railroad president and ex-State judge, a colonel and wealthy planter, a Methodist minister, a doctor, and a farmer. We of the outside were an ex-Rebel general, who sat with the driver; a negro boy, who sat behind on the baggage; and an ex-editor of one of the Augusta papers, an ex-Rebel quartermaster, and the Yankee correspondent, who sat atop. Our driver was a wide-awake young fellow, who put us along at the rate of five miles an hour. Our position on top the coach was pleasant enough, except that the roof was weak, and there was danger of breaking through; the road was in bad order, and there was a fair prospect that we should turn over; the evening was dark, and there was good chance that the numerous low-hanging boughs under which we passed might brush us off or hang us up. However, I made the trip with no worse accident than gaining a hole in my scalp and a bruise over my eye.

The editor and the quartermaster did most of the talking. They gave an hour to the relation of personal incidents of service in the Rebel army. The quartermaster had barely escaped capture on two occasions. At one time he held a white handkerchief in his hand and was ready to surrender, but the soldiers whom he saw didn't see him. He remained in service till the end of the war, and was with Lee at the breaking up of the army of Virginia.

The editor said the war would have closed two years ago but for the women of the South, and the negroes could have closed it in six months at any time by laying down the shovel and the hoe.

The quartermaster expressed surprise that the negroes show so little gratitude to their old owners, and said that those for whom most had been done were now the most ungrateful.

It was about eight o'clock by the time we were unloaded at Sparta, and we left it at three o'clock this morning. The town itself may be very nice, but its hotel is very bad, and the landlord was very drunk last night, and the talk of the loungers in the office was very hostile to the government. The principal sober man about the house seemed to be Sam, a coal-black negro of twenty-five or thereabouts. He was lively and accommodating, and his orders secured us a passably good supper and a lunch before starting this morning.

A ride of twenty-five miles in an old ambulance in company with the colonel, the editor, and the negro boy, brought me into Milledgeville mid-forenoon of the sixth day from Charleston, at an aggregate expense of a good many bruises, a considerable lameness, a bad cold, a very sore throat, a moderate attack of chills and fever, and fifty-seven dollars in greenbacks. When I next make that trip I shall try some other route.

However, the view from the brow of the hill two miles northeast of town was a luxury to eyes and heart aweary of the dull, leaden, eternal monotony of Carolina pine-swamps and Carolina pine-barrens. It was almost a New England scene,—the Oconee River glimmering through green trees, woody hills, and rolling fallow lands on either side; forests and meadows alternating to the right and to the left; a gently rising hill beyond the river; the town embowered in its wealth of trees; windows glistening in the sunshine; a church lifting its spire serenely skyward; the white house corners showing among the trees; countrymen driving into town; cows feeding in the fields beyond; the darling New England charm of blue hills rising in the background; and, over all, the calmest and loveliest of October mornings!

Our driver was William, present freedman, former slave, who marched over our road twelve years ago in a negro-trader's chain-gang. "Dat ting come no mo'," said he, with some emphasis. Curiously enough, he found no trouble in making a living, and had no desire to be re-enslaved!

The two delegates concurred in the opinion that the government ought to pay the South at least one hundred million dollars indemnity money; and one of them expressed the belief that Congress would ultimately take this view of the case, and appropriate the money.

I asked some questions about the Georgia school system, and remarked that I hoped the time would soon come when school-houses would be as numerous in Georgia as in Massachusetts.

"Well, I hope it never will come," said one of them; "popular education's all a d——d humbug, in my judgment."

"I think so too," answered the other. "I used to be in favor of it; but since I've seen what it leads to in the North, I'm opposed to it."

"That's just it," concluded the first; "it's well enough to give boys who are to be professional men a good education; but reading, writing, and arithmetic are full as much as ought to be taught the common people."

The capital of Georgia is simply the capital, and nothing more. It has no manufacturing establishments, and is the center of no trade. Its only railroad connection is with the South.

The quiet and aristocratic little city is regularly laid out, with a deal more show than is necessary; for all its business is done in one block, and most of its residences are on one street. It has three principal features,—the public square, the state-house, and the hotel. The square is large and rolling, and will unquestionably some time be handsome. In its center is the state-house. At one corner is the ruin of the magazine. On one side is the ruin of the arsenal. On another side are the three churches of the place,—small, plain, cheap wooden buildings, occupied respectively by the Presbyterians, the Baptists, and the Methodists. The statehouse is a solid and inelegant pile of brick, hidden beneath a dirty-brown stucco. It is at present very much out of repair, but could never have been either graceful or impressive. It would scarcely be an exaggeration to say that the city exists for the benefit of the keeper of the hotel, who has served his State in the army and in Fort Delaware, and is now anxious to serve it in the Legislature; who keeps a good house, unblushingly pockets twenty-eight dollars per week from each customer, and carries himself with the utmost nonchalance, knowing that, whether you will or no, you must be content with his terms or leave the city.

{XXVI}

Organization and Personnel of the Georgia State Convention

MILLEDGEVILLE, OCTOBER 27, 1865

THE State Convention met on Wednesday, the 25th, in the hall of the lower house of the General Assembly. Unlike the Conventions of either South Carolina or North Carolina, it was called to order by the Provisional Governor. After the list of the various counties of the State had been called, and the delegates had answered to their names, he said, "I am instructed to require of you to take the amnesty oath." There was no such oath-taking in either of the Carolina Conventions. On his making this announcement, the delegates came forward in companies of eight or ten, and the oath was administered by Provisional Judge Harris, of this city.

Herschel V. Johnson was then elected President of the Convention. [His] speech on taking the chair was very brief, and its pith lies in this paragraph:

> "We are convened under extraordinary circumstances, and charged with grave and responsible trusts. The past, with its scenes of chastisement and of sorrow, the present, with its stern and tangible realities, admonish us to act with caution and wisdom. It is not for me to say what you ought or ought not to do. That is your province. Upon you rests the responsibility to a confiding constituency. I may be permitted, however, to suggest that the duty of the Convention is clearly indicated by surrounding circumstances. Let us do what those circumstances indicate. Let us do nothing more, lest, by attempting too much, we should engender schism and excitement. We cannot correct or cure the errors of the past; but it is our duty, as far as possible, to rescue ourselves and our posterity from their consequences. Let us address ourselves to the task with the dignity of manly purpose, humbly relying upon the Father of light to illumine our understandings."

The Convention numbers exactly three hundred delegates,—of whom two hundred and seventy-seven have answered at roll-call. The people have not so thoroughly broken away from their leaders as in the Carolinas. There are also not a few exceedingly rough backwoods fellows who never saw Milledgeville before, and probably never will see it again. On the whole, the body does not give one a particularly favorable impression of the intelligence of the people of the State. It is so large, however, that all this may be true, and yet leave room for the fact that there are many able and intelligent men in it,—though they are not, generally speaking, the ones who do most of the talking.

The journal of the secret proceedings of the Secession Convention which met January 16, 1861, shows that the vote on the test resolution, declaring it the right and duty of the State to secede, was 166 to 130. The vote on the passage of the ordinance of secession was 208 to 89. It will be seen that in the three days intervening between these two votes, forty delegates who originally voted against the right and duty of secession gave way under the tremendous pressure of the time. Three days later in the session the engrossed ordinance was brought in and signed, in presence of the Governor, the commissioners from various States, the judges of the Supreme Court, and a packed gallery of the beauty and wealth of the city. A large number of the eighty-nine gave way under this pressure, but some still remained firm. On the following day six more gave way, though they entered a formal protest on the journal. Efforts then began to dragoon the refractory members into submission. Propositions were made to formally send a list of the delegates who refused to sign the ordinance to the governors of the several Southern States; to distribute photographic copies of the ordinance, with its signatures and blank spaces; to distribute twenty-five thousand copies of a list of the names of the stubborn delegates, etc. So far as appears of record, none of these propositions were actually put to a vote, but they produced their effect; and, day by day, the oppositionists were brought around and gave the document their signatures, so that finally it bore the names of all but about twenty. The position of this little band of the faithful was anything but pleasant. Even those who simply voted against the test resolution of the first day were snubbed on all sides. These others suffered all kinds of indirect, and some kinds of direct, insult; some of them kept a quasi connection with the Convention, but the leaders retired from the city and took no notice of its action.

Twenty-one of the delegates in the Secession Convention are here now.

Of these delegates, [one] was an original Secessionist, but the other twenty voted against the resolution declaratory of the right to secede. Of this twenty there were fifteen who voted against the passage of the ordinance of secession; [five] voted for it; and [one] did not vote at all.

Joshua Hill and James L. Seward [were] in the Federal Congress at the time of the secession of Georgia. A. H. Kenan, and Hines Holt [were] members of the first Rebel Congress.

The inside of the state-house corresponds to its outside. The halls are low, narrow, and dark, with common plank floors. The stairways are of wood, and very narrow and cramped. The basement is a collection of old store-rooms, filled with all sorts of rubbish. In the second story are the library and the executive offices. In the third story are the legislative halls,—in the space between them being numerous apple, cigar, and peanut stands. The Representatives' Hall, in which the Convention meets, is large, square, and squat, the ceiling being about twenty feet. The Senate Chamber is of somewhat more cheerful appearance than the other, and is ornamented with six immense full-length portraits of Washington, Jefferson, Jackson, &c.

"I'll be d——d if I vote for any man who didn't go with the State," said one of the delegates while the canvass for officers was going on; in accordance with which spirit the secretary is a gentleman who was a colonel in the Rebel army, and the doorkeeper a gentleman who lost an arm in the service.

The Governor's message was sent in immediately after the election of officers had been concluded. It is a brief, practical, straightforward document. The Governor says nothing about secession or the war, and what he has to say about slavery and the freedmen is in this paragraph:

> "Slavery has been abolished. Georgia, in Convention, is called upon to put on record an acknowledgment of the accomplished fact, to give assurance to mankind that involuntary servitude shall not hereafter, in any form, exist within her borders; to enjoin on succeeding legislators that they shall guard by law the community from the evils of sudden emancipation; shall secure those emerging from bondage in the enjoyment of their legal rights; and shall protect the humble, the ignorant, and weak from wrong and aggression."

Herschel V. Johnson, late Governor and candidate for the Vice-Presidency, is a man who leaves his mark upon everything he touches. He has a ponderous lower jaw, a cold, steely eye, and a high, retreating forehead. He looks like a man of great abilities, strong force, and immense vitality. His manners are courteous, but he seems reserved, and appears to have very few warm, personal friends, though everybody professes respect for him as a lawyer and a statesman.

Honorable Charles J. Jenkins is the leader of the Convention. The whole business is in the hands of one committee of sixteen, of which he is the head. He has been one of the members of the Supreme Court of the State, is everywhere respected and venerated, and is mentioned in connection with the Governorship and the United States Senate. He is a lame man, who must be considerably over sixty years of age, yet who has still great force and vigor. He ran for the Convention of 1860–61 as a Union man and was defeated, but was sent to this without a show of opposition. His home is in Augusta.

Honorable Joshua Hill is only second in influence to Judge Jenkins. He was a member of Congress in 1860–61, and his course in the stormy days of that session is matter of honorable record. "Had there been three other men as brave as Josh Hill we could have saved the State from secession," said a very intelligent gentleman to me yesterday. Mr. Hill is a fine type of physical manhood, over six feet in height, with deep chest, broad shoulders, erect figure, and a bearing that commands respect everywhere. His intellectual ability is considerable; but his distinguishing characteristic, his friends say, is "plain horse sense." He lives at Madison, the county seat of Morgan County, and is a man of about fifty years of age.

The leader of the lobby, and therefore entitled to mention with the members of the Convention, is ex-Governor Joseph E. Brown. He has three points that the most unobservant observer catches at the first glance,—a large mouth, a long neck, and a narrow and hollow chest. Besides this, he is tall and very slim, has a pleasant face, a courteous smile for everybody, a large and strong nose, dark gray eyes, and a good forehead. He declares himself a firm supporter of the President's reconstruction policy, and has more personal popularity than any other man in Georgia. Everybody seems to concur in the assertion that he managed her finances better than any other Governor they ever had. He still occupies the Executive Mansion, Governor Johnson simply having rooms there.

The Convention attracts more public notice than did those at Columbia and Raleigh,—the lobby representation in the war-debt interest being larger than in either of the Carolina Conventions, and the excitement of the debates furnishing a grateful relief to the monotony of the city's dull life. The daily attendance thus far averages about one hundred and fifty persons, one fourth of them, perhaps, being ladies.

{XXVII}

Secession and Slavery

MILLEDGEVILLE, OCTOBER 28, 1865

THE question of undoing the work of the Secession Convention, which occupied two wrathful days at Raleigh, here scarcely occupied two minutes. The committee of sixteen was named at the opening of the second day's session, and before night Judge Jenkins reported the following ordinance:

"*We, the people of the State of Georgia, in Convention at our seat of Government, do declare and ordain,* That an ordinance adopted by the same people, in Convention, on the nineteenth day of January, A. D. eighteen hundred and sixty-one, entitled 'An ordinance to dissolve the union between the State of Georgia and other States united with her under a compact of government entitled the Constitution of the United States of

America'; also an ordinance, adopted by the same on the sixteenth day of March, in the year last aforesaid, entitled 'An ordinance to adopt and ratify the Constitution of the Confederate States of America'; and also all ordinances and resolutions of the same, adopted between the sixteenth day of January and the twenty-fourth day of March, in the year aforesaid, subversive of, or antagonistic to, the civil and military authority of the government of the United States of America, under the Constitution thereof, be, and the same are, hereby repealed."

As soon as it was read, the chairman of the committee asked its adoption, and it was at once unanimously passed by a viva voce vote without debate, and with little apparent interest.

There was no approving concourse of dignitaries, no ratifying roar of cannon, no packed gallery of beauty and applause, no parchment ordinance for all men to sign, and not even a poor "yea and nay" record on the journal!

Joshua Hill rose as soon as its passage was announced, and gave notice that he should move to reconsider, in order to substitute for the phrase "be, and the same are, hereby repealed," the words "are now, and always have been, null and void." The former is the language in Mississippi and South Carolina, the latter that of North Carolina. Mr. Hill's motion to substitute the strong language of the old North State gave promise of an interesting debate, and the gallery was crowded next morning when he called up his motion. But he bowed down and took upon his neck the yoke of the Secessionists for the sake of, "harmony," and everybody went away disappointed, and to disappointment a few added disgust.

Mr. Hill said: "There are today higher, nobler considerations than the mere discussion of this subject which weigh upon my mind. My labors in this body shall be bent to one single purpose, and that is the earliest admittance of Georgia into the Union, and the restoration of her ancient rights, so far as may be permitted. I am unwilling to be the first to produce dissension in this body, and I therefore withdraw my motion to reconsider."

Possibly Mr. Hill could not have carried his point, but he could at least have made a gallant fight for the sound doctrine. Georgia went out of the Union by a mere repeal, and she comes back by another mere repeal. Is there any abandonment, in her action, of the old heresy of State sovereignty? Did the war settle nothing but the nation's physical supremacy?

The question of the language to use in acknowledging the abolition of slavery, and declaring its prohibition forever, which occupied one long and exciting day at Columbia, here scarcely occupied one minute. In the new Bill of Rights, as it came from the committee of sixteen, is this clause:

> "20. The government of the United States having, as a war measure, proclaimed all slaves held or owned in this State emancipated from slavery, and having carried that proclamation into full practical effect, there shall henceforth be within the State of Georgia neither slavery nor involuntary servitude, save as a punishment for crime after legal conviction thereof; provided, that this acquiescence in the action of the government of the United States is not intended to operate as a relinquishment, or waiver, or estoppel of such claim for compensation of loss sustained by reason of the emancipation of his slaves as any citizen of Georgia may hereafter make upon the justice and magnanimity of that government."

The clause was reached at exactly five o'clock this evening. The clerk read it in his high monotone,—holding the paper in one hand and a candle in the other, for the hall is low and dark; the President responded, as he had nineteen times before in the last half-hour, "If there be no objection, and the chair hears none, the clause will be considered as agreed to, and the clerk will read the next in order." There was no objection, and the clerk went on with his reading. So, without a word to warm the blood of friend or foe, the great Empire State of the South grudgingly took up the banner of liberty and fell into the ranks of progression.

{XXVIII}

Asking Pardon for Jeff Davis

MILLEDGEVILLE, OCTOBER 31, 1865

EARLY in the morning of the second day's session of the Convention, Mr. E. C. Anderson, of Savannah, late colonel in the Rebel army, moved a resolution for the appointment of a committee to memorialize the President in behalf of Jeff Davis and others. Mr. Anderson hoped gentlemen would consider the condition of Mr. Davis and the other persons whose names were mentioned in the resolution. He could see no reason why they were held in confinement, and he thought the great government of the United States should be magnanimous enough to set them at liberty.

Mr. Joshua Hill believed this question should not be forced upon the

Convention. The body had not met to ask pardon for anybody, but to do what was necessary to restore Georgia to the Union. Moreover, the President understands his business and does not ask our advice.

Mr. C. H. Hopkins, of Pierce County, who will run for Congress as an out-and-out Union man, thought the government should be allowed to take its own course in regard to Jeff Davis. If we arrest the trial of Davis now, supposing our petition could have that effect, what would the world say? Why, that we knew he was guilty of treason, and endeavored in this roundabout way to shield him from trial and punishment. If I were him, I would demand a trial, and if found guilty of treason would meet my fate like a man.

Mr. J. D. Matthews, of Oglethorpe, the leader of the impracticables, an ex-colonel of the Rebel army, and a man of most harsh and forbidding manners, would vote heartily for the resolution. The question involved was not one of principle, but of asking pardon for unfortunate gentlemen now languishing in prison. Once they were our representative men on the battle-field and in the council-chamber,—representative of a government to which we were all pledged. That government is so deeply buried that even the second resurrection cannot reach it, and these men now stand only as the representatives of a cause for which we all battled,—a cause which we and they alike thought sacred. (Applause on the floor.) Why should we not ask this favor? We have been pardoned by the national Executive, and by our pardon we become free and sovereign citizens, clothed with all the rights and privileges pertaining to Americans. Among the most sacred of these rights is that of petition; and all we mean to do in passing and carrying out this resolution is to exercise that sacred right. Mr. Davis is no more a traitor than the rest of us. Nor need he nor any of us be ashamed of our records. We have illustrated Southern manhood on a hundred battle-fields, and we have shown that we can honorably submit to the decrees of God. Now let us come up as men, not as criminals for a favor, but as men for our rights, and ask the pardon of our late and beloved leaders.

The resolution was passed by a viva voce vote.

The committee was appointed, and this morning the following memorial was reported:

"TO HIS EXCELLENCY ANDREW JOHNSON:

"The delegates of the State of Georgia, in Convention assembled, do earnestly invoke the Executive clemency in behalf of Jefferson Davis, Alexander H. Stephens, and James A. Seddon of Virginia, A. G. Magrath of South Carolina, David Yulee of Florida, and H. W. Mercer of Georgia, now confined as prisoners, and all others similarly circumstanced.

"Your Excellency has been pleased to restore Mr. Stephens to his liberty. He returns to the grateful people of this State as a solemn pledge of the magnanimity which rules the public councils; and his great name and influence will be potent to revive the amity of the past, and fructify the wise and generous policy which your Excellency has inaugurated. Emboldened by this example, impelled by the purity of our motives, and stimulated by the prayers of a numerous people, we appeal for clemency in behalf of the distinguished persons we have named. Restore them to liberty and to the embraces of their families, translate them from captivity to the light of freedom and hope, and the gratitude of the prisoners will be mingled with the joyful acclamations which shall ascend to Heaven from the hearts of this people.

"Jefferson Davis was elected to his high position by our suffrages and in response to our wishes. We imposed upon him a responsibility which he did not seek. Originally opposed to the sectional policy to which public opinion, with irresistible power, finally drove him, he became the exponent of our principles and the leader of our cause. He simply responded to the united voice of his section. If he, then, is guilty, so are we; we were the principals, he was our agent. Let not the retribution of a mighty nation be visited upon his head, while we, who urged him to his destiny, are suffered to escape. The liberal clemency of the government has been extended over us; we breathe the air and experience the blessings of freedom; we therefore ask that the leader, who, in response to the democratic instincts of his nature, the principles of his party, and the solicitations of his section, became the head and front of our offending, shall not now be bruised for our iniquities or punished for our transgressions.

"Mr. Davis was not the leader of a feeble and temporary insurrection; he was the representative of great ideas and the exponent of principles which stirred and consolidated a numerous and intelligent people. This people was not his dupe. They pursued the cause they adopted of their own free will, and he did not draw them on, but followed after them. It is for these reasons that we invoke the Executive clemency in his behalf. His frame is feeble; his health is delicate; all broken by the storms of state, he languishes out in captivity a vicarious punishment for the acts of his people. Thousands of hearts are touched with his distress, thousands of prayers

ascend to Heaven for his relief. We invoke in his behalf the generous exercise of the prerogative to pardon which the form and principles of the
Constitution offer as a beneficent instrument to a merciful Executive. We
ask the continuance of that career of clemency which your Excellency has
begun, and which alone, we earnestly believe, can secure the true unity
and lasting greatness of this nation. Dispensing that mercy which is incul-
cated by the example of our great Master on high, your name will be trans-
mitted to your countrymen as one of the benefactors of mankind. The
Constitution of our country, renewed and fortified by your measures, will
once more extend its protection over a contented and happy people,
founded as it will be upon consent and affection, and 'resting like the great
arch of the heavens equally upon all.'"

The memorial was adopted without debate or objection. It indicates that the
people of Georgia are not likely to fail of their desires through any excess of modesty.

{ XXIX }

Amending the State Constitution

MILLEDGEVILLE, NOVEMBER 4, 1865

THE CONVENTION has finished the work of amending the Constitution.
The first article embodies the Bill of Rights. The clause heretofore reported
prohibiting slavery is in this article.

The second article relates to the Legislature, and it occupied the attention of
the Convention for two whole days. The number of legislators remains as heretofore,—41 senators and 169 representatives. The sessions of the Legislature are to
be biennial, beginning on the first Thursday of November, and continuing forty
days. The basis of representation is "representative population." Propositions to
change this to "white population," and to "aggregate population," were lost.

The clause respecting the powers and duties of the Legislature in regard to the
freedmen reads:

"5. It shall be the duty of the General Assembly at its next session, and
thereafter as the public welfare may require, to provide by law for the government of free persons of color; for the protection and security of their
persons and property,—guarding them and the State against any evil that

may arise from their sudden emancipation, and prescribing in what cases their testimony shall be admitted in the courts; for the regulation of their transactions with citizens; for the legalizing of their existing, and the contracting and solemnization of their future marital relations, and connected therewith their rights of testamentary capacity; and for the regulation or prohibition of their immigration into this State from other States of the Union or elsewhere."

It will be observed that herein is an implied discrimination against the freedmen, "prescribing in what cases their testimony shall be admitted in the courts." Just how much this may mean depends of course upon the Legislature; but it is clear that the Convention is of opinion that the negro's right to give evidence should be restricted in some degree.

The third article defines the executive powers. A new clause provides that no man shall be eligible for more than two terms [as Governor] till after the expiration of four years from the end of his second term.

The fourth, or judicial, article occupied the attention of the Convention for two days. The judges of the Supreme Court, three in number, whose term of office is not less than six years, heretofore appointed by the Governor, are hereafter to be elected by the General Assembly; while the judges of the Superior, or Criminal Courts, heretofore elected by the General Assembly, are hereafter to be elected by the people on the first Wednesday in January of every fourth year. The election of the State's attorney and the solicitors has also been given to the people. Heretofore the Superior Court has not had jurisdiction in criminal cases relating to negroes, but the restriction is now removed.

The fifth article embodies several general provisions.

The qualifications of electors remain as heretofore,—free white male citizens, of the age of twenty-one years, two years resident in the State, and six months in the county where offering to vote. A proposition requiring that the people shall vote viva voce was defeated by about three to one.

This article and the Constitution ends with the following new and suggestive clause, which was adopted without debate:

"Marriage between white persons and persons of African descent is forever prohibited; and the General Assembly shall enact laws for the punishment of officers who solemnize such marriages, or knowingly issue licenses therefore, and all such marriages shall be null and void."

{XXX}

The Minor Work of the Convention

MILLEDGEVILLE, NOVEMBER 6, 1865

A N ordinance was passed, requesting the General Assembly, at its first session, to provide for the support and maintenance of the indigent widows and orphans of the deceased soldiers of the State.

A resolution was passed requesting the Provisional Governor to provide for the organization in each county of the State of one or more companies of volunteer militia.

There is an excited state of feeling on the subject of Congressional representation, in which all men in the Convention share. "We must have our representatives at Washington on the opening day," says Matthews of Oglethorpe; "and I believe the Administration will sustain us against the radicals and fanatics of the North in our effort to get into Congress." There was a good deal of remark to this effect; but another set of men found voice through a delegate named Kenan, who was in the first Rebel Congress. "I would not be in such haste," said he, "but would take time for due consideration; and when we have elected our best men, let them go there in a dignified manner, not to ask favors of any party, but to demand their rights." However, there was still another class which found voice in what was said by Mr. Wright, of Coweta: "We are living under a military despotism which can't be endured; let us get our rights first, and attend to our dignities afterward."

The State has been redistricted for seven members of Congress.

The Freedmen's Bureau was brought before the Convention by a message from the Provisional Governor, covering a letter from Brigadier-General Davis Tillson, State Commissioner, setting forth the necessity of having an agent of the bureau in each county, and stating that it was with the utmost difficulty that he had been able to get suitable officers for each section, even; and thereupon asking the Governor to authorize such of the county officers as the bureau might select, and as might be willing to serve, to act as its agents. This proposition the Governor endorsed as likely, if accepted and executed in good faith, to tend much toward removing martial law. The message and documents were sent to the committee of sixteen.

During the pendency of the matter, General Tillson met the delegates at the hall one evening, and explained to them the purposes and desires of the government and the bureau in respect to the freed people. He was kindly received, and listened to with great attention.

On the following day the committee made a report, accepting "the wise and liberal proposition" of General Tillson, and authorizing any civil officer, or any citizen of the State, to act, by his appointment and under his direction and instructions, as agent of the bureau "in adjusting difficulties between the white and colored population of the State, in maintaining the police of the country, and in other similar matters."

This goes one step beyond the General's request, but not beyond his desire, in that it authorizes him to constitute any citizen as his agent. Simple as is the whole proposition,—offering to the people a prospect that their own neighbors, instead of military officers, will, in many cases, be put in charge of the freedmen's interests,—their intense hatred of the bureau and the government led some men into opposition to this report.

Matthews, the inevitable, of Oglethorpe, thought he discovered terrible things in it. It was the entering wedge of nigger equality,—it legalized nigger testimony,— it savored of nigger suffrage,—it obliged a white man to stand beside a nigger in the witness-box,—it obliged every court in the State to admit nigger evidence, &c.,— to all of which he and his people were inflexibly opposed.

Several delegates endeavored to make him see the matter in its true light, but without avail; and the report was then adopted, with about twenty dissenting voices.

{ XXXI }

How Repudiation Was Accomplished

MILLEDGEVILLE, NOVEMBER 7, 1865

THE leading question before the South Carolina Convention was that respecting the prohibition of slavery. The leading question before the North Carolina Convention was that respecting the legality of the ordinance of secession.

The leading question before the Georgia Convention was that respecting the assumption of the war debt. Knowing very well what had been required of the conventions of Alabama and North Carolina, and seeing what would probably be required of the Legislatures of South Carolina and Mississippi, in respect to the debt, the delegates here were very touchy on the subject. They would talk calmly enough with an outsider on other questions; but as soon as conversation turned to that many of them became excited, not to say violent, in their language.

When the Convention came together I doubt if there were over seventy delegates out of the two hundred and ninety present who opposed the assumption of that debt. I think there were also at least one hundred to one hundred and twenty-five who favored its assumption at the face value of the bonds and notes in which it exists. The balance of those who favored its assumption would have been content to reduce it to a specie basis on the value of gold at the time the various bonds were issued. In a word, there were at least three to one in favor of assuming that debt.

The Comptroller-General of the State, in his report of the 16th of October, took strong ground in favor of paying the debt, which he said "rested on the highest moral and legal considerations." The Provisional Governor, on the other hand, took strong ground against paying the debt. "It is of no legal or moral obligation, because it was created to aid in the prosecution of a war of rebellion against the United States. The purpose sought to be accomplished was unconstitutional, and all who participated in the effort to sever the country were violators of law, and can therefore set up no claim for money advanced or services rendered."

This report and this message were the standards round which the fight on the debt question raged. The amount of debt contracted during the war was a trifle over seventeen million dollars, of which some four millions were for the civil expenses of the State. Of the whole amount, about eight and a half millions were payable "six months after a treaty of peace shall have been ratified between the United States and the Confederate States."

On the third day of its session an ordinance was introduced declaring void so much of the State debt as was made in aid of the Rebellion against the United States.

[After debate] the ordinance went to the committee [of sixteen].

On the fourth day Mr. J. L. Warren, of Pulaski County, moved for a committee to wait on the Provisional Governor and learn whether he has any information from the President to the effect that the repudiation of the State debt, created during the late civil war, is essential to a resumption of amicable relations with the United States. Mr. Warren was opposed to repudiation, and didn't want any Presidential telegrams sprung on the Convention at the last moment. If the authorities at Washington require this thing of us, we must submit as we did to the emancipation of our slaves; but let us know beforehand what we are compelled to do, so that if we must repudiate the responsibility may rest upon the government of the United States, and not on the escutcheon of Georgia.

Judge Simmons, of Gwinette County, the leading Unionist in the Convention of 1861, earnestly opposed the passage of the resolution. He would not even seem to admit that the debt could be repudiated. We have submitted to a disgrace deep enough and dark enough already. Our meeting here as we do under the proclamation of a military governor is humiliation enough to satisfy any reasonable man. Let us act in a dignified manner and not admit that we are utterly without rights. *Let us repudiate only at the express command of military power; and then, when we are again in the enjoyment of our rights in the Federal Union, and are once more a free and independent sovereignty, let us call another Convention and assume the whole debt.*

Mr. Solomon Cohen, ex-postmaster of Savannah, and probable candidate for Congress from that district, found the whole question of State rights involved in this issue. He honored the President for his course in endeavoring to stay the waves of Northern fanaticism, and would uphold him all he could; but there is a limit beyond which I cannot go, and I never can vote for repudiation, even at the conqueror's command. We know very well what the fanatical portion of the North require of us. They would not be satisfied with repudiation, unless joined with negro evidence, negro suffrage, negro equality, social and political. Do what we may, we cannot get over that test-oath which they have on their statute-book, and which no honorable man in Georgia can take. Charles Sumner and Thaddeus Stevens have already indicated what they require of us. We must meet them somewhere, and I propose to meet them right here. If this test is now made a prerequisite to our restoration, I for one will resign, and let my constituents, if they choose, send another man to fill the seat I now hold.

On the fifth day there came up from the Governor a brief message, enclosing and indorsing the following telegrams:

"WASHINGTON, October 28, 1865.
"TO GOVERNOR JAMES JOHNSON:

"The President of the United States cannot recognize the people of any State as having resumed the relations of loyalty to the Union that admits as legal obligations contracted or debts created in their name to promote the war of the Rebellion.

"WM. H. SEWARD."

"WASHINGTON, October 29, 1865.
"TO JAMES JOHNSON, *Provisional Governor of Georgia:*

"The people of Georgia should not hesitate one single moment in repudiating every single dollar of debt created for the purpose of aiding the Rebellion against the government of the United States. It will not do to levy and collect taxes from a State and people that are loyal and in the Union to pay a debt that was created to aid in taking them out, thereby subverting the Constitution of the United States. Those who invested their capital in the creation of this debt must meet their fate and take it as one of the inevitable results of the Rebellion.

"ANDREW JOHNSON."

To say that this produced consternation is to put the fact very mildly indeed. The fluttering in the gallery was quite as bad as on the floor of the Convention. "D——n the thing!" said a delegate who sat near me. There was nothing for it, however, but to send the message and accompanying documents to the committee of sixteen.

An ordinance was immediately introduced by Mr. Chappell, of Muscogee. The first section declared the whole war debt null and void; the second provided for the payment by subsequent Legislatures of "any particular debts incurred for other purposes than that of carrying on, aiding, or abetting the war, directly or indirectly"; the third provided that "all evidences of debt whatever issued by the State, payable only in Confederate currency," should be forever prohibited from being paid; the fourth made the ordinance a part of the Constitution.

Mr. J. R. Parrott, of Bartow County, a lawyer, a gentleman of thirty-five years or thereabouts, with the blackest of eyes and hair and beard, a man who has served in the Legislature, and was conscripted in the army, alone, of all the speakers, put the question on its true basis. He was utterly and unalterably opposed to the assumption of this illegal and unconstitutional debt, and he would resist here and everywhere all efforts to tax the poor people of the State for the benefit of the Shylocks who hold it. He said no one proposed to pay Georgia's share of the Confederate States debt. No one proposed to pay for the lost slaves, for the burned houses, for the ruined fortunes of the thousands,—no one proposed anything but the payment of these bonds in the hands of men, fat and sleek, who never saw the forefront of battle, and were careful to keep out of harm's way in the hour of conflict. There was one debt the State should pay,—that to the orphans whose property it had, by legislative enactment, forced into State securities; but beyond that it never should, with his consent, pay a dollar of the debt created in the effort to debase the old flag. There are hundreds of men who were in the bullet department of the war, whilst others were in the speculating or stay-at-home department. The

former had no chances at State six-per-cents, the latter class got them all. In many
cases those in the bullet department had their houses burnt, their fencing all destroyed, their horses, cows, mules, hogs, and other property taken from them. In
the name of all that is fair and honest, I ask, gentlemen, if it is right to tax this
bullet department,—man's naked land and the industry of himself and his homeless family, for all time to come,—to put money into the pocket of him of the speculating department or to swell the wealth of the favorites of power? Let gentlemen vote for such injustice if they wish, and go home and meet the condemnation
of an outraged people. Over three hundred millions invested in negroes, over one
hundred and fifty millions of other property, and all our Confederate money, went
down with the war; and now I say, let our State debt created by the war, and for the
war, go with all the balance. Let us have no favorites, let every man, so far as the
war debt is concerned, whether State or Confederate, stand upon an equal footing.
If you will propose any plan by which our people can become educated, the resources of our State developed, our fields cultivated, our barns filled with plenty,
and happiness and prosperity bless the whole people, I will go for it heart and
hand; but my conceptions of honesty and justice will not warrant me in throwing
the burden of the war on the widowhood and orphanage of my State, in taxing
the toiling thousands of my suffering countrymen to pay off a debt which I consider unconstitutional and void, and that should pass away with the unfortunate
war.

Here the war-debt question rested for four days. The subject became one of
grave importance. Committees sat upon it, caucuses deliberated upon it. It was
the common theme of conversation everywhere. The morning was troubled with
it; it disturbed the digestion of noon; and the pillow of night was disquieted by it.
Slowly, but nevertheless very surely, men came to see the matter in a new light.
They were not convinced of the illegality of the debt, and they insisted that their
acquiescence in the results of the war ought not to be judged by their position in
regard to this matter; but they began to admit that it would not do to disregard
the admonitions of the President,—began to see that they could, under certain
circumstances, vote for repudiation.

On the eleventh day the contest was renewed with great vigor; and the battle
raged for four hours.

Judge Jenkins reported from the committee of sixteen that they had been unable to agree upon any report touching the war debt. Mr. Chappell at once called
up his ordinance introduced on the fifth day, declaring the war debt null and void.

Amendments and substitutes [were rejected]. Debate came up on a motion to strike from Mr. Chappell's ordinance the clause making the whole a part of the Constitution. Mr. Chappell wanted the ordinance made a part of the Constitution. If this were not done, the members of the Legislature, sworn to support the Constitution but not the ordinance, would look upon the two in a very different light, and might easily be persuaded that they were under no legal or moral obligations to observe the latter.

Mr. Matthews made another bitter but eloquent speech against the whole ordinance, and against the proposition to incorporate it into the Constitution. He regarded the debt as a debt of honor, a solemn pledge, which Georgia made to the people of the State; and if there is no honor in that transaction, there is no honor under Heaven. I do not wish to be represented here as charging the President of the United States with being a tyrant, but it is little less than tyranny to make this demand upon us. I will not crawl in the dust to lick the hand of power. We are not yet slaves; we are the same men we were four years ago; and I bid my associates stand as we stood when we flung the flag of Rebellion to the breeze, as we stood through the long and bloody years in which we upheld that flag! (Hearty applause.)

Mr. Hill rebuked the gentlemen who kept up the fight in favor of the war debt. He thought the course of the Secessionists who fled the country much more honorable than that of those who remained, got pardoned, and were continually renewing agitation. As for himself, he was not acting at the dictation of the President or any one else, but from his own sense of right and duty. He opposed the motion to strike out the last clause of the ordinance. He wanted it to stand in the Constitution as a landmark for all coming generations of Georgia's children, to warn them against the evils of secession.

The previous question was then called, and the words, "This ordinance shall be a part of the Constitution and fundamental law of the State," were stricken out by a vote of 156 to 107.

On the twelfth day, that is, this morning, the great contest came to a close, and the ordinance as amended passed by a vote of 135 to 117. It is in the following words:

> "*Be it ordained by the people of Georgia, in Convention assembled,* That all the debts contracted or incurred by the State of Georgia, either as a separate State or as a member of the late partnership or confederacy of States styled the Confederate States of America, for the purpose of carrying on the late war of secession against the United States of America, or for the purpose of aiding, abetting, or promoting said war in any way, directly or in-

directly, be, and the same are, hereby declared null and void; and the Legislature is hereby prohibited forever from, in any way, acknowledging or paying the same debts, or any part thereof, or from passing any law for that purpose, or to secure or provide for the said debts, or any part thereof, by any appropriation of money, property, stocks, funds, or assets of any kind to that object.

"*Be it further ordained,* That all debts of the State incurred during said war shall be considered, held, and treated as debts incurred for carrying on the war; Provided, that nothing herein contained shall prevent any Legislature hereafter to assemble from making appropriations of money for the payment of any claim against the State originating after the 19th January, 1861, where it shall be made clearly to appear that such claim was founded upon a consideration disconnected with any purpose of aiding or assisting the prosecution of the late war against the United States, and not incidental to a state of war."

This ordinance was shorn of its strength by the vague words of the proviso, "shall be made clearly to appear," [which] can, in the hands of a Legislature of the proper stamp, be made to cover a very wide range of claims; and leading delegates tell me that they will be made to cover at least half the seventeen millions of the so-called war debt. This proviso was adopted by a large majority, without count.

It is noticeable that the men who voted against assuming the debt live in the mountainous and wire-grass regions of the State, where, indeed, the loyal men of 1860–61 were found. Yet it must not be forgotten that the ordinance finally passed could have received scarcely seventy-five votes on the opening day of the Convention.

{ XXXII }

Review of the Proceedings of the State Convention

MACON, NOVEMBER 8, 1865

THE State Convention adjourned at noon today, having held a session of thirteen days.

It would be a mockery to say that this was a Convention of loyal men. The flag was neither raised on the State-House where the Convention met nor on the hotel where nine tenths of the delegates boarded; and I know, of my own knowledge, that when an outsider remarked one morning to a knot of four delegates that it would look well to hoist the flag on the Capitol, he was answered, "No, I'll be d——d if anybody gets that up there."

The best men were willing to do just as little as would be needful to meet what they supposed are the requirements of the government. The other side only differed from these in the fact that they were anxious to do just as little as would be needful to restore the State to her relations with the Union.

The excessively modest opinion of the Convention in respect to its labors is apparent from the following address, adopted just before the adjournment:

"TO HIS EXCELLENCY ANDREW JOHNSON:

"The people of the State of Georgia, now in Convention, having repealed all ordinances and resolutions by them heretofore adopted with a purpose to separate themselves from the United States, and to enter into another confederacy; and having adopted a Constitution strictly republican, wherein the supremacy of the Constitution, the constitutional laws, and treaties of the United States of America are distinctly affirmed; having therein recognized the emancipation by the United States government of persons previously held as slaves in this State, and ordained, in the fundamental law, that neither slavery nor involuntary servitude (save as a punishment for crime) shall hereafter exist in Georgia; and having, as they conceive, done all things necessary and proper, on their part, to the full and complete restoration of their State to her rights and privileges as a State, and as a member of the American Union, respectfully request that all needful executive and legislative measures be taken to effect such restoration as speedily as possible."

Newspapers came but infrequently to Georgia's out-of-the-way capital, and I have seen little indicative of the opinion held by the sound heart of the North of the Convention's work. For myself, with every disposition to charity of judgment, I must pronounce it very far from being good. The State-rights heresy was as dominant in this Convention, almost, as in that of 1861. True, there is a clause in the new Constitution that acknowledges the Constitution of the United States and all laws created in pursuance thereof as the supreme law of the State; but the natural belief and feeling of members crops out, nevertheless, in the memorial to the President. "With a purpose to separate themselves from the United States and *to enter into another Confederacy*," is the noteworthy language of this document, by

which it is virtually declared that the United States is not a nationality, not a government one and indivisible, but only a "confederacy" that may be broken up at any
moment. Yet, in the face of this language, and in face of the fact that the secession ordinance is only repealed, and of the other grave fact, that no part of the
Convention's work is submitted to the people for ratification, this address to the
President brazenly claims that everything necessary and proper has been done to
entitle the State to a full and complete restoration of her rights in the Union.

It seems to me, in view of the language of all classes of delegates, a very grave
matter that the constitution and the ordinance repealing the act of secession are
not submitted to the people. One of the best of the so-called Union men openly
suggested the repudiation of the war debt by this Convention and its assumption
by another convention, called as soon as the State resumes her privileges in
Congress. Delegate Simmons, representing the element which never acquiesced in
the war, said: "Our meeting here by military proclamation as we do is a disgrace
and humiliation." Delegate Goode, representing the element which opposed secession, but heartily engaged in the war on behalf of the State, said: "The office
of Provisional Governor is a military office, and all his acts and appointments are
of a military character; and with them we as a people have nothing to do except as
we are compelled by military force." Delegate Kenan, representing the element
which favored co-operation in the winter of 1860–61, yet was at heart urgent for
secession, said: "We are living under a tyrannical military despotism; our hands are
tied; we have no free will of our own; we must do whatever the conqueror bids
us do." Delegate Matthews, representing the element which was hot for secession
and is now very malignant, said: "It is an insult to the proud State of Georgia to call
this a free Convention of her people, if we are to be governed in our course by the
views of the President." The argument from all these utterances is plain enough,—
if this was simply a military Convention, how long before we shall have a party
here advocating a repudiation of its action in one or more particulars?

The action of the Convention on the slavery question was consonant with that
on the secession question. It accepted the fact as accomplished by the arms of
the nation, but put in a claim for compensation. We may be thankful for its broad
affirmation that the Presidential proclamation was not the useless paper that
some men would have us believe; but it is scarcely less than an insult to even indirectly assert an obligation on the part of the government to pay for the slaves it
declared free.

The Convention directs the Legislature to provide for government and protection of freedmen, but adds that "the General Assembly shall prescribe in what

cases his testimony shall be admitted into the courts," and thereby impliedly says
he shall yet be a slave in fact if not in name.

It is this indifference to manhood,—low, dwarfed, ignorant, pitifully poor manhood, if you will, but still manhood,—it is this indifference to the man in the negro
that shocks my moral sense everywhere in the South, and nowhere more than
here. There is a lower deep than the Levite reached in going by on the other side,
for he only shunned the wounded man; and these Georgians reach it by ignoring
the very existence of the wounded man.

I am told by a dozen delegates,—am even told by no less than three Superior
Court judges of the State—that there is nothing in the code of Georgia to prevent
the admission of negro evidence in the courts. Indeed, one of these judges, who
has much influence in the State, tells me that when slavery fell everything resting on it fell; and that the negro, by virtue of his status as a free person, has just the
same legal rights that the white man has. The revolting and humiliating feature
of the situation is, therefore, the cool indifference with which everybody ignores
those rights.

The war debt of the State was repudiated, yet here the usual doublefacedness
of the Convention again appeared. In spite of the strong words of the first section
of the ordinance, the final clause, which made it a part of the Constitution, was
stricken out by a vote of 156 to 107, so as to leave the whole subject open for action
at a future session of the Convention. Furthermore, there was inserted, by an almost unanimous vote, a proviso giving the Legislature power to pay any claim
"where it shall be made clearly to appear that such claim is founded upon a consideration disconnected with any purpose of aiding or assisting the prosecution of
the late war against the United States." Will a claim for four years' service as
Governor be allowed under that proviso? Will the two millions necessary to pay the
Legislature for four years' service be disallowed? If the war-debt bondholders can
make it appear that their bonds were issued to pay for corn and bacon to be given
to starving women and children whose husbands and fathers were fighting the
government, will not a pliant Legislature appropriate the necessary money?

There is no hearty acquiescence in the result of the war. There is no love of
the nation as a unit. There is a formal assent to certain terms of restoration, but the
promise is kept to the ear only to be broken to the heart. These delegates prohibit
slavery, but they file their claim for compensation for the emancipated slaves.
They instruct the General Assembly to provide for the protection of the freedman,
but they say he shall have only partial rights in the courts. They declare the war
debt null and void, but they devise a cunning proviso through which speculators

may drive a chariot and four. They admit the supremacy of the Federal Constitution, but they reaffirm the legality of secession.

Have they a right to declare that their new Constitution is "strictly republican" in form? Have they a right to assert that they have "done all things needful and proper, on their part, to the full and complete restoration of their State to her rights and privileges as a member of the American Union"?

{XXXIII}

A Visit to the Home of Judge Lynch

ALBANY, NOVEMBER 10, 1865

I HAVE reached the Southern point of my Southern trip. This town is in the southwestern corner of Georgia, about forty miles from the Alabama line, and about sixty miles above the Florida line.

Winter seems scarcely nearer now than when I left New York on the 1st of September. I write this afternoon in a room with northern exposure, without a fire, and with my two windows wide open. The landlord said to me this morning that he reckoned he would have to get a stove into the office of the hotel pretty soon if this cold snap continued. There has yet been but one frost here this fall, and that was so slight it did no damage. A dozen varieties of roses are in full bloom and fragrance in the gardens and dooryards of the town; wild-flowers blossom in the old fields and by the roadside; the grass still shows freshness and greenness; the leaves of the mulberry are beginning to fall, but those of the oak and china and willow have hardly lost any of their summer color.

Albany contains a population of twenty-five hundred persons. The town is reached from Milledgeville, one hundred and forty miles distant, by fourteen hours of railroad riding, in cars wretched beyond Northern conception, over a road on which not more than an average of one train per day is disabled by breakage or being thrown from the track. Albany has three small churches, two small hotels, half a dozen very large cotton warehouses, a good many groggeries, and one small schoolhouse. Its private residences are neither large nor pretty, and the general aspect of the town is dirty, slovenly, and shiftless. It has a filthy river on the east, and lowland piney woods on the south, west, and north.

I was told by several persons in the upper country that I would find Albany one of the worst places in the State both in regard to morals and Unionism. It was a rabid secession town in 1860–61, and sent many soldiers very early to the war. Such of the returned soldiery as I have met seem, as a general thing, quiet and well disposed; but many of the towns-people who did not go into the field are exceedingly bitter, and do not accept the new order of things in either a wise or kindly spirit. "I have my pardon in my pocket, and have taken the oath three times," said one of them in my hearing last evening, "but I'll be d——d if I a'n't as big a Rebel as I ever was!"

I reached the place at five o'clock last evening. About noon [today] half a dozen of us sat on the hotel steps waiting dinner. I was talking with an ex-Rebel captain. Down the sidewalk, some twenty-five yards from where we sat, we suddenly became aware that a quarrel was progressing. It was between a negro man and a young fellow with his left arm in a sling. I noticed that the latter wore an army blouse, and of course supposed him to be a soldier. He struck out three or four times, but the negro was much the taller of the two and kept out of his reach. Nothing coming of this, he disengaged his arm from the sling and turned and seized a long-handled shovel from half a dozen in front of a store. The negro stepped into the store, the soldier striking a blow at him as he went, and following him. In an instant he shuffled out, one of the clerks striking him about the head and shoulders with a small stick. Thus far the matter had not become serious and no one interfered.

The old negro walked down past the hotel, but soon stopped to excitedly explain the affair to three or four men standing there. While he was doing so, the soldier rushed out of the store above with a large and ugly looking knife in his hand. Seeing this, the clerk of the hotel said to the negro, "Come, come, old Bill, if you don't want to get into trouble you'd better get out of town at once." Old Bill didn't heed the warning, however. Thinking he might be moved by a stranger, and desiring to prevent a possible conflict between the soldiers and the negroes, I stepped to him, took him by the arm, and said, "There, John, that'll do for this time; now go home." He at once started, while I resumed my seat, and half a dozen fellows rushed across from the opposite side of the street, shouting, "Kill him!" "Kill the d——n nigger!" "Somebody shoot him!" He soon turned the corner and was out of sight, the whole affair having occupied scarcely two minutes.

In a moment more one of the three or four men to whom the negro had volunteered his excited explanation stepped up in front of me and demanded why I had interfered in the business. I answered, "Simply to stop the quarrel."

"What business was the quarrel to you?"

"The same as to every good citizen."

"Well, by G–d, we don't 'low any outside interference yerabouts,—do you hear?"

He passed along a few steps, and I supposed he had concluded his advice. Not so, however, for he returned with, "Did you interfere for the white man or the nigger?"

"For neither. I simply interfered to stop a quarrel."

"Well, by G–d! I'm the responsible party in this business, and if you've got anything to say you kin jest say it to me."

"I've nothing to say except to hope that if you are the responsible party, you'll do just what I was trying to do—prevent any fighting."

"You interfered on the side of the nigger, and no one don't do that yere while I'm 'round,—do you hear?"

"Certainly, sir; but you make a mistake,—I interfered on nobody's side. I merely told the negro he had better go home; and I did that only to break up a quarrel and prevent a street fight; and that, I'm sure, anyone, whether a citizen or a stranger, had a perfect right to do."

The fellow would not be satisfied, and I sat for five minutes and heard one unbroken stream of half-drunken taunt and invective. When he said he could jest lay me down and stamp on me, I couldn't help remarking that, as he was four inches the tallest, and weighed one hundred and eighty to my one hundred and thirty, he was probably correct in his judgment in regard to the matter. I thought he might strike me, but he didn't, and I kept my seat. Having assured me that I was no gentleman, and that if I had any pluck I would know how to resent an insult, he allowed a couple of companions to lead him away.

I have been thus minute in detailing this ridiculous affair because of the importance to which it grew in the course of a few hours. Coming out from dinner half an hour later, the landlord told me that the negro had always been free; that the young fellow with the blue army blouse was no soldier, but one of their citizens; and that my assailant was an ex-major of the Confederate service. He added that he was a very fierce man when in liquor, and had recently horsewhipped a person. He further added that perhaps I had better keep out of the way this afternoon. I had hardly taken my seat among the gentlemen on the steps before one of the major's friends passed into the hotel. He soon sent the clerk to call me, and then warned me that the major was always armed, and that I had better keep out of sight unless I was prepared to defend myself. I thanked him for his service, and reiterated that I didn't believe there would be any difficulty. He had scarcely gone before I was waited upon by a citizen of the town, who, in courteous phrase, informed me that

my interference on behalf of the negro as against a white man would not be readily overlooked. I replied to him that I had supposed the white man to be a soldier;
and I presumed no one would undertake to say that I might not interfere between
a soldier and a negro. "But," said I, "there was no interference in behalf of any-
one, my whole purpose being to save the town from a conflict between the soldiers on one side and the negroes on the other side." The explanation was entirely
satisfactory to him, he said, and he would endeavor to put the matter in its proper
light before the major and his friends, of whom I had better keep clear all the afternoon. I said I had been already warned. In less than ten minutes I was waited
upon by citizen number two, who asked my name, residence, and business. I gave
him my card, and told him my business was my own affair. He also warned me to
beware of the major; and added that he had just bought a horsewhip and was drinking pretty heavily. I assured him that I should go about my business as if nothing
had happened. And so I did: that business being, first, to keep an appointment at
head-quarters; second, to write the first part of this letter; and, third, to nurse my
regular tri-weekly turn of chill and fever.

In going to head-quarters and returning therefrom I saw nothing of my friend
the major with the pistol and knife and horsewhip. I met citizen number one,
however, who told me I was doing a very foolhardy thing in being on the street
unless I was prepared to give as well as take. He said the major would horsewhip
me at sight, and finally advised me to leave town forthwith. I answered that I came
here expecting to remain till tomorrow morning, and had not yet seen any reason
for changing my original determination.

Writing quietly in my room, lying buried under a warmthless mountain of bed-
clothes while the ague shook me, sleeping a hot and disturbed sleep while the
fever burned me,—so the afternoon wore away.

I woke a few minutes before six, and found the clerk of the hotel waiting. He
came to advise me as a friend, he said, not to leave my room. I asked him for a detailed account of the situation. The afternoon had been very lively, and the evening
was quite promising. My friend the major had been joined by my friend the colonel
and my friend the Judge and several other high-toned Southern gentlemen, all of
whom were somewhat in liquor and deeply incensed at "the d——d Yankee" for
"taking a nigger's part." Various members of the gang had been to the hotel and
done me the honor of inquiring for my room, and had severally been told that I
was out. Now that supper time was near, they had come in a body, and were anxious to have me show my "d——d Yankee face."

It further appeared that the old negro had made complaint at head-quarters of the man who drew a knife on him,—the little fellow whose arm was in a sling and whose body was in a blue blouse. The captain had sent out a corporal and four men to arrest him, the negro going along to point him out. In front of the hotel the military had fallen in with the major's gang, and a conflict had ensued in which his new horsewhip was worn up on the negro's head and shoulders. The soldiers were powerless to protect the negro, and retired without being able either to effect the arrest of the lame man or the major. The gang now stood in an attitude of defiance, swearing that no one should be arrested by the "d——d Yankees," and the post commandant had taken no measures to assert his authority or to put down the disturbance.

I dismissed the clerk and took the matter into consideration. Clearly, it would be useless to appeal to the military, of whom there are but thirty stationed here. Should I borrow a revolver and use it if attacked?

While I debated the question with myself,—one voice saying "yes" and the other arguing that it would be foolish to get into a quarrel with a gang of drunken ruffians who ruled the town,—citizen number three presented himself. He also came to advise me as a friend. The crowd, he said, was very much excited. If I was seen on the street or in the hall of the hotel I might be shot at once; or I might be seized and carried out of town and "strung up"; or I would at least be assaulted and much bruised unless I shot two or three men at sight. Wasn't this a pretty dish to set before a little Yankee whose only weapons were a pen and inkstand!

Just then the landlord himself entered my room. He asked me if I was going down to supper. I responded that I wanted nothing but a cup of tea, and intended to go down for that. He begged to send it to me, saying that it would not be advisable to appear in the dining-room. I asked him if he expected to allow a gang of drunken brawlers to insult the guests of the house. He replied that he would close the doors against them, but that the excitement was so great he could not be responsible for the consequences. So I consented to take a cup of tea in my room, and my visitors and advisers retired.

While I finished my tea, I heard an excited shout in front of the hotel; and, going into the hall to see what it meant, I met the clerk, who advised me to leave the house as soon as possible, offering, himself, to conduct me by the back way to a safe retreat.

Before I made answer the landlord again appeared. He had been a captain in the Confederate service, and is a very courteous and well-disposed man. He was apparently much embarrassed, but finally made me understand that he, too, thought it advisable for me, on his account as well as my own, to leave the house. He had already been set upon by the gang for declining to show them the way to my room, and expressed the belief that they would "go through the house" before ten o'-clock, unless he could be able to prove to them that I had vacated the premises. He would bolt and block the doors if I insisted on remaining, and would defend his guests to the last; but he hoped I would not deem it necessary to insist upon meeting a gang of twelve or fifteen drunken men. He sincerely regretted that I had been disturbed, and said he had endeavored without avail to explain the affair in its true light. He would have me conducted to a quiet private house, and hoped to see me again on a more auspicious occasion.

Was it worth while to remain and insist upon my rights? I had not seen one of the gang of ruffians; but I had been told that a dozen or more leading men of the town were in it, backed by the usual crowd of idle fellows of the baser sort. Should I allow myself to be forced into a quarrel on an issue that I had not made? I finally concluded to retire from the field.

The clerk, a slight but wiry young man who had served three years as a private in the Rebel army, offered again to see me out of the difficulty. "I know nothing of you," he said, "except that you are the guest of the house, and appear to be a gentleman, and no one shall disturb you unless over my dead body."

It was now eight o'clock, and as we passed into the lower hall I could hear the noisy surging of the drunken crowd in front of the hotel. The landlord reconnoitered at the main door, and reported that it would not be safe to attempt to leave by that. So we filed out through the back yard and the back gate. Reaching the street, we marched in solid column, two abreast; the clerk on the right with pistol in hand, the Yankee on the left with overcoat and blanket, and the negro boy in the rear with my valise on his head.

Through how many back streets did we march? say, rather, through how many did we not march! I had no idea there were half as many in the whole town. I was possessed with a strong desire to sit down and have a hearty laugh; but when I asked my guard if I might shout, he said, "Hiss, there's some of 'em!" Sure enough, there were three tipsyish men blundering along in the darkness scarcely twenty yards away. "I heerd 'em say dey shoot de G–d d——n Yankee if dey gits de chance," said the negro boy in a low voice. I heard the clerk's pistol click, and he pushed me to the middle of the street. "I'll stand by you," he said, and I have no doubt the hot blood jumped in his veins. He breathed more freely when they had passed, and vouchsafed the sole remark, "I know the ways here better than you do." After that we marched in solemn silence through the heavy sand, and finally halted at a large white house just in the edge of the town.

Here he left me, with the simple explanation that the hotel had no accommodations, and wished me to have a bed till morning. The old lady had evidently received lodgers from there before, for she said it was all right, and at once sent me up to this pleasant room in which I write.

AMERICUS, NOVEMBER 11

I am now thirty-seven miles from Albany and my friends of knives and pistols and horsewhips.

It appeared to me that if I was in such danger as my advisers represented, I might be waited upon at the depot about the time of leaving the city. I concluded to take the advice of the hotel-clerk and give my friends the slip, by taking the freight train at half-past five instead of the mail train at half-past seven.

While I walked on the platform of the depot in the breaking morning, laughing at the ridiculous position in which I found myself, one of the train hands spoke to one of the station hands: "Jest be 'round when the mail goes out, an' I reckon you'll see fun." "Why?" said the other. "O, wa'al I do' know, but there's a Yankee he's got in trouble with some o' our folks, an' they's comin' down to see him off this mornin'."

"Thank you, good friends," said I, to myself, "but I shall not be here when you come down." We made the run hither in about four hours, stopping half an hour for breakfast.

I have learned that there was much noise and excitement about the hotel till midnight; that there were twenty or more half-drunken men around there for a long time; that some of the rooms were searched for the offending Yankee. So many of the leading men were in the spree that very little could be done to put down the row, which exceeded any that had occurred there for a dozen years.

Thinking of the affair now and at this distance, it still seems as if everybody had conspired to exaggerate its proportions to me. Three days ago I should have deemed it utterly impossible for anything I could say or do to produce such an exhibition of feeling. While the result indicates the under-current of passion, I cannot believe that any sober citizen of Albany sanctions the work of his townsmen yesterday.

{XXXIV}

The Great Military Prison of Georgia

ANDERSONVILLE, NOVEMBER 13, 1865

A GENTLEMAN who came down from Macon this morning tells me that a private telegram announces the hanging of Wirz on Friday last. The man seems to have no friends even in the little village where he lived so long. That he has passed beyond the praise and blame of men is new hope for the Republic and new source for confidence in the sovereign people.

I sat in the cars talking with an ex-Rebel major, formerly on the staff of Howell Cobb when he had command of the Georgia Reserves. Suddenly he broke into something I was saying with, "There's where Captain Wirz lived," pointing to the right of the track as we came southward. I looked and saw a large unpainted wooden house, two stories high in the ridge, and scarcely one in the eaves,—a plain Southern dwelling of the average country sort, with negro-quarters in the rear and a turnip-patch on the left. A sallow-faced white woman looked from the window, and a large eyed negro child stood on the doorsteps.

"We are near Andersonville, then?" said I. "Yes, Anderson is only a mile and a half distant," he responded. I learned afterwards that the place is generally called Anderson hereabouts, the affix *ville* being of recent origin. Years ago it was simply Station Number Eight, and received its present name, I am told, in honor of General Robert Anderson of Sumter fame.

Five minutes more and there flashed upon us through the trees the white line of the cemetery fence, and in another instant we caught a glimpse of the long rows of white head-boards standing brightly in the noonday sunshine. A score of persons rose to look through the windows and see the famous stockade of dreadful memory.

The great stockade was the central feature of the famous Andersonville prison, technically known to the Rebels as "Camp Sumter." Connected with this were the cook-house, the bake-house, the numerous forts, the officers' stockade, the hospital stockade, the dispensary, the vegetable garden, the Confederate hospital, the general cemetery, the pest-house, and the small-pox cemetery. The great cemetery is nearly north of the large stockade. The whole prison lies east of the railroad.

The main stockade originally contained fifteen acres, about five acres of which were swamp. Eleven acres were afterward added to the northern end, so that it now exists as a parallelogram, rather less than twice as long north and south as it is wide east and west. Some seven or eight acres are south of the little stream which crosses it. The swamp is mostly in that part north of the brook. The extreme southern end is eighteen or twenty feet above the level of the water, and the slope down to it is quite gradual. The bank north of the stream is very steep, and the farther end of the stockade is at least forty-five or fifty feet above the water level.

The stockade has a double wall, the outer one being about one hundred and sixty feet from the inner one, and each being built of logs ten or twelve inches in diameter, set five feet in the earth, and standing twenty feet above the surface. The logs are mostly pine. Those of the outer wall retain the bark. Those of the inner wall are all peeled, and those of the original stockade are also hewn. As if this double wall were not sufficient to guard against escape, a deep ditch was dug along the southern and eastern sides, outside the outer wall of course; and for a part of the distance on the northern and eastern sides there is even a third wall of logs.

The sentry-boxes, built just below the top of the inner wall, are mere frames, covered with a board roof, and reached by rude ladders. The boxes were forty-four in number,—thirteen on each side, seven on each end, and one at each corner. These all remain as though they were but yesterday occupied, except one on the western side near the northern end.

Within the stockade proper there is, as compared with Florence, scarcely [anything] to see. In the days when it was packed with from thirty to thirty-five thousand men, the whole surface was covered with tents and mud-and-stick cabins. Of these not more than fifty remain, and they are all south of the brook.

In the whole stockade there is not a single tree. The ground was originally well-wooded, but Winder cut away everything. In the northwestern corner, near the outer wall, he left a single tall pine, whose grateful shade could never fall within the stockade proper,—left it as if to tantalize the weary and fevered prisoners through the blazing summer days.

How dared any one ever deny the existence of a dead-line here? It is twenty feet inside the inner wall. For a part of the distance it was a palpable thing,—four inch strips of twenty feet siding, nailed on the top of posts three feet high. For another portion of the distance it was, however, marked only by these little posts twenty feet apart. That men in such a packed prison should not crowd beyond this undefined line between these posts was an impossibility. Hellish malignity could not have devised a surer way to lead half-crazed men to swift destruction than was found in thus establishing this unmarked line.

The hospital stockade, sixty or seventy rods south of the general stockade, is an enclosure of eight acres. It is built with logs, only ten feet high, which, considering that no one went to the hospital till he was past walking, seems a needless waste of good lumber that might have been given to the boys in the general stockade for firewood in the winter time. Posts were set within this enclosure for twenty-two buildings, each twenty by one hundred and fifteen feet in size. Seven of these appear to have been finished; that is, roofed and sided. Nine more were roofed, but not sided. The remaining six never got further than the corner-posts. None of them ever had any floor but the earth, and eight never were sided. Of these twelve only nine have chimneys,—mere piles of sticks and clay, with a huge fireplace facing either end of the building. A score of broken bunks are scattered about, but the beds seem mostly to have been spread on the earth.

The dispensary is a plain two-story building west of the hospital stockade. It has three rooms on the lower floor, and two on the upper floor, with a second floor piazza on the western front. The central lower room of the house was the shop. It is arranged with a counter through the middle, and shelves on either side and at the farther end. The medicines in use appear to have been principally such roots, seeds, and barks as could be found in the Confederacy. The floor of this small middle room is covered four or five inches deep with a mass of bark, seed, paper, sticks, and roots. I was able to find the labels of nine different preparations, to wit: prickly elder, pink root, sumach berries, queen's delight, poplar bark, worm seed, wild cherry bark, wild ginger, and Georgia bark. Each was made ready for use by steeping in water, and the dose was from one to three fluid ounces. That there were other medicines than these is evident enough from the fact that I found prescriptions for portions of quinine, camphor, and one or two other articles.

They buried their dead, these prisoners of Andersonville, in the pleasantest field of all the section hereabouts. It is in the heart of the pines, and gives serene resting-ground for men worn down in the battle. All about the graves the wild-flowers of the country blossom,—all around them stately trees keep sturdy guard.

The cemetery covers forty-seven acres, and is nearly square in form. It occupies a tract somewhat larger than the old field, a portion of the timber on the north and the east having also been enclosed. The whitewashed picket fence is completed on three sides; on the eastern side is a rough board fence, which will soon, however, give way to a picket like that on the other sides. The cemetery is [northwest] from the stockade; about one third of a mile from the northern line thereof. [It] is laid out in four nearly equal sections, by cross-roads intersecting near the center of the enclosure. The entrance is by a plain gate about midway in the southern line. Inside the fence, on the right of the gate, on the transverse section of a cross, is the inscription:

NATIONAL CEMETERY
ANDERSONVILLE

On the left of the gate, inscribed upon a similar neat white board, is this impressive and appropriate inscription:

> "On FAME's eternal camping-ground
> Their silent tents are spread,
> And GLORY guards with solemn round
> The bivouac of the dead."

In the southeastern quarter of the cemetery are three sections of graves, separated by broad alleys running east and west. Each of these sections contains about fourteen hundred graves, in long rows of over a hundred each. In the southwestern quarter, are two similar sections, separated also by an alley, and having about the same number of graves in the long rows. Where the first of these alleys crosses the main road, on the right and on the left, are these inscriptions:

> "Whether in the prison drear
> Or in the battle's van,
> The fittest place for man to die
> Is where he dies for man."

> "The hopes, the fears, the blood, the tears,
> That marked the battle strife,
> Are now all crowned by victory
> That saved the nation's life."

Where the second alley crosses are similarly set up, on the right and on the left the following memorial passages:

> "A thousand battle-fields have drank
> The blood of warriors brave,
> And countless homes are dark and drear
> In the land they died to save."

"Then shall the dust
Return to the earth as it was;
And the spirit shall return
Unto God who gave it."

In the northwestern quarter, in the extreme corner of the cemetery, are the graves of the guard, one hundred and fifteen in number, from the 1st, 2d, 3d, and 4th Georgia Reserves. In the northeastern quarter is a solid section of over five thousand graves, in rows of about two hundred each; and here stands the following motto:

"Through all Rebellion's horrors
Bright shines our nation's fame:
Our gallant soldiers, perishing,
Have won a deathless name."

In the center of the enclosure, at the crossing of the roads, is the forty-feet pine flag-staff, erected in July, by the burial party which came out from Washington with Miss Clara Barton, of Massachusetts.

These 12,882 soldiers' and sailors' graves are each marked with a plain white head-board thirty inches high and ten inches wide, inscribed on the inside with name, regiment, rank, and date of death. At first the bodies were buried so far apart that there is often more than a foot of space between the edges of the head-boards; but in the large section in the northeastern corner, where those who died last winter and spring are buried, the space is never more than four inches and in many cases is scarcely two. The first recorded death was February 27, 1864, the last April 28, 1865, giving an average of about nine hundred and twenty deaths per month for fourteen months. In the months of August and September, 1864, the average of deaths appears, however, to have been nearly five hundred per week; and there were many occasions when the number exceeded one hundred per day.

Across the Sweet Water Creek, in the oaks, about a hundred rods distant, and south of east in direction from the hospital stockade, was the pest-house. It simply consisted of three log cabins, each about ten by fifteen feet in size. One has been torn down, but the other two remain, and one of them is occupied by a "cracker" family.

The bodies of those who died of small-pox are buried in an old field about thirty rods northeast of the pest-house. There are sixty-four graves, a large proportion of them being of members of Tennessee regiments. The white head-boards

show that the first death from this disease took place March 12, 1864, within a
month after the occupation of the stockade, and the last on July 19, 1864. The
graves will be enclosed in a little cemetery five rods square.

There were but two storehouses. They are close by the depot, one on either
side of the railroad track. The quartermasters' building is thirty by one hundred
and five feet in size, and eight feet high in the eaves; the commissary building is of
the same height, and forty-five by two hundred and sixty feet in size. It can very
readily be seen that the Rebels were utterly unable to keep a week's full rations
on hand, even when the stockade contained no more than twenty thousand prisoners. These buildings now furnish a temporary home for various persons, and
contain the freight rooms, a shoemaker's shop, a groggery, and the commissary
supplies for the negroes at work in the cemetery.

The forts are nine in number. The largest is at the southwestern corner of the
stockade. It mounted twelve guns, had three magazines, and enclosed the house
and yard of the Widow Turner. At the southeastern corner is a double fort, or perhaps I should say two single forts, one fronting south and the other fronting east,
and each mounting three guns. Midway on the eastern side, not far from the wall,
is a small fort mounting three guns; and far out in front of that, on the hill, the
beginning of a larger one, which never was finished, though two guns were
mounted there. At the northeastern corner is a fort of five guns, and another of
the same size is at the northwestern corner, while between the two is a smaller
one of three guns. On the western side is a long line of rifle-pits, and a square fort
of five guns. Here, then, were forty-one guns, so mounted that nearly every acre of
the stockade could be swept with grape and canister. The forts remain with walls
and ditches and platforms and magazines intact, but the cannon have been removed by the military authorities.

"We had it pretty tough sometimes at Camp Chase," said a young fellow who
had been a Rebel soldier, and with whom I talked at Fort Valley; "we had to tote our
wood nigh onto half a mile in the winter time." Before I could answer, another
young fellow, sitting on the opposite side of the fireplace, responded, "Well, s'pose
you'd been in Andersonville, as my father was, where you didn't have to tote it at
all; where you could see a thousand acres within a quarter of a mile, and wasn't
allowed to have a stick of it!"

{XXXV}

Matters in Southwestern Georgia

FORT VALLEY, NOVEMBER 15, 1865

THIS is a pleasant little town of some sixteen hundred to two thousand inhabitants, situated thirty miles below Macon and about one hundred miles above the Florida line. It is the principal place in Houston County, and is the junction of the Muscogee and the Southwestern Railroads. It is not a point for the cotton trade, but does a large retail business with the surrounding country.

The section of the State below here, of which Albany may be called the center, constituting Southwestern Georgia, is one of the finest cotton-growing regions of the South. It was not much traversed by either army, had no chance at running the blockade, and could get very little shipment on the railroads; consequently the surrender of the Southern army found in the country about all the cotton that had been raised in five years. Various gentlemen whom I met in the Carolinas from time to time told me there was probably more cotton in Georgia at the close of the war than in any other Southern State; and many gentlemen of this State tell me that the great bulk of the amount was in the southwestern section. The estimates of the amount in forty counties of this quarter average about two hundred thousand bales. The estimates of the amount made this year in the same counties average near ten thousand bales.

The men who did the fighting are everywhere the men who most readily accept the issues of the war. "I can whip any three Yankees in town," blustered an ex-Rebel officer at Americus the other day; but when I inquired about his record in the army I found that he was generally "seriously unwell" on the day of battle. So, too, one of the most malignant men I met at Milledgeville served during the war in the home guard, and, afterwards, as the commandant of a prison.

The late Rebel privates of this section are, generally, doing quite well. They mourn over the defeat of their armies, and are very fond of showing that but for this little mistake, or that little accident, or that other little blunder, the Confederacy would now be a great nation; but they appear, on the whole, to accept the issue of the war in good faith and with a determination to do their duties hereafter as orderly citizens. I should add, however, that there are more exceptions to this general fact than I found in South Carolina.

However strongly the Carolinian clings to his State-rights doctrine, he knows and feels that his State has been punished as a criminal for upholding that dogma. The people of this section hold to the old faith on the abstract question, and do not seem to recognize that they have been beaten in the contest; and hence there is much scolding at what is termed "Presidential interference in the affairs of the State." Most noticeable as this is, there are very few who desire any further war on the subject. "I am as good a Calhoun man to-day as ever I was," said a gentleman to me at Smithville, "but you Yankees are too strong for us; and now I propose to keep my opinions to myself and do my duty as a good citizen."

An Americus merchant told me he was a hot Secessionist all through 1860, and, though sixty years of age, shouldered his musket early in 1861 and saw two years of service before he broke down. "We staked everything on the result, and for my part I submit to the issue without a murmur"; but before our conversation closed he said, "We have all taken the amnesty oath; we have just as many rights now as Mr. Johnson himself has; Georgia is again a member of the Federal Union, and I should like to see any Massachusetts or New York congressman get up and deny her sovereignty!" and, warming with his subject, he soon added, "We're not going there to ask favors, by G—d, but to demand our rights!"

There is a pretty general contempt everywhere for the "Yankees," the word standing for the resident of any Northern State. Passing by a piazza in Americus on which three or four men sat, I overheard one of them remark, "Well, hell's the place for Yankees, and I want 'em all to go thar as soon's possible, and take the niggers 'long with 'em." Talking with a very intelligent Macon gentleman, I asked him how Northern men would be likely to succeed in business if they were to come into the State this winter; and his answer was, "I think they would get along well enough in the upper-country, but in the lower part of the State there is such ignorance and prejudice that I reckon they would see hard times a long while before they made a living." I must add, that in a general way I hear much expression of a desire for an influx of Northern energy and Northern capital. "Yet when the Yankees come down here," said a man from Columbus, whom I sat next to at the tea-table, "they'll have to be Georgians if they reckon to make money."

I have seen not a little of feminine bitterness since coming into the South; but the women of this section have favored me with some unusual exhibitions during the past week. One who took the train at Montezuma remarked to an acquaintance that the Yankees had all left that place, and she hoped to the good gracious that none would ever be seen there again; to which her friend responded, "I wish we could git shet of 'em forever up to our place." When we went down past Andersonville the other day, a genteel young lady who sat in the seat in front of mine said to the gentleman who was her seatmate, "Do you know, I'm not sorry so many Yankees died here, for they'd no business to come down and fight the South!"

I found many negroes below here who were run out of the northern part of the State and out of South Carolina, on the approach of Sherman's army. The beauty of the old "patriarchal institution" appears in the fact that none but the able-bodied negroes were brought away,—the love of the late masters for their servants so prevailing that the aged and infirm were left to the tender mercies of the Yankees!

These refugee negroes generally seem anxious to return to their former homes, though the whites profess to think it an indication of shiftlessness that they desire to see fathers and mothers and children. I saw a party of eleven one morning just starting out to walk over to Barnwell District, South Carolina, a distance of at least two hundred and fifty miles; and the members of another gang of fourteen told me they were going to start for North Carolina so as to get there by Christmas.

The idea that the whites and the blacks cannot live together is unusually prevalent throughout all this section. "The negroes were the ignorant cause of the war, and are bound to be exterminated before the conflict closes," said one gentleman, a member of the late Convention; and I have heard the same idea a dozen times expressed within a week. "We must go down or they must," says another man; and his associate responds, "D——d if it's us, though." The colonization scheme has no supporters, I judge; I've not heard it mentioned since coming into the State.

I sat an hour or more in the Freedmen's Bureau agency office at Albany one day last week. A planter from Mitchell County came in with the stereotyped phrase, "Niggers won't work, and everything is all going to ruin." He wanted the captain to send him a dozen good fellows who would work right along. I don't at all wonder that he has trouble with his negroes,—white men wouldn't work for him if he talked to them as he said he did to his present hands. While he sat there, in came a planter from Lee County, an ex-Rebel colonel, who works twenty men and twelve women. He said he had found no trouble with his negroes. As soon as he came home from the army he called them together, explained to them that they were free and could go where they pleased; said to them that he would like to have all of them remain on the place, and would pay them fairly for their work. He gave them a week for consideration, and then every one was ready to contract with him. The contract gives them house room, firewood, medical attendance, and one third of the crop. None of his hands have left him, and all are ready to contract for the next year. In the statement of these two cases lies the whole problem: give the negro fair treatment and there will be very little cause for complaint against him.

The cases in which the planters turn the negroes off the plantation as soon as the crops are gathered are numerous. Here is one that comes under my own observation. The planter worked seven men and six women. I met the men on the street one forenoon, wandering aimlessly about. When I talked with them they told me their story. "Ole mass'r had 'greed to give we one tird de craps, an' we dun got 'em all up,—got de corn shucked, an' de tatees digged, and de rice trashed; an' ole mass'r he dun gone sold all de craps, an' he bringed we all up yere yes'erday, an' gif we seven dollar fur de man an' he wife to buy de cloth wid to make we clofes, an' he say may be he gif we some shoes; an' he dun gif we'n none o' de craps, none o' de rice, none o' de corn, none o' de tatees, on'y de seven dollar fur de man an' he wife; an' den he tell we ter come on de plantation no mo'; an' he say we all bof mus' make livin' on we'ns freedom; an' we got not'ing fur all de work on'y de seven dollar fur de man an' he wife, an' we got no corn nor no'ting for de winter." I have some satisfaction in knowing that this wretch is ordered to appear before the provost-marshal at two o'clock tomorrow afternoon.

An intelligent boy of about twenty touched his old cap to me, and asked the way to head-quarters. I went there with him and heard his story. He was a refugee from C'lina,—brought down last spring by his old master, who had since died. He had been doing job work this season, and had got fifty dollars laid up. He was a blacksmith, and worked at his trade. "A month ago, sah,—next Monday's four weeks, sah,—I goes to work fur Mr. Bell; an' he promise to do well by me; an' I make no reg'lar bargain with him, but jes' work right 'long ev'ry day from sun to sun; an' he say to me yes'day mornin', sah, 'Henry, you go up to town with me an' I reward you well for your work'; an' I dun cum up in his wagon, an' he drive round town an' say ag'in he gwine to reward me well; an' when he git ready to go home, he jes' give me dis yer old pipe an' say he don't want me no more; an' when I ax'd him where was de reward he gwine to give me, he cut at me wid de whip an' tell me to go 'bout my business; an' den I comed yere, an' I tell you de whole story." That old pipe did not seem to the captain a sufficient compensation for a month's work at blacksmithing, and Mr. Bell was also ordered up for settlement with Henry, the aforesaid freedman.

In the South Carolina Convention one of the leading up-country delegates, during the debate on the slavery-prohibition clause of the Constitution, said, substantially, that the condition, as well as the name, of slavery should be prohibited; and in this view he took exception to the phrase, "neither slavery nor involuntary servitude shall exist except as a punishment for crime," &c.; for, he argued, it will be very easily possible for the Legislature, if so disposed, to re-establish the condition of slavery by a system of crimes and punishments impliedly authorized by that clause.

Down here in Southwestern Georgia is the man who furnishes the practical illustration for this argument. He is called General John T. Morgan, and he has been making a speech on the negro question, which the editor of his county paper indorses as "sensible." "He urged that, as the Constitution gives the power to indict involuntary servitude as a punishment for crime, a law should be so framed as to enable the judicial authorities of the State to sell into bondage again those negroes who should be found guilty of certain crimes; and in conclusion said he thought that this, in connection with the whipping-post and the pillory, would do more to check vagrancy, theft, robbery, and other crimes among the negroes than all the penitentiaries which could be built."

I cannot doubt that some simple-minded persons really apprehend trouble with the blacks about Christmas. I have talked with hundreds of the negroes since I left Milledgeville, but am utterly unable to find any feeling among them that seems to me to threaten a revolt. On the contrary, they appear to believe that their only chance for decent treatment during the winter lies in the protection which the presence of the military will give them. If the troops are all removed they fear just what this General Morgan advocates,—a virtual re-establishment of slavery.

{ XXXVI }

The State Elections

COLUMBUS, NOVEMBER 17, 1865

THE general election of this State took place yesterday. In this city and county it passed off quietly enough.

The election of Judge Charles L. Jenkins, of Augusta, to the governorship of the State is cause for congratulation. Judge Jenkins appreciates the present situation much better than the majority of the people of the State. He was defeated as a Union man, in spite of the great repute in which he was personally held, for the Convention of 1861. His position on the bench kept him aloof from active affairs during the war; but though, like almost every one else, he "went with the State," it was known by all who cared to inquire his views, that he never ceased regretting the course of the South. He was elected to the late Convention without opposi-

tion. His course in that body is well known. As chairman of the committee of sixteen, he reported the obnoxious clause of the new Constitution which sets up the
claim for compensation for emancipated slaves, but one of his friends asserts that
he very decidedly opposed the adoption of that clause in committee. As chairman
of that committee, he also reported the bill repealing the ordinance of secession;
but I have his own assurance that he desired to declare it null and void. As chairman of that committee, he also reported the equivocal measure respecting the
rights of the freedmen in the courts. How far it concurred with his own views I
am unable to say. He voted against the repudiation of the war debt; his position
being that the people ought to be left free to do as they pleased in regard to its
payment. A better man for the office and the crisis might possibly be found, but it
is a good deal to get one into that position of such stamp as he is.

Without waiting for the returns, I can safely say that the local elections in
nearly all the counties of the western and southwestern sections resulted in favor
of the men who "went with the State." I do not hear of the success of a single candidate who opposed the war or was even lukewarm in its support, while as between war men the result is generally in favor of the most radical.

In most of these counties wherever an issue was made during the canvass for
delegates in the late Convention, the election resulted in favor of men who were
co-operationists in 1861 and against those who were original Secessionists. There
was a certain disagreeable work to do in the Convention, and the people seemed
to think that *quasi* Union men were the proper parties to haul the chestnuts out of
the fire. Now the case is different. The Legislature will be composed of men of another stamp,—generally of men of more ability, but also of less original Unionism
than those in the Convention.

I everywhere encounter more or less of the feeling which a Cuthbert man expressed in this terse and forcible language: "I hope every district in the State will
elect a man for Congress who can't take that d——d test oath; I want to see the
Yankees try it on; if Georgia isn't a free sovereign State, I think, by G–d, it's time
we knew it!" This practical reaffirmation of the dogma of State rights is something
of every-day witness to any one traveling here. The people hold to it just as strongly
today as they did five years ago; and the moral of this election is, that the supremacy of the State is above that of the nation.

{XXXVII}

Matters in Western Georgia

NEWNAN, NOVEMBER 20, 1865

As I looked up the streets of Newnan from the windows and platform of the railway car, it seemed a charming place,—a gentle slope toward the east, three or four white stores, the corner of the court-house with its surroundings of luxuriant trees, the hotel with its broad and high piazzas, a wealth of trees and shrubbery everywhere, on all sides handsome cottage houses embowered in greenness and rose blossoms, to the right and left numberless oaks with their crimson and golden frost-touched leaves, and then in the dim background the dreamy and uncertain outline of wooded hills with their blue beauty shimmering in the low sun of a glorious Indian summer afternoon!

Yet Newnan is just like every other Southern town,—streets full of mud-holes and wallowing swine, fences in every stage of tumble-down ruin, sidewalks in every condition of break-neck disorder, yards full of sticks and stones and bits of every conceivable rubbish,—everywhere a grand carnival of sloth and unthrift and untidiness and slovenliness,—everywhere that apathy of shiftlessness so pitiful to the soul of a New-Englander!

'T isn't Nature's fault. She is infinitely more bountiful than under our Northern skies. Wild-flowers beautifying every grove and creek-side, and roses and half a dozen strange blossoms tempting into every garden,—and snow on our Massachusetts hillsides! One may well say the war did not produce its full and proper fruitage if the year 1870 does not show this fair South-land redeemed from the careless mistreatment of all these long years,—this Southern people educated to a love of order and cleanliness, and an appreciation of thrift, industry, and the royal dignity of labor!

Newnan is the county seat of Coweta County, and it has a population of about twenty-seven hundred. It is on the line of railroad from Atlanta to Montgomery,—forty miles below Atlanta, thirty miles from the western line of Georgia, and rather above the middle of the State north and south. It is the home of very many rich planters, boasts numerous handsome suburban residences, is said to have a more elegant and cultured society than any other place in the western part of the State, prides itself on its early and constant devotion to the cause of secession, and has just elected radical Secessionists and unconquered Rebels to the Legislature.

Surprised as most of them are at the result, not one man in fifty seems to have any true conception of the real significance of the late elections in the North. The merchant of Columbus who said in the public parlor of the hotel one evening so loudly that half a dozen persons heard him, "I'm in favor of having our men go to Congress and take their seats any way, whether the d——d Yankees are willing or not," only to put in strong phrase an idea I have heard half a dozen times in more cautious language. If there are fifty good Union men in all the towns where I have stopped within two weeks they live so quietly that neither observation nor inquiry can find them; and the great mass of the people characterize the result of the recent political campaign in the North as sectional.

Through this part of the State the moral standing of the citizen seems to be measured by his war record. The chief requirement in respect to any man is that he shall "go with the State." The supremacy of the Constitution of the United States is formally acknowledged, but the common conversation of all classes asserts the supremacy of the State. The Calhoun doctrine is pushed to its last conclusion. There is not merely a broad assertion of the rights of the States, but an open enunciation of the supremacy of the State over the general government,—an enlarged reaffirmation of the doctrine declared in simply repealing the ordinance of secession.

A gentleman whom I met in the eastern part of the State said to me: "If there had been three bold and true leaders in the winter of 1860–61, we could have saved the State from secession, in my judgment; but Benj. Hill forsook us, and then Alex. Stephens forsook us, and we had only Josh. Hill left, and the State swung into Rebellion."

Benjamin H. Hill lives at LaGrange, some twenty miles below here. He has long been one of the leading men of the State. He acquiesced in secession, but did not go into the army, I believe. Pending the recent election, he was asked his opinion as to the duty of the people in the present emergency, particularly with reference to the expediency of electing gentlemen to Congress who cannot take the test oath. The following letter is his answer:

"The oath is unconstitutional, because it adds to and varies from the oath required by the Constitution.

"The oath is unwise, unnatural, and unprecedented, because it is retroactive in its requirements. It does not seek to procure proper conduct in the officer while discharging the duties of his office; but does seek to exclude him from the office altogether by reason of something done or not done long before the office was conferred.

"If Congress can prescribe one test it can prescribe another test, and thus, by legislation, destroy the right of representation.

"I would vote for no man to represent Georgia who *could* take this oath, because it is the highest evidence of infidelity to the sentiments of the people of the State.

"I would vote for no man, anywhere, who *would* take this oath, because it is the highest evidence of his infidelity to the Constitution. The man who takes that oath admits a power in Congress to destroy every department of the government as well as every right of representation.

"I am a candidate for no office, and will seek none and desire none. The man who wishes now to be a representative in Congress from the South either does not comprehend the very unpleasant and very heavy duties of that position, or has made up his mind to hold the position without discharging the duties. In either case he is not fit to be trusted.

"There is no danger now from any spirit of resistance in Georgia. The only danger comes from an opposite direction,—servility. I intend to be loyal myself, and I have not been faithless to any obligation I ever assumed, even when unwillingly assumed. I resisted secession until resistance was hopeless, and then I resisted subjugation until resistance was hopeless. I would not, if I could, change my record.

"But I will help no man to represent Georgia whose fidelity to the State is doubted, or whose ability and willingness to maintain and vindicate the honor of her people, living and dead, is suspicious. I will vote for no man to administer the Constitution who, in the very beginning of his work, would take an oath which admits a power in Congress to subvert that Constitution.

"Each house of Congress is *sole judge* as to whether persons seeking seats have the qualifications prescribed by the Constitution, and have been elected and returned according to the laws. THE PEOPLE are the *sole judges* of every other qualification. Otherwise, Congress can nullify or even *destroy* the right of election secured to the people alone, and thus make a congressional despotism.

"The right of the States to representation in Congress is the clearest of all rights under the Constitution. It is the right without which no other right can exist and no obligation can be imposed. I have an abiding faith that the President will not permit its destruction by test oaths or otherwise. He was for the Union against the South; and it is my opinion that he will show himself for the Union against *Massachusetts* when the time comes."

The italics of this remarkable letter are Mr. Hill's. I believe it expresses the feeling of four fifths of the men and all of the women of Georgia. If it is not a formal declaration of war against the nationality of the government I am unable to comprehend the force of its very explicit language; and if it does not indicate an insolence and dictatorial spirit without precedent I have read history to little purpose.

Let Congress dispense with the test oath, and give us back the good old times! Let it admit all these Rebel generals and colonels and politicians, and so restore universal harmony! Let us all join hands and cover the nakedness of the land, and assure the world that it is not scarred with a million graves, and that there has been no war for lofty principles and the natural rights of man, but only a friendly contest of strength and endurance, in which the victors concede everything to the vanquished on the sole condition that the latter pronounce the former magnanimous!

Whether the North Carolina "dirt-eater," or the South Carolina "sand-hiller," or the Georgia "cracker," is lowest in the scale of human existence would be difficult to say. The ordinary plantation negro seemed to me, when I first saw him in any numbers, at the very bottom of not only probabilities, but also possibilities, so far as they affect human relations; but these specimens of the white race must be credited with having reached a yet lower depth of squalid and beastly wretchedness. However poor or ignorant or unclean or improvident he may be, I never yet found a negro who had not at least a vague desire for a better condition, an undefined longing for something called freedom, a shrewd instinct of self-preservation. These three ideas do not make the creature a man, but they lift him out of the bounds of brutedom. The Georgia "cracker," as I have seen him since leaving Milledgeville, seems to me to lack not only all that the negro does, but also even the desire for a better condition and the vague longing for an enlargement of his liberties and his rights. Such filthy poverty, such foul ignorance, such idiotic imbecility, such bestial instincts, such grovelling desires,—no words can make plain the scene in and around one of these "cracker" habitations. Time and effort will lead the negro up to intelligent manhood; but I almost doubt if they will be able to lead this "white trash" even up to respectability.

Ex-Governor Herschel V. Johnson closed the late Convention with a brief speech. I have often been referred to it as an epitome of Georgia feeling and judgment. He speaks of the freedmen as follows:

"We are now to enter upon the experiment whether the class of people to which we are in future to look as our laboring class can be organized into efficient and trustworthy laborers. That may be done—or I hope it may be done—if we are left to ourselves. If we cannot succeed, others need not attempt it; and I trust that in the future we will have the poor privilege of being let alone in reference to this class of our people."

There spoke the true Georgian. He is sublimely ignorant of the fact that the negro is also a child of the Republic; sublimely ignorant of the other fact, that the war has restored to him certain human rights. He only sees so many machines, the mission of which it is to do his work; and he asks you to let him alone in their management. He begs of you to give him this "poor privilege," and gravely tells you that they cannot be made to work at all if this be denied him!

I also bear sorrowful witness that every Georgian despises the negro. As a slave he was well enough; but as a man he is only a poor, pitiful creature, from whom little or no good can be expected. Secessionists and Unionists are just alike, so far as I can see, in contempt for him, and alike in wanting him out of the way.

From the average Georgia stand-point, he is half insane who talks of educating the negro. "What, build schoolhouses for the niggers!" exclaimed a citizen in the public room at the Macon hotel. Some of the leading men see that the interests of the State will be promoted by educating the freemen; but nine tenths of the people sneer just as the Macon man did. Yet within four blocks of that same hotel I saw the negro porter of a store laboring at his spelling-book in the corner, when no customers were in; and a young negro woman with her spelling-book fastened to the fence, that she might study while at work over the wash-tub. Still I'm everywhere told that the nigger can't learn, and money spent in educating him would be money thrown away!

Georgia is the richest and most enlightened of the Gulf States. It asks Northern capital, but it holds out no inducement for the development of the mental and moral capital dormant in its negroes and poor whites. For which of these classes there is the best chance in the coming years it is hard to say. There certainly can be no more wretched human beings than the "crackers." The adults of this class can have no hope for this life, and the children will grow to the estate of their parents unless the spirit of caste is broken down and common schools are built up. The universal prophecy that the negro will not work is undermining his humanity and forcing him to its partial fulfillment. The universal contempt in which he is held is driving him into hatred of his contemners and such vagabondage as leads by swift steps to the grave.

{XXXVIII}

Matters in Northwestern Georgia

ATLANTA, NOVEMBER 23, 1865

ATLANTA is built on something less than a hundred hills; and, excepting Boston, is the most irregularly laid out city I ever saw. In fact, the greater portion of it seems never to have been laid out at all till Sherman's army came in here. That did the work pretty thoroughly.

Coming here has dispelled two illusions under which I rested: first, that Atlanta was a small place; and second, that it was wholly destroyed. It was a city of about fourteen thousand inhabitants two years ago, and it was not more than half burned last fall. The entire business portion, excepting the Masonic Hall building and one block of six stores and a hotel, was laid in ruins, and not a few of the larger residences in all parts of the city were also burned. But the City Hall and the Medical College, and all the churches, and many of the handsomer and more stylish private dwellings, and nearly all the houses of the middling and poorer classes, were spared; and on the first of last June there was ample shelter here for at least six or eight thousand persons. Of course, when the entire business portion of the place had disappeared, the city had been practically put out of the way for the time being, even if nothing be said of the fact that it was depopulated by military orders.

The marks of the conflict are everywhere apparent. The ruin is not so massive and impressive as that of Columbia and Charleston; but as far as it extends it is more complete and of less value. There is yet abundant evidence of [the fire],—not so much in crumbling walls and solitary chimneys, as in thousands of masses of brick and mortar, pieces of charred timber, half-burned boards, scraps of tin roofing, engine bolts and bars, ruined articles of hardware, thousands upon thousands of tons of debris of all sorts and shapes. Moreover, there are plenty of cannon-balls and long shot lying about the streets, with not a few shell-struck houses in some sections; and from the court-house square can be seen a dozen or more forts, and many a hillside from which the timber was cut so that the enemy might not come upon the city unawares.

From all this ruin and devastation a new city is springing up with marvelous rapidity. The narrow and irregular and numerous streets are alive from morning till night with drays and carts and hand-barrows and wagons, with hauling teams and shouting men, with loads of lumber and loads of brick and loads of sand, with piles of furniture and hundreds of packed boxes, with mortar-makers and hod-carriers, with carpenters and masons, with rubbish removers and house-builders, with a never-ending throng of pushing and crowding and scrambling and eager and excited and enterprising men, all bent on building and trading and swift fortune-making.

Chicago in her busiest days could scarcely show such a sight. The four railroads centering here groan with the freight and passenger traffic, and yet are unable to meet the demand of the nervous and palpitating city. Men rush about the streets with little regard for comfort or pleasure, and yet find the days all too short and too few for the work in hand. The sound of the saw and plane and hammer rings out from daylight till dark, and yet master-builders are worried with offered contracts which they cannot take. Rents are so high that they seem fabulous, and yet there is the most urgent cry for store-room and office-room. Four thousand mechanics are at work, and yet five thousand more could get immediate employment if brick and lumber were to be had at any price. There are already over two hundred stores, so called, and yet every day brings some trader who is restless and fretful till he secures a place in which to display another stock of goods.

Where all this eagerness and excitement will end no one seems to care to inquire. The one sole idea first in every man's mind is to make money. That this apparent prosperity is real no outsider can believe. That business is planted on sure foundations no merchant pretends. That there will come a pause and then a crash, a few prudent men prophesy.

Meantime Atlanta is doing more than Macon and Augusta combined. The railroad from here to Chattanooga clears over one hundred thousand dollars per month, and could add fifty thousand more to that enormous sum if it had plenty of engines and rolling stock. The trade of the city is already thirty per cent greater than it was before the war, and it is limited only by the accommodations afforded, and has even now spread far out on streets heretofore sacred to the privacy of home.

Wonderful as is the new growth of the city, its original existence is still more wonderful. It is two hundred and fifty miles from the sea-coast, in the midst of a country but moderately productive, not in the vicinity of any navigable river, and without facilities of any kind for manufacturing purpose; yet it was founded less than twenty years ago, is now the fourth place in population in the State, and bids fair to be the second in less than five years.

It can never be a handsome city, but its surrounding hills and slopes offer beautiful sites for elegant residences. Many of the buildings now going up are of frail and fire-tempting character, but in several instances owners are putting in solid one or two-story brick blocks,— intending at some future time to add two or three stories more. Few of the present merchants were here before the war,— few of them are yet to be considered as permanent residents of the city. The streets never were either neat; now, what with the piles of building material and the greater piles of debris and rubbish, and the vast amount of teaming and hauling over them, they are simply horrible. The former residents are coming home, and in the private portions, as well as the business section, there is great activity of repair and refurnishing. The place has no decent hotel,—no one has yet found time to build a large house. Of small and wretched fifth-rate hotels there are half a dozen; but better than any of these are several of the very numerous so-called private boarding-houses, which send their porters and runners to every train, receive all classes of transient guests, charge the usual four dollars per day, and are hotels in everything but name. The city handsomely supports two of the largest daily newspapers in the State, has five or six churches, a medical college, two or three select schools, and is talking about an academy.

These northwestern counties were all strongly opposed to secession in 1860–61, and this Congressional district furnished several hundred soldiers to our armies. Its disposition toward the government is now, as a whole, probably better than that of any other district in the State. Its slaves constituted less than one fourth of its aggregate population before the war, and in general there is much less complaint here than elsewhere as to the disposition of the freedman. The people pretty generally quietly accept the decision of the sword, and the men who prate of State supremacy are far less in number than in the district below.

The social condition of affairs is deplorable in the extreme. It results mainly from the bitter feud between the two classes of people,—those who "went with the State," and those who remained true to the Union. While the country was under the control of Johnston and Hood, the Union men suffered almost every conceivable wrong and outrage. Their families were turned out of doors, their wives were abused and insulted, their daughters were maltreated and ruined, their farms were pillaged and desolated, their houses were sacked and burned, and they themselves were imprisoned and tortured; nay, many of them were hunted down like wild beasts, and shot like dogs when at the point of death by starvation. That the Union men now seek to strike a balance for the indignities and barbarities of other days is only most natural. Whence a constant turmoil in all sections, which results in the sudden death of not a few persons and the arrest and imprisonment of large numbers.

The people of this section are generally hardy and industrious, and in many respects are so much unlike those of some other sections of the State, that "Cherokee Georgia" is a term of contempt and reproach with the aristocrats and land monopolists of the southern and southeastern parts. I found the delegates from this quarter lacking in something of the polish of those from the cities, but no class of men in the late Convention showed a wider range of general information. I find the common people no more ignorant than elsewhere in the State, and it is certainly to be said in their favor that they are not sitting in sullen indifference nor idling in helpless poverty. Poor they are, having little left but lean bodies and homespun garments; but I judge that the whites of these twenty counties in the northwest have done more work since the close of the war than the whites of any fifty counties below the middle line of the State.

I am very certain that the President's course in granting pardons so freely to leading Rebels in this State has not strengthened the faith nor upheld the hands of these mountain men who were always our friends. They should receive such favors as government has to give; but I am everywhere told that the golden apples are cast into the laps of men not yet cleansed of love for the Rebellion, while the original Unionists, who kept the faith unto the end, are generally sent away empty handed. As I have already said, hundreds of these men suffered every possible outrage at the hands of the Rebels. You needn't undertake to tell them who is to blame for their treatment, for they know that Joe Brown and Howell Cobb could have prevented it by a word.

Scores of women, whose husbands were abused or imprisoned, went to Brown or Cobb for protection or relief, only to be insulted or coldly turned away. Now when these men and women see Joe Brown put forward and accepted as Presidential adviser for this State, and see Howell Cobb restored to all his rights of person and property, is it any wonder that they manifest little love for the government,—nay, any wonder that some of these men swear roundly, and exclaim "D——n your government, if it has no favors for anybody but black-hearted Rebels!"

{XXXIX}

Matters in Central Georgia

GREENSBORO, NOVEMBER 26, 1865

FINALLY I have found what I began to fear I should not see in this Southern trip,—evidence that it is possible for at least some persons in this section of the country to know and appreciate order and beauty and taste and neatness and home-like comfort.

Greensboro is the only place of thirty or forty in which I have stopped that may challenge comparison with Northern towns on the score of general appearance. It has a population of sixteen hundred to two thousand persons, and is often mentioned in the State as the place where Mr. Secretary Seward once taught school. It is situated on the Georgia Railroad, about midway between Atlanta and Augusta, in the heart of a high, rolling, productive country, in which there are many good farms under fair cultivation. It formerly had a cotton factory, which is now used as barracks for the one hundred and fifty soldiers stationed here; a handsome brick college in grounds luxuriant with vines and flowers and evergreens, in which an academy is now kept; and two or three small hotels, which are now all closed. It has half a dozen substantial brick stores, and is doing a moderate trade with the well-peopled surrounding country. Its court-house is the best I have anywhere seen in the State; and two of its half-dozen churches are buildings both tasteful and costly. Its beautiful yards and gardens are not so numerous as in some other towns I have visited, but there is everywhere a noticeable absence of that glaring showiness so common in the South. In general, the little town has a very Northern appearance,—looking not indeed so much like a New England town as like a quiet county seat of Northern New Jersey or Central New York.

Finally, I have also found what I began to fear I should not see in this Southern trip,—evidence that it is possible for at least some Southern women to know and appreciate the dignity of domestic life, and to comprehend the subtle mysteries of thrifty and orderly and cleanly housekeeping.

The house of this widow lady, in which I am domiciled for a day or two, is the one house of all in which I have stopped that may challenge comparison with the house of any New England dame under the sun. It is a small corner-lot house, set round with vines and evergreens and china trees, and having the usual cook-house and servants' quarters in the rear. Every one of its four rooms below and its three chambers above is as neat and tastefully furnished as any house I ever saw in Massachusetts. There is a place for everything, and everything is in its place. The room assigned to me is without carpet, but its bare floor is as clean as water and soap and scrubbing-brushes can make it; its furnishing is old and quaint, but every way proper and in order; its bed will bear the most careful inspection, from the snowy counterpane to the solid cotton mattress,— evidence of well-ordered household economy! I confess that I am charmed and delighted,—for how much sloth and apathy and filth and shiftlessness and slovenliness has vexed and saddened my New England soul for twelve long weeks!

Nor is the comfort and good order of the household due wholly to the servants, either. There appear to be a couple of them, and they well do their work, but the head of the house is the widow lady herself; and she and the married daughter living with her superintend household affairs to their minutest detail; and I am sure that if the servants were to leave tomorrow, the home would neither fall in pieces nor go into bankruptcy. The table is well supplied, and the manner in which it is served demonstrates the capacity of a negro woman to be a good cook. The ladies of the house are ladies in the good sense of the word. It is a private boarding-house, at which chance travelers are always at liberty to ask for accommodations, and I expect to pay the usual four dollars per day; but the boarders are apparently at home, and I am treated like the guest of the family. The mistress of the house owned a few slaves, and is not very hopeful regarding free negro labor; but in that respect she does not differ from every other native resident of the State, and I am very sure no one can be kinder to this black man working out his great destiny than she was to her slaves.

Does all this matter seem merely personal or unimportant? It is neither. The son and son-in-law of the house were both soldiers, and both suffered long imprisonment at our hands. They are now good citizens, who live by honest work. If any member of the household has any bitterness of feeling because of the war, I have failed to find it, after a good deal of conversation on all branches of the subject. They mourn the loss of property, but they accept that as part of their defeat. They wish the soldiers were out of the way; but peaceable citizens of no town like the presence of the military. They have some prejudices against the Yankees, but they are not offensively apparent, even to one who avows himself a Yankee of the Yankees. It is not a small matter that there is even one town in the whole of this great State that may court measurement by a Northern standard; for herein is the promise of many more such towns to be built up, when the land is purged of the spirit of slavery. It is not a small matter that one traveler has found a pleasant stopping-place; for in that fact is proof enough how little slavery cared either for the comforts or the economies of home, and proof also of the future homes that shall rise here under the new heavens. It is neither merely personal nor unimportant that twelve weeks of travel in three of the late slave States should find but one village and one household that would lose nothing in comparison with fifty villages and some hundreds of households in Massachusetts alone. Give this people Freedom and all her handmaids, and the traveler of a dozen years hence will not need to draw such pictures as I have drawn of Southern shiftlessness and slovenliness.

Visiting many of the wretched towns of this State and the Carolinas, and seeing how all the inhabitants live, one can scarcely wonder that the negroes sought early opportunity to break away from their old homes, and begin life on their own account. If they said, "Anything will be better than this," they exaggerated very little. The new life might bring them poverty and trouble, but it at least gave them freedom, and the poverty was no strange thing. In such towns as Greensboro, one cannot help seeing most vividly the other side of the question involved in their course. That freedom should bring desire for change was most natural, as all human experience testifies. Yet, seeing what that change has worked in many of the best towns of Central Georgia, one cannot help wishing the poor negro could have been content, for a time, in his old situation.

His removal has reduced hundreds of these Southern women to even such necessary work as will support life, and thousands more to a certain amount of manual labor. Let no one regret this. If there is one thing more needed in the whole South,—in the three States, I mean, which have come under my observation,—more needed here than loyalty, it is respect for labor as labor; not merely as a means of sustaining life, but respect for it as a branch of Divine economy, respect for it as a means of human elevation. And if there is one thing more needful than to teach the men of the South that labor is noble, it is to teach the women of the South that labor is not degrading. Therefore, as one who would see the problem of man's capacity wrought out in this country to most beautiful results, I welcome the necessity which the course of the negro has forced upon so many women here. Let them work,—let them begin as children, and learn to do housework.

It is pitiful that, in this age and in this country, one should find occasion to say what is thus impliedly said; but we shall not see the full fruit of the war till labor is dignified in every town and village of the whole South; and if the negro must ignorantly many times sacrifice his own ease and comfort now for the good of this people, as they have heretofore sacrificed his freedom and his life for their pleasure, there will only be given another proof that "God works in a mysterious way His wonders to perform."

Yet that the negro should thus ignorantly sacrifice his ease and comfort is none the less touching. That he does do this is apparent to any one who looks upon the situation with unprejudiced eye. He does it everywhere in individual cases, however hard that fact may be of acceptance to any of our theorists; but in all Central Georgia he does it on a wholesale scale. He is a human being, and it was not easy to believe that he would do what all experience had proved human beings would not do except in isolated cases; yet thousands of negroes in this section, where slavery was less a burden than in almost any other part of the South, have left homes wherein they had every needful care and comfort, for the uncertain chances of life by themselves. Go where you will in Central Georgia, and you cannot fail to come to this conclusion.

In the Carolinas and in other parts of this State I found a few negroes who had clearly let go the bird in hand without any prospect of finding even one in the bush; here I find thousands of such. I know very well that every white man, woman, and child in the whole State is ready to swear that every negro is worse off now than before he was freed. I accept no such evidence; but hundreds of conversations with negroes of every class in at least a dozen towns of this section have convinced me that the race is, on a large scale, ignorantly sacrificing its own material good for vagabondage.

In South Carolina, as I have already said, where slavery reached its lowest estate, it was not easily possible for the negro to make his condition worse by striking out for himself. There was scarcely more than a choice between two evils, and he chose that which promised him most independence. Hereabouts his situation was different, and he has too often made the bad choice.

This must also be borne. For if the privileges of freedom are given to the negro, must he not also take its duties and responsibilities? If his exercise of the privilege of choice leads him into want and suffering, will you again enslave him with the requirement that he shall live with the old master or mistress who treated him well? You may advise him to such course, but you cannot compel him thereto. If you would secure his freedom to him, you must let him have his own way in this regard, even if you see that it will bring him to the utmost misery.

I went into the outskirts of Macon and hunted up many of the negroes who had left old homes in the city and surrounding country. I did the same thing at Madison and Milledgeville. Hundreds and hundreds of them will feel the pangs of cold and hunger this winter who might have kept every necessity and many of the comforts of life, if they had chosen to remain with those who formerly held them as slaves. Who shall have the heart to blame them? For they were in search of nothing less noble and glorious than freedom. They were in rags and wretchedness, but the unquenchable longing of the soul for liberty was being satisfied.

Near Milledgeville I found a crowded cabin, in which lived a man and his wife and seven children, the eldest of whom could not have been over twelve or thirteen years of age. He was an intelligent fellow, and there was a certain air of spruceness about his cabin rather uncommon. I had much talk with him. He came up from Fort Valley country, he said, and he reckoned he could get something to do after a bit. 'T was rather hard times, he knew, an' good many black people was comin' to de city, but he reckoned they'd all git through the winter some way.

"But don't you think," said I, "that it would have been better for a great many of them to remain on the plantations or with their old masters and mistresses in town?"

"Wa'l now ye see, sah, das a Scriptur' what says if de man hab a little to eat, an' he eat with a 'tented mind, he be better off dan de man what hab de fat ox an' isn't 'tented."

There seemed no further occasion to argue the case with this man at least. Elsewhere in the same neighborhood I talked with other negroes. Many of them had left comfortable homes, but all seemed to think they could get along somehow through the winter. It was a warmish day, and many of the women were sitting on the ground on the sunny side of their huts, engaged, as so many negro women everywhere are, in knitting socks or stockings.

This morning I walked out to the little negro village near Greensboro, where are living many blacks who were house-servants in the town, as well as some who have come in from the country. Their average condition is better than that of those in the neighborhood of large cities, but yet it is impossible but that many of them must either suffer or steal before spring. I am convinced that many of those who were servants in town had pleasant homes, and did not want for any of the simple comforts of life.

"Well, Auntie," said I to one of them, a weather-beaten old creature, who looked as though she had seen at least sixty years, but was as vigorous about her small housework as a girl of twenty,—"how do you get along in your freedom?"

"No reason to make complaint, sah. I has sum soin' and some washin', and 'pears like I had nuf ter do."

"But you are getting to be an old woman, and your old mistress would have given you a good home as long as you live. Wouldn't it have been better to stay with her?"

"Well, now, honey, ye don't see only one side 'pears like. I be an ole woman as ye say, but I's mighty peart yet, and I don't reckon I'll want fur nothing dis yer winter; and when de wa'm season cum agin, mebbe I go back to town ter live."

"What did you leave the old place for, Auntie, any way?"

"What fur? *'Joy my freedom!*"

The directness and exultation of this answer half puzzled and half disconcerted me. I knew how this old woman had lived,—knew what a favorite she had been in the family in which she had formerly been owned,—knew what large liberty had been always given her in everything. What is the "freedom" that war has brought this dusky race?

{ X L }

Matters in Eastern Georgia

AUGUSTA, NOVEMBER 28, 1865

AUGUSTA is a fine point for business; and when it is once more brought in connection with Charleston and Savannah by railroad, Atlanta, busy as she is now, and confident as she is of the future, will need to have sharper eyes and even yet more restless energy if she would not be distanced.

The close of the war found more cotton, probably, stored in and about this city than at any other point in the South. One feels justified, from all that is said, in estimating the amount at fully fifty thousand bales; and many dealers put the figure at sixty thousand. Very little of this was burned, and most of it was in the hands of private parties. Consequently, there has been a large business here in the article all the fall.

In this Congressional District, the contest at the recent election was more animated than in any other district in the State,—and one of the worst Rebels in the district carries the Day[:] Colonel James D. Matthews, of Oglethorpe County, a lawyer by profession, a colonel in the Rebel army[,] the noisiest and bitterest Rebel in the late Convention, and about as badly disposed toward the government and the new order of things as any man I have met in all my tour.

In the stage between here and Milledgeville I rode a month ago with two gentlemen of considerable local weight and prominence, who were both anti-

Secessionists in 1860–61. They talked of the approaching Convention. "Well, Colonel," said the younger, himself a man of over forty years,—"what will be our proper course when we are once more fully restored to the Union?" The answer came, "We must strike hands with the Democratic party of the North, and manage them as we always have." There was a pause while we rattled down the hill, and then the questioner responded, "That's just it; they were ready enough to give us control if we gave them the offices; and I reckon they've not changed very much yet." There was then conversation on other matters; but half an hour later, after a mile or so of silence, the Colonel suddenly resumed, "Yes, sir, our duty is plain; we shall be without weight now that slavery's gone, unless we do join hands with them. Andy Johnson will want a re-election, and the united Democratic party must take him up; it shall be a fair division, we want the power and they want the spoils."

At Atlanta I saw a family of seven persons, from the county above this, on their way to [Texas], at Greensboro I saw a family of thirteen, including the old folks, with daughter, son-in-law, and grandchildren, and having a wagonload of trunks, bound for that State; at Berzelia, twenty miles west of here, I fell in with a man who had just returned from an inspection tour, and would start for there next week at the head of a company of twenty. I asked him if he didn't like it in this State. To which he answered, "I am going to see if I can't get shet of the Yankees." I have heard of very few persons who fall in with the Alabama scheme for emigrating to Brazil; but I am convinced that in the Central and Eastern sections of Georgia there are many who purpose moving to Texas, and only in one or two instances have I heard any reason assigned but a desire to get away from the Yankees.

Yet not all the people of this section are of such antagonistic spirit,—not all of them are so at war with common sense and the conquering Yankee. "I'm d——n glad the war's over, any how," said a Madison gentleman to me. He was dressed like a gentleman and mostly spoke like one, but profanity is much more common down here than in the North. "I did all I could for the revolution, and now I'm going to do all I can for the Union. You mustn't ask me to give up my idea of State rights,—that's in my bones, and never can be got out; but I assure you it shall never give any more trouble, so far as I am concerned."

When Federal soldiers died in the South, while held as prisoners, they were very rarely given burial in the cemeteries of the town or city in which they died, but were generally packed away outside the walls, if, indeed, their bodies were not ignominiously buried in by-places. Here, however, the bodies of such men were all given decent burial in the large and beautiful city cemetery,—a fact which must be infinitely grateful to the friends and relatives of the two hundred boys who finished their warfare in this city. They lie in three long rows in the southeastern corner of the cemetery, and can readily be identified by a reference to the sexton's books. When the first ones were laid there, now two years ago, some of the extra-finished Rebels of the city were very much offended, and complained of the sexton for his action in the matter, saying that it was an insult to bury Yankees there. With gratitude and admiration I set down the answer of the sexton: "If you ever get to heaven, you'll find plenty of Yankees there; and 't won't hurt anybody to lie alongside a Yankee in here, I reckon."

I saw Alexander H. Stephens today,—a little old man with most marvelous eyes, looking not so much like a human being as like a character from one of Dickens's stories. Yet if Georgians reverence anybody it is Mr. Stephens; and there isn't the least question but that his presence in the State is beneficial in the best sense. He resists all importunities to make a public speech; but I am told that he converses freely with all who call upon him, and that he urges everybody to accept the issue of the war in the most cheerful and liberal spirit.

I hear much talk about Wirz during the last three or four days, because the last of the illustrated papers chronicles his execution, I suppose. Winder is generally considered the chief brute, but Wirz is held to have been a willing tool. Of course the people don't readily own that the Andersonville cruelties were practiced in their State, and occasionally I find a man who seeks to justify them. The great majority of the people, however, condemn them; and I am constantly assured that such models of Christian manhood as Howell Cobb and Robert Toombs did all they could to improve the condition of the prisoners. On the whole, I believe there is a general sense of relief at Wirz's execution. "There's one wretch the less left to remind us of the terrible war," said a very intelligent Macon gentleman.

I have talked with many of the planters of this section. Most of them complain of the negroes; and General Tillson, State Commissioner of the Freedmen's Bureau, says he is satisfied that the blacks are not generally doing more than about half the work they might, though he considers this quite a good proportion when all the facts of the situation are taken into account. Many of the planters, however, are making arrangements to introduce white labor. I have, within the last four days, heard of no less than nine leading men, in their respective localities, who either have already made contracts for white labor or are soon going North to secure it. One of these planters left here yesterday for New York, to arrange for sixty men for himself alone, and for thirty more for some of his neighbors. He will get Germans if possible, and does not doubt but that they can readily be taught to make cotton with proficiency. "The only way in which we can control the labor of the free negro is to bring him in competition with the white laborer," is the language of scores of men.

WAYNESBORO, NOVEMBER 29, 1865

"There are two places in the State," said an acquaintance to me at Augusta, "where they'd as soon shoot a man as a dog,—Albany and Waynesboro." Remembering Albany, I am giving it due heed.

Waynesboro isn't a lovely place, by any means. In fact, I don't see why anybody should desire to live here; and a forced residence of half a year might very well make a man long to be shot. From Greensboro to Waynesboro is about one hundred miles, but those miles space the distance from civilization to barbarism. Not to be unjust to Waynesboro, let me say that it has a hotel, and a church, and two or three stores, and a good many dram-shops, and at least a hundred residences.

There is hereabouts a strong surface hatred of the Yankees. As a curious specimen of what one hears, take the following little speech made by an apparently intelligent man to a group of half a dozen persons, of whom I was one:

"I've sent an advertisement to the paper for a job of overseeing some plantations next year. I reckon I could do that right lively. Can't lick free niggers, but I don't know if there's any law ag'in cussin' 'em, and I believe it does 'em a heap o' good. It's next best to lickin'. Jest cuss one o' 'em right smart for 'bout five minutes, and he'll play off peart. Probably the Yankees don't like that style, but I ha'n't no use for a Yankee no how. I had a lot of likely negroes, but they're all gone; had Confederate money, but that's all gone; and I've got a heap o' Confederate bonds, but they a'n't worth a damn. I reckon God Almighty fought on the other side in this war. He used to smile on us, but He hasn't given us anything but frowns lately. I don't care a damn, but I don't like to see my friends all so cut up about it. I can git along well enough. I should like to lick a hundred free negroes jest once all 'round. If I didn't bring 'em to know their places, I'd pay ten dollars apiece for all I failed on. Free-damn-cusses I call 'em."

The State-rights doctrine flourishes here much more vigorously than in the northern part of the State. I asked one of the delegates to the late Convention what the war had settled, and his answer was, "Well, it settled that the North was the strongest, and that the negroes are free."

"But did it settle nothing in regard to State rights?" I continued.

"It settled that you are able to enforce your belief on that question, but I don't believe it has changed the opinion of a single Southern man," said he; and after a moment he added, "but I've no idea we shall ever go to war on that point; we down here have had war enough, and you may hold your opinion just as I hold mine."

The planters hereabouts are not generally hopeful in regard to the availability of free negro labor. I had some conversation with a knot of them, in which the question of white labor came up.

"We shall have to have control of the free nigroes, or import white men to do the work," said one of them.

I asked if the negroes wouldn't work if they were treated exactly as white men would be in the same circumstances.

"No, a free nigroe is a free nigroe, any how."

"But," said I, "that way of talking and feeling cannot be beneficial either to him or to your interests. Why not use him fairly, like a man?"

"The trouble is," said another, "he don't know his place. If you let us alone, we'll teach him, and then I reckon we'll git along with him better."

"But what do you mean by teaching him his place?" I asked.

A third man took up the question, and answered: "Our people are restive at what they call outside interference. The negro isn't to blame for his freedom. He served us faithfully all through the war, and I sincerely believe very few planters have any desire to see him injured. We know his ways; and if you give us time, I think we shall be able to get him back into his place again,—not as a slave, but as a good producer."

They kept up a conversation among themselves, till the first again responded, "A free nigroe is a poor cuss, any how."

To which a fourth one answered, "I'll tell you how 't is: a free nigger's jest like any low-down white fellow,—pull off your coat and work with him, and he does well enough; put it on and go off to town, and he shirks." Numbers one and two seemed a little puzzled at this, and he continued: "Now I don't have a d——n bit of trouble with my fellows when I work right 'long with 'em."

"But your people don't generally go into the field and work, as our Northern farmers do," said I.

"That's just it," said the third; and the fourth concluded, "Yes, that's just it; we've had too many d——n fine notions, and one of our new notions is, that we must have white labor; I go in for white labor,—yes, I do; and I'm agoin' to put some on my plantation. I'm goin' to work myself!"

{XLI}

Matters in Southeastern Georgia

SAVANNAH, DECEMBER 2, 1865

THE destruction of railroads in this State was as complete as in South Carolina, but the energy of the people in repairing damages is much greater, and, therefore, communication between the different sections ever reached by the cars is much more readily made here than there.

I have traveled over most of the stage lines in the State; and while I can't say that either the vehicles or the animals are respectably good, I can fairly own that neither are quite so bad as those in Carolina.

In many towns there are no hotels, chance travelers finding accommodations at so-called private boarding-houses. The almost invariable charge, whether at these houses or at regular hotels, is four dollars per day,—three and a half being the rate in only two of the many towns I have visited. In the large cities, and in one or two of the large towns, I have found the table reasonably well supplied, that is, from a Southern stand-point; but elsewhere the standard is hardly up even to that of the Carolinas.

Western Georgia and Northern Georgia I found full of "runners" from Louisville and Cincinnati. They represented all branches of trade, and pretty generally reported that they were getting many orders. In this section I find more representatives of Eastern houses. I believe the delivery of goods already ordered will give a stock in the State sufficient for the coming year. Everybody seems to have a passion for keeping store, and hundreds of men are going into trade who should go into agriculture. If the coming season brings a "smash" in many towns, the prophecies of numerous business men will not be unfulfilled.

Business in the city has been very brisk all the fall, and a merchant said to me yesterday, "There's been more done in the last six months than I believed last winter would be done in two years." I have found no other place in the South where early faith in the recuperative energies of the people has met with such large reward as here. Many men seem inclined to believe that the promise will not be kept, and are prophesying a dull season next year. Others are more hopeful, and say that when the railroads connecting with Augusta, Macon, and Thomasville are repaired, the trade of the city will be fifty per cent greater than ever. This latter view seems to me the correct one; but it can hardly be appreciated by any one who is un-

informed as to the numbers of Northern, and particularly Northwestern men moving into the upper and western sections of the State.

There are already many Northern men in business here, and I am told of many
more who propose coming out during the winter. A considerable portion of these
are men who were in the army, and not a few of them are ex-soldiers who did more
or less duty in the city, and of course come here now with some social and business
relations already formed. The feeling toward persons from the North is very far
from being what is desirable, but several who have been here through the year say
it is improving.

I record with pleasure that I have found two men who are eminently sound
on the State-rights question. One of them has been a Rebel sergeant, and is now a
railroad fireman. He stood by while three or four of us were carelessly chatting
about the subject. "Dun know anything 'bout the matter myself, but old Uncle
Sam says as how States ha'n't any right to kick out o' the traces, and that's enough
for me." The other is a planter, and he put this word into the conversation of a
couple of his neighbors who were hair-splitting about reserved rights, &c.: "Well,
I reckon it's one of the reserved rights of the Federal government to put down a
rebellion, and I don't happen to know any man down to my section who proposes
to dispute that right agen."

I also record with pleasure that I have found one man who is eminently sound
on the negro labor question. He keeps a hotel,—the most systematic and orderly
house, with one exception, that I have found in the South. He has no help but that
of negroes. I asked him how he got along so admirably with them, when so many
persons complained that nothing could be done with them. "Why, I treat 'em just
as I would white men; pay them fair wages every Saturday night, give 'em good
beds and a good table, and make 'em toe the mark. They know me, and I don't
have the least trouble with 'em."

There is much want and suffering among the residents of Southeastern
Georgia. I judge they did not very readily accept the situation last spring. However
that may be, there is no question about two facts,—they were despoiled of nearly
all their property by the Rebel army, and have made but insignificant crops of all
kinds during the present season. I am told that there are at least two thousand respectable white persons in and around Savannah alone who must live mainly on
charity through the winter. I know, too, from conversation with many of the
Convention delegates from this section, that there are numbers of such persons
in nearly all the twenty-five or thirty nearest counties.

Of course this general destitution affects the negroes even more seriously than the whites. Hundreds of them have already died in and about Savannah of actual starvation. What the combined effect of increased scarcity of food and increased severity of weather will be in the course of the next three months is easily conjectured. The military authorities and the officers of the Freedmen's Bureau have done, and will continue to do, all that is possible to relieve this widely-spread suffering; but they work at a double disadvantage,—the prejudice of the whites and the ignorance of the blacks hindering their labors.

The negroes are badly treated in some of the counties west and northwest of the city. I fell in, yesterday, with a gentleman who has been making a horseback tour in six or eight of them, in search of cotton. He says hundreds of negroes have been turned off the plantations during the month, with little or no money, and but a few bushels of corn, and that many of them will be actually forced into thieving to support life. He saw one negro woman horse-whipped very severely for some offense, and saw a negro man who had been shot in the arm for declining, at first, to be turned off the plantation where he had worked all summer. He also tells me that some of the members elect of the Legislature are pledged to resist all efforts to give the negro the right to sue or be heard as evidence in the courts.

I hardly need add that the freedmen throughout this section are somewhat disinclined to make contracts for another season. The rice plantation negroes are very slow to comprehend that freedom does not mean idleness,—being the most degraded specimens of the race I have anywhere found. They generally seem without conscience in respect to the sin of theft, and almost infinite patience will be required to bring them out into an intelligent appreciation of their rights and responsibilities. One large planter tells me that he has offered twelve dollars per month for the season, without being able to get all the labor he wants. This case, however, I believe to be exceptional.

I have fallen in with a gentleman of middle age who was in the Rebel army about three years. He is a lawyer, and is among the leading members of the bar in his section. He has been in the Legislature, and before the war was one of the most popular speakers in his district. He is a man of such ability that he was often invited to speak with leading politicians. He claims to have been always a Union man, and says his service in the army was compulsory. He is now, at least, acting the part of a quiet, well-disposed citizen; and his advice is found of value by the officer in command in his city. I do not deem it advisable to give either his name or his residence. On a certain Sunday morning we fell into some talk on the condition of the State and the prospects of the future. I found him, after a time, quite ready to speak, and he found me equally ready to listen. And this is what he said:

"Giving suffrage to the negro would not accomplish the ends you desire to reach. Perhaps I'm prejudiced against him, but I doubt if suffrage would secure his freedom to him, for I know too well how he can be wound round the finger of a plausible white man.

"The negro's first want is not the ballot, but a *chance to live.* You say the government has given him freedom, and that many good men in the North believe he must have the ballot to secure that freedom. I tell you he's not got his freedom yet, and isn't likely to get it right away. Why, he can't even live without the consent of the white man! He has no land; he can make no crops except the white man gives him a chance. He hasn't any timber; he can't get a stick of wood without leave from a white man. We crowd him into the fewest possible employments, and then he can scarcely get work anywhere but in the rice-fields and cotton plantations of a white man who has owned him and given up slavery only at the point of the bayonet. Even in this city he can't get a pail of water from a well without asking a white man for the privilege. He certainly can't live in a house, unless a white man gives his consent. What sort of freedom is that?

"He has freedom in name, but not in fact. In many respects he is worse off than he was before you made him free, for then the property interest of his master protected him, and now his master's hand as well as the hand of everybody else is against him. True, he has the military here for his protection; but there are a thousand things done here every day under the colonel's very nose that he don't know anything about, things he couldn't remedy if he did know about 'em. 'T isn't whippings that most wrong the negro; it's the small, endless, mean little injustice of every day that's going to kill him off. He's only partially protected now; take the troops away, and his chance wouldn't be as good as a piece of wood in a house on fire.

"I know a good many of these men they've sent to the Legislature; and I know there'll be private talk this session, even if there isn't open effort, to make the penal code take him back into the condition of slavery. It'll be called 'involuntary servitude for the punishment of crime,' but it won't differ much from slavery. Why, I know men right here in this very town who believe in making the breaking of a contract a crime for which the nigger may be sold. They can do it. They can establish any system of crimes and punishments they please. Get the troops away and the State into Congress, and I give you my solemn word that I believe three fourths of the counties in the State would vote for such a penal code as would practically reduce half the negroes to slavery in less than a year.

"I haven't much faith in the idea that capital and labor will reconcile themselves. Our capital is all in the hands of a few, and invested in great plantations. Our

labor is all in the hands of a race supremely ignorant, and against whom we all
have a strong prejudice. In my opinion, you can't reconcile these two interests unless you put the labor in subjection to the capital, that is, unless you give the white
man control of the negro. Of course that can't again be allowed, and therefore
there's an almost impassable gulf between the negro and freedom unless the government aids him.

"I'll tell you what I think you should have done. The policy of confiscation
should be rigidly carried out at once. Mercy to the individual is death to the State;
and in pardoning all the leading men, the President is *killing the free State he might
have built here.* The landed aristocracy have always been the curse of the State,—
I say that as a man born and reared in Georgia and bound to her by every possible
tie. Till that is broken down there can be no real freedom here for either the negro
or the poor white. The result of the war gave you a chance you never will get again
to overthrow that monopoly. The negroes and the poor whites are bitter enemies
in many respects, but they agree in wanting land. You should have divided up the
great plantations into fifty-acre lots, and sold them to the highest bidders, that
would have thrown some of the land into other large plantations, but it would
have been fair, and would have given the poor whites and the negroes a chance.
Give a man a piece of land, let him have a cabin of his own upon his own lot, and
then you make him free. Civil rights are good for nothing, the ballot is good for
nothing, till you make some men of every class landholders. You must give the negroes and the poor whites a chance to live, that's the first thing you should do. The
negro has a great notion to get a piece of land, and you should help him along.
What does he want of a vote? He wouldn't know how to use it, and 't wouldn't
bring him anything to eat or wear if he had a dozen. Give him land, and you touch
his case exactly. He can get none now. There isn't one planter in a thousand who
would sell him any; but if you'd carried out your confiscation policy he could have
bought it like anybody else.

"I said in a speech on last Fourth of July that we had always boasted of our
country as the land of the free, while in fact it had been the home of the slave. I
said, too, that I hoped the war had made it possible for men to be free without regard to color, so that we might boast more truly than England that our flag floats
over no slave. I spoke very cautiously, but what little I said was enough to kill me
politically in this county. I have sometimes thought I would go North and urge
your people to take the first fruits of the victory, but I should not dare to come
back here after speaking up there. I've wanted to write a letter to some leading
newspaper; but if I should say what I honestly believe, I should be killed if it ever

got out that I wrote it. There isn't any freedom of speech here, or anywhere in the State, unless you speak just as the Secessionists please to let you. I should be shot before tomorrow morning if I were to publicly say what I've said to you. Take the troops away, and off the great lines of travel there would be a reign of terror in a month."

I have not met many men in this State who are more competent to speak upon the condition of the people than this captain. His remarks do not apply to this section alone. It seems to me that they are a powerful argument out of the mouth of a Southern advocate of the opposite policy, that the ballot in the hand of every man, white and black, is the only method of securing the rights of the humbler classes of all colors in the South. It will give them the power and eloquence of numbers. It will give them what party leaders will covet, and what the bitterest slave oligarchist in the whole list will not be above stooping to secure. To be sure, some should be owners of land; but the citizen, with the ballot in his hand, is a king in his own right, to whom all things are possible. Ownership of land in fee-simple does not necessarily include command of the ballot; but put into the negro's horny palm the simple right to vote, and he is at once installed into ownership of houses and lands and comforts and luxuries, from which only his own idleness or improvidence can dispossess him.

{ X L I I }

Summary of Five Weeks' Observations in Georgia

SAVANNAH, DECEMBER 4, 1865

VERY much of Georgia reminds one of Central New York. Not that there are pretty villages and prosperous towns, nor that there are churches and school-houses and multiplied evidences of thrift and industry and intelligence; but that Nature has been very kind in her gifts of soil and surface, setting rich acres into a beautiful and comfortable diversity of hill and valley, upland and lowland, open country and timber. The extreme southern section is much like the Carolinas in its general features,—sand and swamp, piny woods and barrens; but even there the soil is richer and more easily worked than in the country farther up the coast. Elsewhere, however, with local exceptions, the State is much more inviting than any part of the Carolinas to the man from the North or the West. Given perfect freedom of speech and a hearty acquiescence in the new order of things, and even the New England farmer could easily find a home within Georgia.

I note, also, that for one Northern man coming into the Carolinas to live there are at least twenty coming into this State. They come mainly from the States of Ohio, Indiana, and Illinois, though I have met men from New York, Connecticut, Michigan, and Wisconsin. The greater proportion of all these are men who were soldiers; and among those yet in service I found not a few who declare their intention of coming back here before winter is over if they are mustered out prior to Christmas.

Atlanta seems to be the center from which this new life radiates; it is the great Exchange, where you shall find everybody if you only wait and watch. I saw it with wonder. The very genius of the West, holding in the one hand all its energies and in the other all its extravagances, is there, standing in the nervous tension of expectant movement. What is thus affirmed of Atlanta is to a less extent true of twenty other places in that quarter of the State.

I believe the contempt for labor and the laborer is at least quite as strong in Georgia as even in South Carolina. In the office of head-quarters at Americus I met an ex-colonel, a man of forty-five years, who had a plantation and worked thirty-four negroes. I asked him how he and his neighbors were getting on with the fall work. "I know nothing about the work, sir," said he with a lofty air, in which there was a sneer. At Macon I found a man who mourned for the State because her "gentlemen" had all been ruined, and she must hereafter be the home of "greasy workingmen."

It has not been held degrading to "be in trade," and accordingly hundreds of men are opening little stores in localities where those already existent find but precarious support. Since the war it has not been held degrading to superintend a plantation, and accordingly many men are looking for easy supernumerary places among the planters. But woe to the upper-class white man who proposes to come down from his proud idleness and put his own hand into farm work! And woe to him of that class who talks of learning a trade!—"What, work with niggers and Yankees!"

The people, as a class, are much more intelligent than those of the other Southern States I have visited, though an exception in this regard must be made respecting the residents of several counties in the lower section. The State once had a good system of common schools, and it was productive of much benefit for a time. There is also noticeable here a certain degree and quality of energy that I did not find to the northeast. It does not manifest itself in varied industries so much as in the victory over despondency consequent upon the downfall of the

Confederacy. Give the people a right mind upon the question of the dignity of labor, and you shall see here what Governor Johnson covets,—"a great, happy, powerful, and prosperous State."

I also find here, in a certain proportion, what gives the North its superiority,— a middle class of people. The Georgia aristocrat is not always, as in Carolina, a great landholder; but his aristocracy takes even a more lordly tone than that of any other State. The poor white, the "cracker," is certainly as low in the scale of human existence as anything can be in this country. Between these two far-apart extremes is a great class whose presence assures the future of the State. Altogether too many of its members despise manual labor and covet a professional life; but time will bring them good sense, and with that will come the new era in which Georgia may rightly call herself the "Empire State of the South."

The prevailing vice of the whole people seems to be whiskey drinking. I have seen three times as much here in a month as I saw in the Carolinas in two months. That the native, on starting out for a ride in the cars or stage, should take a bottle of "Bourbon" or "old rye" or "sod corn" or some other similar liquid, is a deal more in keeping than that he take a lunch or a clean shirt. Not to drink is to separate yourself from the mass and frequently bring upon yourself personal criticism of an unpleasant sort.

There is scarcity of food everywhere; in many whole counties, the merest necessaries of life are all any family have or can afford, while among the poorer classes there is great lack of even these. Of course this poverty falls most hardly on the negroes. The Freedmen's Bureau reports something less than two thousand pauper blacks in the State; but I know it will find ten thousand as soon as the cold weather comes, if it has agencies in most of the counties. But the suffering will not by any means be confined to the blacks. Hundreds of the "cracker" families will have a hard fight to keep starvation from the doors of their wretched cabins; and not a few of those who before the war never knew any want, will now know that sharpest of all wants,—the want of food.

The people accept the repudiation of the Rebel war debt quite cheerfully, considering the doleful prophecies of the gentlemen of the Late Convention. So many of the delegates there earnestly assured me that their constituents were exceedingly anxious to pay that eighteen millions of dollars, that I was half led into believing that the President had imposed a hard condition upon the Georgians. Haply, I didn't waste much sympathy, for I find that it was all a grand game of speculation. Men who had bought the bonds at ten to twenty cents on the dollar were anxious the State should be held to the payment of their face value, but I haven't found a single man, except those thus pecuniarily interested, who finds fault because of the repudiation!

The feeling toward Northern men is very far from being liberal or kindly. Many of them are, as I have already said, coming in here; they are tolerated, but, generally speaking, not welcomed. Having once fought to overcome resistance to the government, they must fight again to overcome prejudice against the spirit of the nation. There are many counties in the State in which Northern labor and capital would not be safe but for the presence of the military. I know that this is a broad and serious assertion. I make it with full consciousness of its meaning.

The worst feature of the political situation is that the secondary character of the authority of the general government is everywhere virtually asserted. "Our defeat was the necessary result of superiority of numbers and resources," says ex-Governor Johnson gravely, without any recognition of the fact that he and they had warred against the supreme law of the land. The general sentiment asserts that every man's fealty is first due to the State. Not to have "gone with the State" in her late struggle is now to be scorned and contemned.

That a State has the right to secede is a doctrine not so generally held in Georgia as I supposed. Of course it follows from the doctrine of State supremacy, but the common people have not pushed this latter dogma to its conclusion. The average and common talk designates the late war as "the revolution," this being a phrase I did not more than once or twice hear during my trip in South Carolina, and a phrase very little used even in North Carolina.

The idea broached by one of the speakers in the late Convention—that a subsequent Convention could undo its work—seems to have many supporters in the State. How far any of these would like to have that work undone is more than I can say. I only know there are plenty of men who argue that it is not of binding effect because done under duress. The Convention was called in violation of the Constitution, they say, and did its work at the point of the bayonet. It is not the voice of a free people, and may be repudiated as soon as we are in the Union again.

The citizens of the State are excessively anxious to be let alone with regard to the freedman. In South Carolina, nearly everybody spoke of the negro as though he had become the special charge of the Yankees; here, however, there is much of this talk which indirectly asserts the continued supremacy of the whites over the blacks.

That many of the leading men desire to see the negro have a fair chance is beyond all question. I have met some such men. They take pains to tell me that he was very docile and trustworthy during the war, that he is not to blame for being free, and that he ought to be justly treated now. A few men even go so far as to urge that he must be educated. This is the bright side of the picture.

The complaint that the free negro will not work is even more common than in South Carolina. There I found many persons anxious to argue the point, anxious to show me why he would not work; but here the fact is assumed in a somewhat lofty manner that precludes discussion. That the negro will not work simply because he is free is the most insolent of all the humbugs of Southern society.

Everybody tells the Northern man that the negroes all expect a gift of lands or mules at Christmas. I have made numberless inquiries among them, bearing upon this point, and I declare that the assertion is untrue. There are some negroes in the southern, or perhaps I should say the southeastern section, who do expect some division of land at that time; and there are some in the western part who appear to have hopes that Christmas will bring them mules and carts; but the aggregate number of both these classes is comparatively small, and is very far from warranting the talk which one everywhere hears.

The truth in respect to the situation is, that the negroes are uncommonly ignorant of their rights and responsibilities. The State is very large, and the regular agents of the Freedmen's Bureau are very few in number. The old negro at Macon, who said to me, "One say dis, an' one say dat, an' we don' know, an' so hol' off till Janerwery," expressed the feeling of his people. The negro is lazy, he is improvident, and he prefers job work to season-contract work; but where he is honestly informed and fairly treated, I believe he does quite as well as any one had a right to expect that he would.

The negroes of this State seem more suspicious and distrustful of the whites than those of the Carolinas. I judge that the Western troops did not use them quite fairly, and failed to strengthen their confidence in the Yankees. Moreover, not a few of the numerous post-commandants have been men utterly unfit to deal with the blacks, while I fear that some of them have been only less pro-slavery than the natives themselves. The appointment of local agents of the Freedmen's Bureau will give the blacks an opportunity to appeal to some responsible authority; and when these are good men, it will do much to bring about a proper relationship between the two classes of people.

In some sections a new method of crime is developing. In almost any of the larger places it is a matter of daily report that negroes have been guilty of theft for which bad whites are primarily responsible. In a few counties there are reported gangs of which white men are leaders and negroes are members, whose purpose is systematic plunder. I believe this state of affairs prevails more generally in the northwestern section than elsewhere.

The negro's prospects are not, on the whole, as good as they ought to be in this great State. He has freedom in name, but it will be some time before he gets it in fact. His hope lies in the continued military occupation of the State and the continued existence of the Freedmen's Bureau. Even with these for his aid and protection, his condition is bad enough; take these away, and in a good portion of the counties he would very soon not even have left the name of freedman.

{ XLIII }

Some General Conclusions on the Situation in Georgia and the Carolinas

ON SHIPBOARD, DECEMBER 7, 1865

MY fourteen weeks' tour is at an end, and I am returning to New York. I have traveled over more than half the stage and railway routes in the States of North Carolina, South Carolina, and Georgia. I have been generally treated with civility and occasionally with courteous cordiality. I judge, from the stories told me by various persons, that my reception was, on the whole, something better than that accorded to the majority of Northern travelers.

I went South to study the political situation. I sought conversation with all classes of Southerners,—my object being to gather information at first hand and to keep my reports free from the bias and prejudice of Northern sojourners. I was not obliged to write in the interest of any party or any person, and was not required to furnish arguments for upholding or breaking down any particular theory of reconstruction. In a word, my duty was that of a reporter. I meant to tell the truth, and I hoped to find the truth pleasant to tell.

Yet the conclusion of the whole matter is, that a very grave mistake, not to say a criminal blunder, has been committed, if the Southern representatives have been admitted into Congress.

It will not be safe to admit them to their seats at present. Some of them ought never to be admitted. They have no business in a Congress of the United States, for they are either of bitterly rebellious spirit or are encased in the poisonous bigotries of State supremacy. Against these the doors of our legislative halls should be forever closed. Other men there are of better disposition and larger views; but the time has not come for even their participation in the national counsels. If they are really fit for the places to which they have been chosen nothing will be lost if they prove anew that those also serve who stand and wait.

Public sentiment is changing very rapidly in the South, and not wholly in the right direction. The President went to the extreme limit of magnanimity; but the more he gave the more was demanded. I have recently seen an article in one of the Southern papers in which the removal of Secretary Stanton is asked as a good-will offering to the people of the South; and a knot of gentlemen at the hotel in Augusta argued to me that the unconditional release of Jeff Davis was necessary to prove the kindly disposition of the North! So far as the people of Georgia and South Carolina, and a large proportion of those of North Carolina, are concerned, the endorsement of President Johnson, of which so much is said in their newspapers, is merely a grateful sense of favors to be received.

Possibly we were wrong to hope that one season could sow the grain of reconstruction and gather its fruitage of good order and fair respect for human rights. At least this season has not done that. I am sure the nation longs for nothing else so much as for honest and heroic peace; yet let not the representatives of the nation mistake this longing for weakness of faith or faintness of purpose in respect to the final triumph of justice.

It cannot be said that freedom of speech has been fully secured in either of the three States which I have visited. Personally, I have very little cause of complaint, for my role was rather that of a listener than that of a talker; but I met many persons who kindly cautioned me, that at such and such places, and in such and such company, it would be advisable to refrain from conversation on certain topics. Among the members of the better class of people, resident in the cities and large towns, I found a fair degree of liberality of sentiment and courtesy of speech: but in traveling off the main railway lines, and among the average of the population, any man of Northern opinions must use much circumspection of language.

It follows, of course, that safety of person is not assured. Very likely one might travel through every county of either State without harm; but any Union man must expect to hear many insulting words; and any Northern man is sure to find his principles despised, his people contemned, and himself subjected to much disagreeable contumely; while any man holding and openly advocating even moderately radical sentiments on the negro question, stands an excellent chance, in many counties of Georgia and South Carolina, of being found dead some morning,— shot from behind, as is the custom of the country.

The leading men generally invite immigration, and are honest and sincere in their expression of desire for the influx of new life. They will, I am sure, do all they can to make the States safe and inviting for immigrants. In time even South

Carolina will be as free as New York; but at present the masses of the people have little disposition of welcome for Northerners.

The late private soldiers of the Rebel army are the best class of citizens in the South. Generally speaking, they are disposed to go to work, though few of them know what work to do or to undertake. The bad classes are nearly all the women, who are as rebellious and as malignant as ever; most of the preachers, who are as hostile now as they were three years ago; many of the Rebel ex-officers who didn't see active service; and more than half the young men who managed in one way or another to keep out of the army.

I often had occasion to notice, both in Georgia and the Carolinas, the wide and pitiful difference between the residents of the cities and large towns and the residents of the country. There is everywhere a rigid spirit of caste. The longings of South Carolina are essentially monarchical rather than republican; even the common people have become so debauched in loyalty that very many of them would readily accept the creation of orders of nobility. In Georgia there is something less of this spirit; but the upper classes continually assert their right to rule, and the middle and lower classes have no ability to free themselves. It will sadden the heart of any Northern man, who travels in either of these three States, to see how poor and narrow a thing life is to the country people. Even with the best class of townsfolk it lacks very much the depth and fruitfulness of our Northern life, while with these others it is hardly less materialistic than that of their own mules and horses. Thus Charleston has much intelligence and considerable genuine culture; but go twenty miles away and you are in the land of the barbarians. So Raleigh is a city in which there is love of beauty and interest in education; but the common people of the country are, at least, forty years behind the same class of people in Vermont. Moreover, in Macon are many very fine residences, and the city may boast of its gentility and its respect for the nourishing elegances of life; but a dozen miles out are large neighborhoods not yet half civilized. Till all these hateful walls of caste are thrown down, we can have neither intelligent love of liberty, decent respect for justice, nor enlightened devotion to the idea of national unity.

It has been the purpose of the ruling class apparently to build new barriers between themselves and the common people rather than tear away any of those already existing. I think no one can understand the actual condition of the mass of the whites of Georgia and the Carolinas, except by some daily contact with them. The injustice done to three fourths of them was hardly less than that done to all the blacks. Negro slavery was only more wicked and debasing than white slavery. Nine of every ten white men in South Carolina had almost as little to do with State affairs as the negroes had. Till civilization has been carried down into the homes and hearts of all classes, we shall have neither regard for humanity nor respect for the rights of the citizen.

Any plan of reconstruction is wrong that does not assure toleration of opinion and the elevation of the common people to the consciousness that ours is a republican form of government. Whether they are technically in the Union or out of the Union, it is the national duty to deal with these States in such manner as will most surely exalt the lower and middle classes of their inhabitants. The nation must teach them a knowledge of their own rights, while it also teaches them respect for its rights and the rights of man as man.

Stopping for two or three days in some back county, I was always seeming to have drifted away from the world which held Illinois and Ohio and Massachusetts. The difficulty in keeping connection with our civilization did not so much lie in the fact that the whole structure of daily life is unlike ours, nor in the other fact that I was forced to hear the Union and all loyal men reviled, as in the greater fact that the people are utterly without knowledge. There is everywhere a lack of intellectual activity; while as for schools, books, newspapers, why, one may almost say there are none outside the cities and towns!

Had schools abounded six years ago, I doubt if the masses of the South could have been forced into the war. "Why, d——n it," said a man to me, "the Union never hurt me, but I was the hottest Secessionist I reckon you ever saw. Howell Cobb made me so." Talking with a Columbia gentleman about sectional characteristics he said, "We had one advantage over you: your people knew all about the war, while ours only knew they were fighting for their homes."

In the important town of Charlotte, North Carolina, I found a white man who owned the comfortable house in which he lived, who had a wife and three half-grown children, and yet had never taken a newspaper in his life. He thought they were handy for wrapping purposes, but he couldn't see why anybody wanted to bother with the reading of them. In that State I found several persons—whites, and not of the "clay-eater" class either—who never had been inside a school-house, and who didn't mean to 'low their children to go inside one.

The Southern newspapers are all local in character, and most of them are intensely Southern in tone; while as sources of general information, and particularly of political information, they are beneath notice. The Southern colleges have mostly suspended operations on account of the war. Efforts are making to reopen them, and those in Georgia will probably be in working order by next spring. But that best fruit of modern civilization, so plentiful in the North,—the common-

school house,—is almost wholly unknown in the Carolinas and Georgia. I have
scarcely seen a dozen in my whole journey, while a trip of the same number of
miles in New York and New England would probably show me five hundred.
Underneath this one little fact lies the whole cause of the war.

There is small desire for schools and books and newspapers. The chief end of
man seems to have been "to own a nigger." The great majority of the common people know next to nothing either of history or contemporaneous affairs; either of the
principles of government or the acts of their own government; either of the work
or thought of the present age; either of the desires or the purposes of nations. They
get their information and their opinions mainly from the local office-seekers. You
can touch the masses with few of the appeals by which we move our own people.
There is very little aspiration for larger life; and there is almost no opportunity
for its attainment. That education is the stairway to a nobler existence is a fact
which they either fail to comprehend or to which they are wholly indifferent.

Where there is such a spirit of caste, where the ruling class has a personal interest in fostering prejudice, where the masses are in such an inert condition,
where ignorance generally prevails, where there is so little ambition for better-
ment, where life is so hard and material in its tone, it is not strange to find much
hatred and contempt. Ignorance is generally cruel and frequently brutal. The political leaders of this people have apparently indoctrinated them with the notion
that they are superior to any other class in the country. Hence there is usually very
little effort to conceal the prevalent scorn of the Yankee,—this term being applied
to the citizen of any Northern State. Any plan of reconstruction is wrong that
tends to leave these old leaders in power. A few of them give certain evidence of a
change of heart; but the others, the men who not only brought on the war, but
ruined the mental and moral force of their people before unfurling the banner of
Rebellion,—for these there should never any more be place or countenance among
honest and humane and patriotic people. When the nation gives them life and a
chance for its continuance, it shows all the magnanimity that humanity can in
such case afford.

In North Carolina there is a great deal of something that calls itself Unionism.
It is a cheat, and any man who trusts it will meet with overthrow. In all sections of
the State I found abundant hatred of some leading or local Secessionist; but how
full of promise for the new era of national life is the Unionism which rests only
on this foundation?

In South Carolina there is very little presence of love for the Union, but everywhere a passionate devotion to the State; and the common sentiment holds that

man guilty of treason who prefers the United States to South Carolina. There is no occasion to wonder at the admiration of the people for Wade Hampton, for he is the very exemplar of their spirit,—of their proud and narrow and domineering spirit. "It is our duty," he says, in a letter which he has recently addressed to the people of the State,—"it is our duty to support the President of the United States so long as he manifests a disposition to restore all our rights as a sovereign State." That sentence will forever stand as a model of cool arrogance, and yet it is in full accord with the spirit of the South-Carolinians. The war has taught them that the physical force of the nation cannot be resisted, and they will be obedient to the letter of the law; but the whole current of their lives flows in direct antagonism to its spirit.

In Georgia there is something worse than sham Unionism or cold acquiescence in the issue of battle: it is the universally prevalent doctrine of the supremacy of the State. In South Carolina, a few men stood up against the storm, but in Georgia that man is hopelessly dead who doubted or faltered. The common sense of all classes pushes the necessity of allegiance to the State into the domain of morals as well as into that of politics; and he who did not "go with the State" in the Rebellion is held to have committed the unpardonable sin. There is everywhere only cold toleration for the idea of national sovereignty, and but little pride in the strength and glory and renown of the United States of America.

Much is said of the hypocrisy of the South. I found but little of it anywhere. The North-Carolinian calls himself a Unionist, but he makes no special pretense of love for the Union. He desires many favors, but he asks for them generally on the ground that he hated the Secessionists. The South-Carolinian demands only something less than he did in the days before the war, but he offers no pleas of Unionism as a guaranty for the future. He rests his case on the assumption that he has fully acquiesced in the results of the war, and he honestly believes that he has so acquiesced. His confidence in South Carolina is so supreme that he cannot yet believe that destiny has decreed his State a secondary place in the Union. The Georgian began by believing that Rebellion in the interest of slavery was honorable, and the result of the war has not changed his opinion. He is anxious for readmission to fellowship with New York and Pennsylvania and Connecticut, but he supports his application by little claim of community of interest with our other States. His spirit is hard and uncompromising; he demands rights, but does not ask favors; and he is confident that Georgia is fully as important to the United States as they are to Georgia.

The fact that such a large proportion of the offices in the gift of the people of

these States have been filled with men who were officers in the Rebel army does
not in itself furnish any argument against the good disposition of the people. The
sentiment which voluntarily confers honor on a man who has shown personal
bravery, who has been plucky and daring and gallant, is one we cannot afford to
crush,—it is one of the strong moral forces of a nation, and deserves nurture rather
than condemnation. Moreover, in not a few cases these ex-officers are of better
will and purpose toward the government than any other men in their respective localities. It may not be pleasant to us to recognize this fact; but I am confident that
we shall make sure progress toward securing domestic tranquility and the general
welfare just in proportion as we act upon it.

The other fact, that almost every candidate was defeated who didn't "go with
the State" during the war is one of serious import. It indicates a spirit of defiance
to the nation, of determined opposition to the principle of national unity. So long
as this spirit prevails, we can hope for no sound peace. It will not again marshal
armies in the field. Such a thing is utterly beyond the range of possibilities so far
as this generation or the next is concerned. A few untamed fire-eaters will bluster,
and local politicians will brag, but the leaders are wiser than they were, and the
people have had enough of war. But there are things quite as bad as open war; and
one of these is a sullen and relentless antagonism to the idea of national sovereignty,—from which will breed passionate devotion to local interests, unending
persecution of the freedmen, never-ceasing clamor in behalf of State rights, and
continual effort to break away from the solemn obligations of the national debt.

That is the true plan of reconstruction which makes haste very slowly. The one
sole needful condition is, that each State establish a government whereby all civil
rights at least shall be assured in their fullest extent to every citizen. When Georgia
and the Carolinas establish governments republican in fact as well as in form, they
will have brought themselves into harmony with the national will, and may justly
demand readmission to their former political relations in the Union. It is no time
for passion or bitterness, and it does not become our manhood to do anything for
revenge. Let us have peace and kindly feeling; yet, that our peace may be no sham
or shallow affair, it is painfully essential that we keep these States awhile within national control, in order to aid the few wise and just men therein who are fighting
the great fight with stubborn prejudice and hidebound custom. Any plan of reconstruction is wrong which accepts forced submission as genuine loyalty or even
as cheerful acquiescence in the national desire and purpose.

Prior to the war we heard continually of the love of the master for his slave,
and the love of the slave for his master. There was also much talk to the effect that

the negro lived in the midst of pleasant surroundings, and had no desire to change his situation. It was asserted that he delighted in a state of dependence, and throve on the universal favor of the whites. Some of this language we conjectured might be extravagant; but to the single fact that there was universal good-will between the two classes every Southern white person bore evidence. So, too, during my trip through Georgia and the Carolinas they have generally seemed anxious to convince me that the blacks behaved well during the war,—kept at their old tasks, labored cheerfully and faithfully, did not show a disposition to be lawless, and were rarely guilty of acts of violence, even in sections where there were many women and children, and but few white men.

Yet I found everywhere now the most direct antagonism between the two classes. The white charge generally that the negro is idle and at the bottom of all local disturbance, and credit him with most of the vices and very few of the virtues of humanity. The negroes charge that the whites are revengeful, and intend to cheat the laboring class at every opportunity, and credit them with neither good purposes nor kindly hearts. This present hostility of each class to the other is a fact that will sorely perplex any Northern man traveling in either of these States. One would say, that, if there had formerly been such pleasant relations between them, there ought now to be mutual sympathy and forbearance, instead of mutual distrust and antagonism. One would say, too, that self-interest, the common interest of capital and labor, ought to keep them in harmony; while the fact is, that this very interest appears to put them in an attitude of defiance toward each other. I believe the most charitable traveler must come to the conclusion that the professed love of the whites for the blacks was a monstrous sham.

Individual cases of real attachment to individual servants were doubtless common enough before the war, and an honest observer finds not a few of them even now. But, having seen the present relations of the two classes, I wonder that any-one could ever have believed that the common white people, as a class, had any real love for the blacks as a race. Some of the better men are now willing to concede to them the minor rights of humanity, but not one man in five thousand proposes to give them all the rights of men and women, and scarcely one in twenty thousand would invest any of them with the rights of citizenship. To dream that any of these States will voluntarily grant the ballot to the negro during this generation seems to me to qualify yourself for the insane asylum. The plainest of all requirements is that the freed negro shall have the right to be heard in the courts; and the fierce and bitter opposition to meeting this requirement gives the unequivocal lie to all professions of love for him.

The negro is no model of virtue or manliness. He loves idleness, has little conception of right and wrong, and he is improvident to the last degree of childishness. He is a creature,—as some of our own people will do well to keep carefully in mind,—just forcibly released from slavery. The havoc of war has filled his heart with confused longings, and his ears with confused sounds of rights and privileges: it must be the nation's duty, for it cannot be left wholly to his late master, to help him to a clear understanding of those rights and privileges, and also to lay upon him a knowledge of his responsibilities. He is anxious to learn, and is very tractable in respect to minor matters; but we shall need almost infinite patience with him, for he comes very slowly to moral comprehensions.

Going into the States where I went,—and perhaps the fact is also true of the other Southern States,—any man would almost be justified in concluding that the end and purpose in respect to this poor negro was his extermination. It is proclaimed everywhere that he will not work, that he cannot take care of himself, that he is a nuisance to society, that he lives by stealing, and that he is sure to die in a few months; and, truth to tell, the great body of the people, though one must not say, intentionally, are doing all they well can to make these assertions true. If it is not said that any considerable number wantonly abuse and outrage him, it must be said that they manifest a barbaric indifference to his fate which just as surely drives him on to destruction as open cruelty would.

There are some men and a few women—and perhaps the number of these is greater than we of the North generally suppose—who really desire that the negro should now have his full rights as a human being. Unfortunately, in these Southern communities the opinion of such persons cannot have the same weight it would in ours. The spirit of caste, of which I have already spoken, is an element largely against them in any contest involving principle. The walls between individuals and classes are so high that the men and women who recognize the negro's rights and privileges as a freeman are almost as far from the masses as we of the North are. Moreover, that any opinion savors of the "Yankee"—in other words, is new to the South—prevents its consideration by the great body of the people. Their inherent antagonism to everything from the North—an antagonism fostered for half a century by the politicians in the interest of slavery—is something that no Northern man can understand, till he sees it with his own eyes. That the full freedom of the negroes would be acknowledged at once is something we had no warrant for expecting. The old masters grant them nothing, except at the requirement of the nation, as a military or a political necessity; and any plan of reconstruction is wrong which proposes to at once or in the immediate future substitute free-will for this necessity.

Three fourths of the people assume that the negro will not labor except on compulsion; and the whole struggle between the whites and the blacks is a struggle for and against compulsion. The negro insists, very blindly perhaps, that he shall be free to come and go when he pleases; the white insists that he shall only come and go at the pleasure of his employer. The whites seem wholly unable to comprehend that freedom for the negro means the same thing as freedom for them. They readily enough admit that the government has made him free, but appear to believe that they still have the right to exercise over him the old control. They cannot understand the national intent as expressed in the Emancipation Proclamation and the Constitutional Amendment. I did not anywhere find a man who could see that laws should be applicable to all persons alike; and hence even the best men hold that each State must have a negro code.

I think the freedmen divide themselves into four classes: one fourth recognizing very clearly the necessity of work, and going about it with cheerful diligence and wise fore-thought; one fourth comprehending that there must be labor, but needing considerable encouragement to follow it steadily; one fourth preferring idleness, but not specially averse to doing some job work about the towns and cities; and one fourth avoiding labor as much as possible, and living by voluntary charity, persistent begging, or systematic pilfering. It is true that thousands of the aggregate body of this people appear to have hoped, and perhaps believed, that freedom meant idleness; true, too, that thousands are drifting about the country or loafing about the centers of population in a state of vagabondage. Yet of the hundreds with whom I talked, I found less than a score who seemed beyond hope of reformation. It is a cruel slander to say that the race will not work except on compulsion. I made much inquiry wherever I went, of great numbers of planters and other employers, and found but very few cases in which it appeared that they had refused to labor reasonably well when fairly treated and justly paid. Grudgingly admitted to any of the natural rights of man, despised alike by Unionists and Secessionists, wantonly outraged by many and meanly cheated by more of the old planters, receiving a hundred cuffs for one helping hand and a thousand curses for one kindly word, they bear themselves toward their former masters very much as white men and women would under the same circumstances. Their souls are filled with a great but vague longing for freedom; they battle blindly with fate and circumstance for the unseen and uncomprehended, and seem to find every man's hand raised against them either for blows or reproaches. What wonder that they fill the land with restlessness!

However unfavorable this exhibit of the negroes in respect to labor may appear, it is quite as good as can be made for the whites. It is the boast of men and women alike, that they have never done an hour's work. I met hundreds of hale and vigorous young men who unblushingly owned to me that they had not earned a penny since the war closed. Nine tenths of the people must be taught that labor is not debasing. It was pitiful enough to find so much idleness, but it was more pitiful to observe that it was likely to continue indefinitely. The war will not have borne proper fruit if our peace does not speedily bring respect for labor as well as respect for man. When we have secured one of these things, we shall have gone far toward securing the other; and when we have secured both, then, indeed, shall we have noble cause for glorying in our country,—true warrant for exultation that our flag floats over no slave.

There are at least five things for the nation to do: make haste slowly in the work of reconstruction; temper justice with mercy, but see to it that justice is not overborne; keep military control of these lately rebellious States till they guarantee a republican form of government; scrutinize carefully the personal fitness of the men chosen therefrom as representatives in the Congress of the United States; and sustain therein some agency that shall stand between the whites and the blacks and aid each class in coming to a proper understanding of its privileges and responsibilities.

INDEX

Aldrich, A. P.: 20, 21, 25, 26; opposes revision of constitution, 37

Aristocracy, in South Carolina: 19-20, 38, 98; and Whig party, 67

Atlanta, Georgia, 164-66, 173

Augusta, Georgia, 114, 173

Barton, Clara, 151

Black Codes, proposed: in South Carolina, 28-29; in North Carolina, 78; in Georgia, 127-28

Boyden, Nathaniel, 68, 69, 70, 72-73, 80, 89

Brown, Joseph E., 122, 167

Business, revival of, 2-4, 16, 165, 178-79

Buttons, Confederate, 14, 19

Calhoun, John C., 5, 68, 154, 160

Charleston, South Carolina: destruction of, 1-2, 5; political power of, 23, 36, 38; voting in, 98

Cobb, Howell, 147, 167, 175, 191

Colonization, 10, 75-76, 84

Columbia, South Carolina, destruction of, 14, 16

Compensation, for slave property, 29, 106-7, 117, 138

Crime, general, 10, 53, 187

Davis, Jefferson: pardon of, 26, 39, 115, 124-27, 189; discussed, 87, 88, 105-6

Debt (War): 80-82, 122; in Georgia, 130-36, 138, 139, 185-86

Democratic Party, 21, 66-67, 174

Education: African American, 63, 91, 163; general, 112, 117-18, 191-92

Emigration, white, 174

Fort Sumter, 1, 25

Freedmen's Bureau: problems of, 11, 129-30, 187; cases before, 12, 155; contracts, 45-46; and white southerners, 51, 85, 89-90; praised, 61; chastised, 107; on black workers, 175; on poverty, 185

Freedpeople: described, 10, 64-65, 89-90; and work, 11, 15, 46, 84-85, 91, 175; restrictions on, 29, 100, 128; and political representation, 33-34, 38, 80; political actions, 64, 85, 116; and education, 163; and mobility, 170-73

Freedpeople, quoted: on war, 1; on postwar conditions 4; on working, 6, 7, 9, 110, 156, 187; on whites, 13, 99; on freedom, 32, 172-73; on land distribution, 45; on prisoners, 49-50, 97; on militia, 55; on Freedmen's Convention, 5, 60; on justice, 79, 100-101; on testifying in court, 90; on slavery, 117

Galloway, A. H., 57, 60

Grant, Ulysses S., 115

Greenbacks, 16-17, 55, 86, 117

Haiti, 61

Hampton, Wade, 18, 98, 193

Harris, John H., 60, 64

Hill, Benjamin, 160-62

Hill, Joshua, 120, 121-22, 123, 124-25, 135, 160

Holden, W. W., 65-66, 80, 81

Howard, Oliver Otis, 101, 103-104, 115

Jenkins, Charles J, 121, 134, 157-58

Johnson, Andrew: 2, 24, 25, 79; communications to, 26, 42, 125-127, 137; favorable view of, 30,

66, 116, 122; as Unionist, 54; visited, 72-73; communications from, 81, 132-33; and reelection, 88, 174; and abandoned lands, 101-104; and Jefferson Davis, 106; policies of, 167, 189
Johnson, Herschel V., 119, 121, 162-63, 185

Land: distribution expected, 45, 108, 187; government grants of, 101-104
Language (dialect), 112-14
Lee, Robert E., 115, 116
Liberia, 61
Lincoln, Abraham, 29, 57, 61

Manly, M. E., 68, 69-70, 73
Massachusetts: 2, 4, 32, 60, 91; superior civilization of, 44, 109, 169-70; education, 117; rights of, 80, 154
Matthews, J. D., 125, 129, 130, 135, 138, 173
Military rule: 4, 21, 29-30, 138; and elections, 19; removing, 129; and debt, 132
Militia, 55-56
Moore, B. F., 68, 80, 82

Northern civilization, 2, 9, 14, 109, 168-70
Northerners (Yankees): 2; contempt for, 5, 7, 52, 154, 176; fanatic, 26, 30, 132; and elections, 82-83, 160; in prisons, 96; violence against, 108, 141-46

Orr, James L.: 19, 24, 25, 29; on political representation, 33; on black suffrage, 42; as candidate for governor, 44, 98

Perry, Benjamin F., 23, 24, 44
Pickens, Francis W., 20, 25, 27
Poverty, 17-18, 111-12, 179-80, 185

Railroads: 6, 14-15; 46, 51, 165; destroyed, 98, 105, 178
Randolph, John Jr., 57, 60, 64
Republican Party: 21, 22, 61; "black Republicans," 35, 82

Saxton, Rufus, 11, 101-2
Secession: convention, South Carolina, 18, 19, 24; ordinances repealed, 25-26, 69-73, 122-23; convention, North Carolina, 65, 67-68; convention, Georgia, 119-20
Segregation, 61, 128
Sherman, William Tecumseh: 3, 14-16, 52, 96, 115; and railroads, 105; and slaves, 155
Slavery, 2, 37, 62, 107; spirit of, 18, 84, 111; abolition of, in South Carolina, 21-22, 27-32; abolition of, in North Carolina, 66, 74-75, 90; abolition of, in Georgia, 121, 123-24, 127, 138; attempts to restore, 156-57
Soldiers, African American: 5, 14, 108; and civilian demoralization, 45, 100
Southerners, white: attitudes toward African Americans, 10, 40, 85, 155; violence against African Americans, 14, 46, 56; 84, 99-100, 107-8, 116, 141; on postwar period, 17; on renewal of hostilities, 18, 20, 21, 24; unrepentant, 20, 136-40; on political representation, 34-35, 79-80, 127, 129; on black testimony in court, 41; and free labor, 44-45, 47, 84-85, 170; on northern politics, 83; poor whites, 83-84, 162, 163, 185; and Freedmen's Bureau, 85; described, 86-87; laziness of, 87-88, 110-11; class conflict, 98, 133-34, 136, 167, 190-92; and abandoned lands, 103-4; war experiences, 116
Southerners, white, quoted: 9; on northerners, 2, 16, 36, 83, 153-54; on African Americans, 8-9, 12, 13, 40, 87, 117, 180-83; on violence toward African Americans, 13, 176; on white conflict, 23, 52, 79; on war experiences, 25, 152; on black suffrage, 34-35, 41, 75; on southern illiteracy, 39; on secession, 43, 121, 191; on renewal of hostilities, 43, 89; on prisoners, 50; on militia, 55; on Freedmen's Convention, 56; on colonization, 76; on representation, 79-80, 129, 160; on Johnson, 81; on Workingmen's Association, 99; on labor, 110, 176, 177, 179, 184; on education, 117-18, 163; on state loyalty 121, 158; 174; on military rule, 138; on rebellion, 141, 154, 167;

on politics, 174; on emigration, 174; on Wirz,
    175; on states' rights, 176-77, 179
States' rights: as cause of war, 30; persistence of,
    in North Carolina, 66, 68; in Georgia, 123, 132,
    137-38; 154, 158, 160, 174, 176, 193; opposed,
    179
Stephens, Alexander H., 125-126, 160, 175
Stevens, Thaddeus, 30, 132
Suffrage, African American: 21-22, 41-42, 47, 183;
    and representation, 33-35; in North Carolina,
    75, 90; in Georgia, 130, 132
Sumner, Charles, 61, 132
Supreme Court, U. S., 22
Swett, Isham, 64, 79

Testimony, African American, 41, 90-91, 128, 138,
    39
Tillson, Davis, 129-130, 175
Tilman, George D., 38
Toombs, Robert, 175

Unionism: 5, 48; in South Carolina, 20, 98; in
    North Carolina, 52-55, 72, 79, 80, 88, 192; in
    Georgia, 136, 166

Whig Party, 66-68
Wirz, Henry, 147, 175
Women, southern, white: 5, 7-9, 168-170; on
    Yankees, 17, 154; on defeat, 43, 116; on freed-
    women, 89-90.
Wood, John W., 58-59
Workingmen's Association, 98-99

Yankees. See Northerners